THE
WORLD ATLAS
OF STREET
FASHION

CAROLINE COX

MITCHELL BEAZLEY

NORTH AMERICA

LATIN AMERICA AND THE CARIBBEAN

CONTENTS

EUROPE

AFRICA

ASIA

AUSTRALIA AND NEW ZEALAND

The septuagenarian sapeur La Mame, nicknamed 'the Parisian Kiboba', poses at his home in Brazzaville in 2014.

INTRODUCTION

In the city there are ways of making your mark, provoking a reaction and standing out from the crowd. Street fashion exists to turn heads and create comment, morphing into what historian Elizabeth Wilson calls 'the poster for one's act'. The message can be one of resistance, subversion, musical affiliation or a combination of all three, and a group of likeminded individuals can create a powerful sartorial force moving beyond fashion's mere billboard for the latest brands. Since the late 19th century the city's pavements have become a runway where idiosyncratic modes of dressing are presented, often to the consternation of the general public, as exemplified by the Peaky Blinders of Birmingham, UK, in the 1880s. Named after the peak of their caps and recognized by their donkey jackets, bell-bottomed trousers and heavy boots, they were described at the time as 'foul-mouthed young men who stalk the streets in drunken groups insulting passers-by'.

Street fashions are consumed and exported, their original messages often re-framed to fit each culture's codes. The teddy boy (see page 185) is a case in point – a young working-class dandy from London's East End, who co-opted a style of suit originally designed by Savile Row tailors for young upper-class men in the late 1940s. The drape suit was a retrospective look harking back to the menswear of the Edwardian era (1901–10) and reflected the same direction being taken in womenswear by couturier Christian Dior. Dior unveiled fashion's New Look in 1947 with a tailored collection featuring jackets in shantung silk with sculpted basques and heavily boned, wasp-waisted gowns with tiers of pleats and huge Victorian inspired crinoline skirts that mocked wartime sobriety and the restrictions on the use of materials. In the hands of the teddy boy, the drape suit became a symbol of rebellion by a boy who may not have had the money or 'class' of his 'betters', but could certainly look as good.

From its heyday to its deconstructed disarray, the incendiary street-style of punk (see page 360) has created a visible set of sartorial symbols – such as the studded and painted black leather jacket and mohican hairstyle – that make up a generic language of anarchy. In 2012, journalist John Harris described contemporary punk as tending to fall into self-parody in its homelands. UK punk is nowadays something of a street fashion cliché, but when redeployed in Berlin and Jakarta the style takes on a compelling local flavour, emerging as an important way of showing dissent under repressive regimes by refusing to conform. As Jakarta punk Onie said, 'punk is about freedom. People can choose what they want to do and what they want to say.' Such spirit inspires crackdown; in 2011, in Aceh, a conservative province of Indonesia, the local police arrested 65 punks at a concert and forcibly shaved their Mohican hairstyles because of the perceived rejection of Islamic values. As Harris puts it, 'to jaded western eyes, many of the groups and fans appear to be straight out of central casting, and the music can sound hopelessly derivative, rather clumsy, and in thrall to influences whose cultural charge faded three decades ago. Some of the musicians' chosen western reference points are almost comically unlikely. But that is our problem, not theirs: to paraphrase Johnny Rotten, they mean it, man.'

Thus the styles of the street can be overtly political, as in the case of the sapeurs (see page 270) of Kinshasa, who use dressing up as a way of escaping their social position, or the chola (see page 44) gangs of East Los Angeles, who took strength from the Chicano Movement of the 1960s, which called for the recognition of the indigenous Mexican, the original inhabitant of the city. Some more recent street fashions are a visual manifesto of eco-awareness, taking inspiration from the hippies and psychedelics (see page 30) of the 1960s and the longstanding ferals (see page 370) of Australia. Embodied in looks such as boho (see page 216), with references to global culture in fringed, printed and patchworked clothes and exhortations to 'make love not war', these styles hold resonance in our post-Trump, 'post-truth' era and chime with a new generation of youth who are reworking anti-fashion looks as a form of protest. Grunge (see page 16) has enjoyed a revival and normcore (see page 92), at first an ironic stance purportedly invented by the Internet, has become a way of showing one's rejection of fashion branding and a means of questioning the fashion system itself.

Street fashion can be created by obsession; the K-pop (see page 304) enthusiasts of Seoul and the Philippines inhabit the lives of stars to such an extent that they re-create publicity stills through carefully constructed cosplay, which are then distributed through Internet communities of like-minded fans. Such scenes can develop cachet by being underground for longer, available only for 'those in the know', giving integrity to a look that is absent from the vagaries of mainstream fashion. Street fashions are not just for the young – they are also multi-generational. One of the key proponents of Advanced Style (see page 196), an anti-fashion movement originating in New York, is the innovative Iris Apfel, a nonagenarian known for her trademark owl glasses and eclectic ensembles of antique, vintage and modern fashion, who felt written off by fashion designers. The pachuco (see page 60), many of whom have dressed in the same way for decades, draw on a rich cultural heritage as a form of important self-affirmation.

The products of catwalk fashion have been endlessly documented by the world's top photographers for presentation as fantasies in the pages of fashion magazines such as *Vogue*. Street fashion has a history of being photographed, too, but its portrayal is more gritty. Chief cartoonist at *Punch* magazine and amateur snapper Edward Linley Sambourne began photographing his subjects (rather voyeuristically) with a concealed camera in 1905; by the 1960s, Bill Cunningham, who is considered the first street fashion photographer, was chronicling the dress of his subjects for *The New York Times* column 'On The Street'. Significantly, Cunningham – who had an avowed disinterest in the red carpet poseurs of the celebrity world – was the first to spot the flamboyant appearance of Advanced Style's

poster girl, Iris Apfel. The writing and photography of American anthropologist Ted Polhemus has been pivotal in understanding post war subcultures and identity, in particular the book and exhibition *Streetstyle: From Sidewalk to Catwalk* (1994), which provided one of the first taxonomies and analyses of street fashion. In 1997, Shoichi Aoki began documenting Harajuku street fashion in his magazine *FRUiTS*, thereby introducing Japan's immense contribution to style through looks such as gothloli (see page 334), decora (see page 320), ganguro (see page 322) and kogal (see page 328). Scott Schuman founded the seminal street fashion blog *The Sartorialist* in 2005, displaying his shots of innovative street fashion worn by 'real people', which spawned thousands of copies and changed the hierarchy of fashion. Today, brands know that idiosyncratic street fashion has cachet and are prepared to pay its innovators to wear their latest looks. In 2002, branding specialist Tom Julian told *The New York Times* journalist Ruth La Ferla that 'People still think street style is a voice of purity, but I don't think purity exists any more'. In 2013, fashion doyenne Suzy Menkes wrote that 'Today, the people outside fashion shows are more like peacocks than crows. They pose and preen, in their multipatterned dresses, spidery legs balanced on club-sandwich platform shoes, or in thigh-high boots under sculptured coats blooming with flat flowers.'

Selfie culture has given voice to street stylists, providing them with the tools to present their own image to the world by cutting out the middle man. The carefully staged self-portrait is a format that can be spread across a global network in an instant, and allows much play with fashion and identity. The front-facing camera of a smartphone allows detailed self-scrutiny, where looks can be tried out, manipulated and sent. It has become an important tool for micro communities on social networking sites such as Qzone, the home of the Beijing shamate (see page 300), and photo-sharing sites such as Fotolog, which became the meeting place for the Bueno Aries flogger (see page 150).

As Ted Polhemus explains, 'group affiliations define human experience'. *The World Atlas of Street Fashion* examines street fashion in all its international diversity by tracing the many and varied ways in which it has developed in different regions of the world. Within its meticulously researched pages the skinheads (see page 356) of Kuala Lumpur moonstomp alongside the funkeiros (see page 138) of Sao Paolo; the raggare (see page 160) of Stockholm mingle with the junglists (see page 110) of Whistler; the fantasy world of the fairy kei (see page 316) is joined by the Muslim moshpits of Taqwacore (see page 342). This is world street fashion.

NORTH AMERICA

SEATTLE PORTLAND SAN FRANCISCO OAKLAND
LOS ANGELES LAS VEGAS EL PASO HOUSTON
CHICAGO KENTUCKY GARRETTSVILLE BOSTON NEW YORK
PITTSBURGH WASHINGTON, DC MIAMI VANCOUVER
WHISTLER TORONTO MONTREAL

GRUNGE HEALTH GOTH HELLS ANGEL DEADHEAD PSYCHEDELIC
MODERN PRIMITIVE SCRAPER BIKER SWING KID CHOLA GANGSTA RAPPER PSYCHOBILLY
ROCKABILLY NEW RAVE PACHUCO BANDIDOS RIVETHEAD SEAPUNK OTHERKIN JUGGALO
PREPPY FLY GIRL B-BOY GHETTO GOTH NORMCORE FURRY STRAIGHT EDGE CHONGA
FETISH BRONY JUNGLIST MOD CYBERGOTH

She was as 'new as the night's batch of bathtub gin, as shiny as the firehouse-red roadster just driven from the showroom floor. Effervescent, giddy, with rolled-down hose to show her bee's knees, the new-collegiate heroine drank, smoked, made love in cars and was as happy-snappy as bubble gum.' The girl was Clara Bow and the birth of modern cinema had made her a film star, one of the household goddesses of 20th-century consumer culture. She was the 'It girl', the embodiment of the American 'tootsie' and the archetypal New York flapper on film, a role she extended into her off-screen life with wild parties featuring drugs, Latin gigolos and her seven dogs dyed to match her red hair. Zooming around in her red convertible, Bow was one of many stars who earned vast wages and lived a life of luxury and excess. Rudolph Valentino's exploits took place in a black marble and leather bedroom, Pola Negri had a Roman plunge pool in her living room, and Gloria Swanson owned a limousine upholstered in leopard skin. Bow's 'bathtub gin' was born of Prohibition (1920–33), an era that created its own street fashion inextricably linked to the criminal underworld. In 1922, the *Boot and Shoe Recorder* reported on the unsightly trend for the Russian boot, noting, 'It can hardly be said to be a fitting and beautiful part of the costume of the modern American girl, whose skirts are short and whose feet in Russian boots are far from being petite.' Little did the journalist know that the Russian boot was being used by the heavily painted molls of Chicago's notorious gangsters to smuggle illegal liquor into speakeasies, hence the term 'bootlegging'.

The sexual lure and fashion influence of Hollywood stars made stages of streets, with people appraising and being appraised, checking their reflections in the windows of shopping arcades for their real life 'close-ups'. In the 1930s, the Depression made cinematic imagery more keenly felt as the movies provided a window into another world for a lost generation whose every effort was taken up with finding employment, a living wage and sustenance. The arrival of black, Mexican and Puerto Rican migrants in North American cities brought musical forms and ways of dressing that had a profound effect on street fashion. Academic Michael Brake describes their influence: 'In a society where black people were kept out of desirable suburban residences and decent schools and their civil rights were restricted, symbols of affluence were important. Clothes, cars and other goods were deliberately and openly flaunted. Whether it was the zoot suit, the conked hair, the city clothes of the hep cat or Superfly...these were all signs of money, often where no visible income was present.'

After World War II, the economic boom in North America led to a renegotiation of the class system, as recognized by Vance Packard in *The Status Seekers* (1959) who wrote, 'With the general diffusion of wealth, there has been a crumbling of visible class lines now that such one-time upper-class symbols as limousines, power boats and mink coats are available to a variety of people.' This new post-war wealth was displayed in the domestic environment, with his 'n' hers bathrooms, push-button curtains and maître d' kitchens. As one magazine article promised in 1956, in 'a time not very far away, your home will be a push-button miracle [in which]...electronic maids will cook and clean by magic'. However, for the Beat Generation, such futuristic possibilities were the province of the suburban 'man in a grey flannel suit', and instead they advocated the concept of 'dropping out' or living with no fixed income in deprived areas of the city populated by the urban working class.

The bobbysoxer and the sweater girl were two street fashions actively born of consumer culture; the bobbysoxers were teenage fans of Frank Sinatra who hit the headlines in 1943 after thousands congregated outside New York's Paramount Theatre before one of his concerts, screaming for their hero. The sweater girl look was popular through the 1940s and 1950s, a colourful, brash, anti-maternal style comprising a skin-tight sweater, tight pencil skirt or capri pants and stiletto mules. Film star Jayne Mansfield (opposite), a glamorous blonde whose vital statistics were boosted by a whirlpool-stitched bra, epitomized the look. Not everyone was prepared to indulge in consumer culture, however, and there was an undercurrent of dissent apparent in rock 'n' roll. Anti-authoritarian stars such as Elvis Presley, Little Richard and Buddy Holly provided an alternative representation of masculinity to the traditional rugged anti-emotional heroics of the American cowboy embodied in John Wayne.

Cultural shifts and rebellious attitudes were expressed in hair, too: the conk of the African-American hipster, the duck-tailed pompadour of the pachuco (see page 60), the cropped mod (see page 112) and the long-haired beatnik and hippy. In the 1960s, a 'natural' look was exhorted through the Black is Beautiful movement, which encouraged African-American men and women to reject their enslavement to white beauty ideals by straightening their hair. Authentically black hairstyles such as the natural or afro, as it began to be called, were worn as a badge of pride. A hair androgyny also swept the United States, worn by demonstrators against the war in Vietnam, student protesters in Quebec and promoters of drug culture; it was also fetishized in the hippy musical *Hair*.

GRUNGE

The joke goes that it rains so much in Seattle that the only thing to do is stay indoors and form a band. The city's musical creativity was showcased in 1986 on the compilation album *Deep Six*, released by Chris Hanzsek and Tina Casale on their C/Z label. It featured six local bands including the Melvins and Soundgarden, who were the antecedents of the Seattle Sound – aka grunge. In 1991 Nirvana's iconic album *Nevermind* made lead singer Kurt Cobain the (albeit unwilling) voice of his generation and his appearance in the 'Smells Like Team Spirit' video in the same year codified the grunge look, with his flannel shirt becoming the signifier for 'slacker' culture. Grunge street fashion was a direct rejection of the logo-mania of the 1980s and the yuppie (young, upwardly mobile professional) who, as a by-product of Reaganomics, appeared as the physical embodiment of cynicism and greed. Grunge demanded authenticity and revived a whole host of rugged non-fashion workwear brands such as Filson, Woolrich and Pendleton, whose shirts and Mackinaw jackets were combined with wool beanies, ripped and faded jeans, thrift store T-shirts and heavy boots. Seattle's proximity to the logging industry made workwear readily available in the local thrift stores and army surplus outlets, and the city's changeable climate made layering a functional way of dressing. Courtney Love, lead singer of the band Hole and Cobain's wife, combined vintage baby-doll and tea dresses with oversized cardigans, white knee socks and Mary Jane shoes, overthrowing ideas of 'prettiness' and creating a powerfully subversive physical presence. Her experiments took the meaning of grunge beyond that of a musical mash-up of punk (see page 360) and heavy rock to one that questioned the tropes of masculinity and femininity and their association with appearance.

1 Kurt Cobain, Krist Novoselic and Dave Grohl of Nirvana wear the downbeat, undone, anonymous grunge look as a protest against 1980s logo-laden excess. 2 US band Soundgarden in 1989. 3 Courtney Love created an innovative style, mixing traditionally 'glamorous' vintage finds with both punk and childlike references.

4 New York fashion blogger Lua P does recession chic in new grunge, the latest incarnation of the original Seattle style. **5 & 6** Marc Jacobs's grunge-inspired collection for Perry Ellis (1992).

Grunge has always had an uneasy relationship with high fashion, as evidenced by the overwhelmingly negative response to Marc Jacobs's grunge-inspired collection for Perry Ellis in November 1992. Jacobs sourced plaid flannel shirts from thrift stores, replicating them in pure silk, and woollen beanies were refashioned in expensive cashmere without, it appeared, any sense of irony. Fashion buyers were unimpressed and in 1993 *New York* magazine declared that 'Grunge has run its course...For many, Marc Jacobs's grunge fashion collection was the final shove.' Kurt Cobain appeared to agree with the sentiment, having in the previous year been photographed sporting a T-shirt with the slogan 'Grunge is Dead'.

Grunge's anti-authoritarian stance continues to have huge effects on street fashion, however, and in the recession of the 2010s a new generation of teenagers is finding inspiration in its rejection of consumerist excess. The scene has an authenticity that many have found lacking in contemporary fashion culture, with its emphasis on high glamour, hyper-grooming and artificiality in the form of fake tans, acrylic nails and hair extensions. High fashion brands are referencing the new grunge trend, too, and Saint Laurent featured Courtney Love in a 2013 fashion editorial photographed by Hedi Slimane. Love styled herself in her 1990s incarnation complete with tiara, panda eyes and tattoos.

HEALTH GOTH

PORTLAND
COUNTRY USA
DECADE OF ORIGIN 2010s

Portland has a history of micro-communities, including an important hardcore punk and indie music scene in the early 1980s. In 2013 an esoteric example was created via a Facebook page set up by the hi-tech R&B duo Mike Grabarek and Jeremy Scott (aka Magic Fades) with artist Chris Cantino. They proceeded to upload a selection of images with an aesthetic described by Wyatt Schaffner on the website of AMDiscs as an 'anti-nostalgic dystopian present'. In an interview for the online magazine *Complex* in 2014, Grabarek and Scott described their keywords as 'mesh, moisture-wicking fabrics,

BioWare, body enhancement tech, prosthetics, shoe dipping, various fashion and performance wear brands, transparent clothing, chains and light weaponry, tactical gear, elemental aesthetics, corporal modification, and rendered environments'. Fashion images included combat gear and monochromatic or clear-shell hi-tech performance sportswear from Hood By Air (see ghetto goth, page 88), British menswear brand Cottweiler, the 'future-forward urban wear' of Whatever 21 (a health goth take on Forever 21) and A D Y N (whose name is a stylized acronym of 'androgynous'). These labels shared

1 & 2 Sandro Dal Bianco captures the futuristic health goth aesthetic in his images of urban streetwear.   3 & 4 Nasir Mazhar's S/S 2016 collection plays with sportswear references to accentuate masculinity.

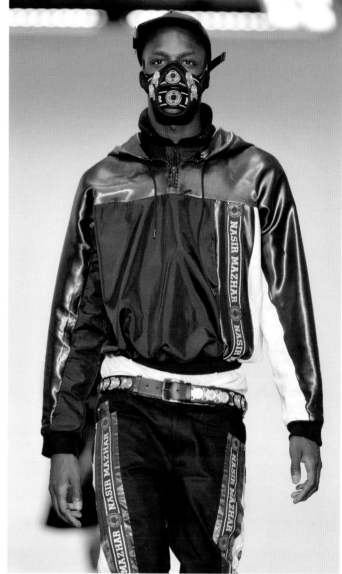

a vision: to create a form of fashion that rejected the nostalgia of retro styles and the ironic referencing of the hipster (see page 192).

The term 'health goth' was used to describe the overall online aesthetic, but the style could also be found in Portland's underground, most notably at Club Chemtrail, a rave run by resident DJs SPF666 and Massacooramaan, both with a background in the city's punk (see page 360), squatting and DIY movements. Its online presence was also given a fillip by Johnny Love's healthgoth.com, a site that encourages fitness and healthy eating within the goth (see page 164) community.

Love says, 'Clothes fit and look best on a well-maintained body; no one wants to see a Grover belly poking through your Under Armour compression shirt. After your body is right then you can swaddle it in all the semi-futuristic, minimal, monochrome sportswear you desire, and then it'll look good.' In his erudite analysis of health goth for online magazine *The Fader*, underground music critic Adam Harper responded, 'It seems to me that saying that health goth is gymming for goths is like saying that cyberpunk is Johnny Rotten doing spreadsheets on a Dell.'

SAN FRANCISCO

From its lawless days as a frontier town to its deification as the site of the 1967 Summer of Love (see image 1), San Francisco has always been the bohemian heart of the United States. The area's original inhabitants were the Yelamu, a branch of the Ohlone people who lived in tribal groups and moved seasonally around the huge natural harbour of the Bay, hunting, foraging and, according to one of their songs, 'dancing on the brink of the world'. In 1774 Juan Bautista de Anza became the first explorer to find an overland route from Mexico to the Pacific Coast of California, where he established a Spanish mission in 1775 with an anchorage at Yerba Buena Cove, enabling ships to land and trade safely. In 1846 naval captain James B Montgomery declared Yerba Buena to be US territory, and its name was changed to San Francisco a year later.

San Francisco's fortunes were transformed by the construction of the Central Pacific Railroad and the population rapidly increased until 1906, when the city was decimated by a huge earthquake that killed three thousand of its inhabitants (see image 2). There was a rapid rebuilding programme that continued into the 1930s with the construction of the spectacular Golden Gate Bridge, and the city became a centre for war production and the embarkation of troops during World War II. San Francisco's booming economy, reputation as a union town that stood for workers' rights and decent wages, and general air of liberalism persuaded many to move there. African-Americans, beatniks, homosexuals, hippies and students breathed life into areas of the city such as Fillmore, the home of bebop and pool hustlers, Haight-Ashbury, the hippy hang-out, and Castro, an increasingly gentrified area that became the focus of a collective affirmation of gay culture (see image 3), as immortalized in the novels of Armistead Maupin. The City Lights Bookstore (see image 4) at North Beach, founded in 1953 by Lawrence Ferlinghetti and Peter D Martin, became a literary hang-out for Beat pioneers including Jack Kerouac and Allen Ginsberg. After Ferlinghetti heard Ginsberg's first public reading of 'Howl' on October 1955 at the Six

Gallery in North Beach, City Lights published the poem. The ensuing obscenity trial, which the proprietors successfully defended, brought the San Francisco Beat Movement into the national spotlight, inspiring artists and writers to hitch their way to the West Coast.

In the 1960s the run-down Haight-Ashbury district (see image 5) began to transform after the San Francisco State College moved its campus to the coast. Students colonized the area, taking advantage of its cheap rents and substantial Victorian houses. In 1966 brothers Ron and Jay Thelin opened the Psychedelic Shop on Haight Street, which was swiftly followed by boutiques and head shops catering to the counter-cultural crowd. Haight-Ashbury, or 'Hashbury' as it began to be known, became the go-to destination for Janis Joplin, Timothy Leary and George Harrison of The Beatles, and all those seeking enlightenment in the war against the 'uptight' of the suburban United States. Haight became a hippy Mecca of head shops selling roach clips and hash pipes, the headquarters of the underground newspaper the *San Francisco Oracle* and home of The Free Store run by The Diggers (aka The Free City Collective). The Diggers, named after a group of 17th-century peasant revolutionaries, were committed to 'non-violent anarchy' and communal ownership. The global success of Scott McKenzie's 1967 psychedelic ode to flower power, 'San Francisco

(Be Sure to Wear Flowers in your Hair)' made the district the first stop on the West Coast tourist trail and Gray Line began running tour buses advertising their Hippie Hop Stop as 'a safari through Psychedelphia'.

The Gay Liberation Movement of the 1970s was a political force that shaped the city and the first openly gay public official, Harvey Milk – affectionately known as the Mayor of Castro Street – was elected in 1977. After his and Mayor George Moscone's assassination by Dan White in 1978, thousands marched to City Hall in a silent candlelight vigil led by Joan Baez singing 'Amazing Grace'.

Rock group Jefferson Airplane hailed from San Francisco, as did Grateful Dead founder Jerry Garcia, who grew up in the city's Mission District. During the 1970s and 1980s San Francisco became a major focal point in the North American and international punk (see page 360) scene, as chronicled in *Search & Destroy* magazine. The front man of the Dead Kennedys, Jello Biafra, famously ran for city mayor in 1979 coming fourth out of a field of ten with 6,591 votes on a ticket that promised to ban cars citywide and to require businessmen to wear clown suits within city limits. In 1991 queercore band Pansy Division was formed in the city by Jon Ginoli to confront the stereotypical view that as an openly gay man he was expected to love show tunes rather than 'The Ramones, Buzzcocks and early Beatles' songs'.

HELLS ANGEL

SAN FRANCISCO
COUNTRY USA
DECADE OF ORIGIN 1940s

In 1948 the first Hells Angels Motorcycle Club, named after a US World War II fighter squadron, was founded in Fontana, San Bernardino County. California became the centre of a network of clubs that moved beyond the boundaries of the state, into Auckland, New Zealand, in 1961 and London in 1969. The 1960s was a significant decade in the United States, as traditional values and modes of social behaviour were rejected by the young. Rebellious identities challenged suburban life and the black leather jacket marked the outlaw, an outsider who was tearing up the rules. Originally derived from the uniform of military aviators in World War I, the black leather jacket – a cut-down version of the full-skirted fleece-lined leather coat – was first sported by roustabouts, longshoremen and construction workers in the 1920s and Hells Angels in the 1950s. The jackets of full members were decorated with the Hells Angel death's head logo, the words 'Hells Angels' on the top rocker (patch) and the

1 The Devil's Henchmen motorbike gang.
2 The black leather jacket has moved from the street to high fashion. 3 The death's head motif and black leather are paired with sheepskin. 4 Blogger Paul Conrad Schneider layers black leather with high fashion items.

5 Model Stella Maxwell wears a modern take on the leather jacket, here studded with silver and gold in 2016. **6** Marlon Brando as Johnny in *The Wild One* (1953) made a profound impact on teenagers across the world. **7** A modern Hells Angel wears a leather vest.

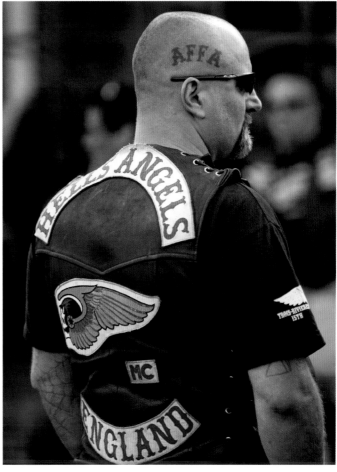

location of the club on the lower rocker. The number 81 was also used – 'h' is the eighth number of the alphabet and 'a' is the first. According to Angel lore, the desecration of these 'colours' is punishable by death. The original Angels inspired a generation of teenage rebels when their subcultural uniform was worn by Marlon Brando as juvenile delinquent Johnny in *The Wild One* (1953). In the film's most famous exchange, Brando is asked, 'What are you rebelling against, Johnny?' and in reply he drawls, 'Whaddaya got?'

In 1965 *Life* photographer Bill Ray spent several weeks on the road photographing the Angels, describing them as 'a new breed of rebel. They didn't have jobs. They absolutely despised everything that most Americans value and strive for – stability, security. They rode their bikes, hung out at bars for days at a time, fought with anyone who messed with them. They were self-contained, with their own set of rules, their own code of behaviour. It was extraordinary to be around.' The rebellious nature of the Hells Angel fitted perfectly with the counter-culture of San Francisco's Haight-Ashbury. Despite their differing stances on the Vietnam War and the bikers' capacity for violence, hippies and Hells Angels gravitated towards each other. In 1965 psychedelic pioneer Ken Kesey invited the local chapter to his ranch in La Honda, California, an event described by 'gonzo' journalist Hunter S Thompson in *Hell's Angels: A Strange and Terrible Saga of the Outlaw Motorcycle Gangs* (1966), Tom Wolfe in *The Electric Kool-Aid Acid Test* (1968), and Allen Ginsberg in the poem 'First Party at Ken Kesey's with Hell's Angels' (1965).

Today, Hells Angels chapters have a justified reputation for extremism and violence, but still assume a romantic outlaw status in culture. This image has inspired everything from TV series such as *Sons of Anarchy* (2008–14), with its depiction of an outlaw motorcycle club, to designers such as Alexander McQueen, who in 2010 was successfully sued by the Hells Angel Motorcycle Corporation for copyright infringement after using the winged death's head logo.

DEADHEAD

SAN FRANCISCO
COUNTRY USA
DECADE OF ORIGIN 1960s

In 1971 a sleeve note appeared on the cover of the Grateful Dead's second live album (*Grateful Dead*), reading, 'DEAD FREAKS UNITE: Who are you? How are you? Send us your name and address and we'll keep you informed.' The return address was a PO Box in California under the name 'deadheads', a moniker that was taken up by the fans of the psychedelic rock band.

The most committed deadheads chose a nomadic lifestyle, moving from venue to venue, and by the 1980s had created their own 'car park' community where bootleg tapes were shared and stalls set up on 'Shakedown Street' to sell vegetarian food, ethnic jewellery and distinctive tie-dye clothing. American academic Robert Sardiello, who

Dana Suchow, @DoTheHotpants, www.DoTheHotpants.com

studied deadheads over a number of years, observed that 'the larger the scale of production and distribution, the less it is tolerated in deadhead subculture. This became evident at a concert in 1989, when a vendor was seen using a credit card machine to sell clothing. A nearby vendor became irate, shouting that this was not a deadhead and that this was a violation of community norms. He then proceeded to smash the credit card machine on the ground.' The anti-consumerist ethic of the deadheads was endorsed by the band itself, which openly allowed the taping of concerts; in 1971 The First Free Underground Grateful Dead Tape Exchange was set up by Les Kippel (later founder of *Relix* magazine) as a means of circulating concert tapes. The band also inspired a religion – the Church of Unlimited Devotion – which was formed by a deadhead subgroup known as 'the Spinners' or 'the Family', who used the Grateful Dead's music in their services and spun in ecstasy during the band's live performances.

Deadhead style reflects Grateful Dead's hippy and psychedelic heritage in the Haight-Ashbury area of San Francisco in the 1960s, and features long hair for both men and women and tie-dyed clothing that uses rainbow spiral effects and motifs such as hearts and peace signs. The 'stealie' logo – which appeared on the cover art for the 1976 live album *Steal Your Face* – features regularly, and consists of a red-and-blue skull containing a lightning bolt.

PSYCHEDELIC

In 1964 writer Ken Kesey and his band of Merry Pranksters set off across the United States in a hand-painted bus, initiating passers-by into the psychological benefits of LSD. Kesey presaged the work of Timothy Leary, an academic and drug advocate who, in 1967, exhorted an audience of thirty thousand hippies at San Francisco's Human Be-In to 'turn on, tune in and drop out'. As he put it, 'a psychedelic experience is a journey to new realms of consciousness'. Psychedelia was the name given to the visual effects of LSD on the human brain and the melting, folding shapes owed much to the laudanum-induced fantasies of Art Nouveau. The psychedelic or 'acid' colour palette was intense, incorporating vivid pink, searing yellow and lime green, and was given a brash modernity through its inclusion in 1960s mod styles (see page 112) and Op art by London's New Psychedelics, and later by the Paisley Underground of Los Angeles in the 1980s. In the 2000s, Psy-trance, a form of rhythmic, electronic dance music synthesizing sounds from traditional instruments, used a combination of cosmic and psychedelic elements in its light shows and artwork.

The communal nature of psychedelic counter-culture found expression in the 'happening', a spontaneous event featuring live music, a light show and performance art. The concept was spearheaded in London by photographer John Hopkins, whose UFO Club of 1966 featured Pink Floyd and Soft Machine. The audience was encouraged to become a spirited participant in the act of artistic creativity. This same philosophy underpins many of today's festivals, including Burning Man, a huge celebration of alternative culture that

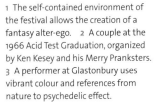

1 The self-contained environment of the festival allows the creation of a fantasy alter-ego. 2 A couple at the 1966 Acid Test Graduation, organized by Ken Kesey and his Merry Pranksters. 3 A performer at Glastonbury uses vibrant colour and references from nature to psychedelic effect.

4 Singer Paloma Faith in a contemporary version of psychedelic fashion.   5 Icelandic singer Bjork is renowned for her avant-garde stage outfits.   6 A Burner outfit with a cinematic 'warrior queen' feel.

takes place in a petrified lakebed known as the 'playa' in the middle of the Nevada Desert. San Francisco holds a Gathering of the Tribes Festival, a one-day psychedelic happening and Glastonbury Festival in Somerset, UK, has evolved from a free gathering to a huge performing arts festival attracting international headline acts. Festival outfits are prepared in advance and the enclosed environment allows the creation of fantasy personas. At Burning Man, tutus, top hats and fibre-optic accessories are favourites, along with utilitarian boots and goggles to protect the eyes from the sandstorms. Participants – known as 'Burners' – view the event as one of the world's biggest and most inventive costume parties, many sourcing their outfits from San

Francisco's hippy district of Haight-Ashbury. The Piedmont Boutique (aka the Burner Store) is one of the most popular, established in 1972 in Castro before moving to Haight-Ashbury in 1981. Designer Mary Hogue at Praxis on 24th Street makes one-off costumes for Burners and says they have to 'be comfortable to wear in either the heat or the cold'. Another criterion for the festival is that clothes do not shed detritus or MOOP (matter out of place) in the form of feathers, or sequins in particular. Jesseca Diskobaal of Sea Dragon Studio, who specializes in handmade Burner wear, has solved the problem by using her signature holographic Lycra that 'lights up the night and flashes with the brightness of a thousand suns by day'.

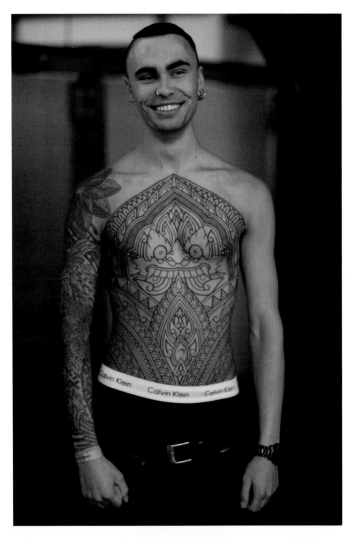

MODERN PRIMITIVE

San Francisco has always been a breeding ground for nonconformity and rebellion, an important centre of dissent, counter-culture and bohemian communities. In 1989 RE/Search publications released the book *Modern Primitives*, introducing the tattooed, pierced, branded and scarified modern primitives of San Francisco, a disparate group of body modification and S&M enthusiasts whose mouthpiece was body artist Fakir Musafar. Musafar coined the term 'modern primitive' in 1979, using it to describe a 'non-tribal' person who responds to 'primal urges and does something to the body'. His 1970s mash-up of all things 'primitive' included Maori tattoos, Native American flesh-hanging and the stretched necks of the Padung women of Thailand, and his thesis contended that by indulging in such practices one could achieve a form of spiritual enlightenment and self-discovery. Tattooing and piercing parties were held by fans such as Hollywood businessman Doug Malloy (born Richard Simonton), where 'body play' was encouraged under Musafar's direction.

Musafar aside, San Francisco already had a reputation as a port city of celebrated tattooists, such as 'Brooklyn Joe' Lieber who had a roster of naval, maritime and working-class clients. In 1974, Don Ed Hardy, a print-making graduate from the San Francisco Art Institute, opened his first studio, Realistic Tattoo. He followed it in 1977 with Tattoo City in the Mission District, which specialized in Chicano work. Around the same time Lyle Tuttle crested the wave of the hippy movement in the city with his peace and yin-yang symbols and dolphin and butterfly ankle tattoos, introducing a middle-class, female audience to the formerly macho world of the tattoo.

The post-hippy sensibility of the city fostered experimentation with identity and a rejection of consumer culture. As San Francisico's modern primitive looked, like the hippy, to world culture for inspiration, their romanticized espousal of all things 'tribal' began to flood into the mainstream. Today all forms of piercing, even dermal punching, have become accepted practices evoking little comment and tattoos can be seen on every high street.

1 The word 'tattoo' derives from the Tahitian 'tatu', meaning 'to mark something'. The earliest tattoos date back to ancient Egypt.   2 A tattoo artist at the London Tattoo Convention in 2016.
3 A contemporary modern primitive with a bifurcated or split tongue. Tongue splitting is a ritualistic practice in many tribal societies.

SCRAPER BIKER

'I've seen homicides, I've seen dead bodies on the curb, I've seen people die in front of my own eyes in the hood I'm only 21 years old...Oakland's no joke, you definitely learn how to stand your ground early, it's crazy.'
– Tyrone 'Babye Champ' Stevenson (aka The Original Scraper Bike King)

East Oakland was the centre of car production in Northern California and home to a number of light industries. The closure of two car factories in the 1960s meant that the area became increasingly deindustrialized, ending up as the poorest neighbourhood of the city. Like Compton, East Oakland became an important hip hop location, producing rap artists Too Short, MC Hammer and Keak da Sneak as well as its own distinctive addition to the gangsta rap genre, 'Hyphy' or Hyper-Fly. The scraper bike movement evolved in response to gang culture, to give young people a more positive peer group and a sense of community. Tyrone Stevenson, founder of The Original Scraper Bike Team, believes that by building bikes 'kids feel they're part of something – two hours off the streets can save their lives'. Following the traditions of scraper car customization – so called because the modified rims are so big they scrape against the wheel walls – scraper bikers refurbish old bike frames using cardboard, paint and tin foil to mimic chrome plating. Materials are cheap, disposable and close to hand, and include duct tape and colourful Skittles and Oreos wrappers that, when wrapped around the spokes, create patterns when the wheel spins. 'Put the correct material on the spokes, spray your bike a beautiful colour, something that means something to you in a decorative way,' says Stevenson. 'That makes you a scraper biker.'

1–4 The Original Scraper Bike Team pose with their creations. The movement went viral in 2007 with the YouTube music video 'Scraper Bike' by rap group Trunk Boiz.

LOS ANGELES

'Ask anyone in California where the craziest people live and they'll say Los Angeles.' — Joni Mitchell

From the hippies of Laurel Canyon in the 1960s through to the rappers of Compton in the 1980s and the grunge excesses of the Viper Room in the 1990s, Los Angeles has been a crucial centre of counter-cultural activity, with grit running counter to the constructed glamour of Hollywood. The nascent city of El Pueblo de Nuestra Señora la Reiná de los Angeles was founded in 1781 under the Spanish governance of Felipe de Neve. After Mexico's independence from Spain, the settlement remained a trading post until 1848 when it was ceded to the United States. The Californian Gold Rush drew prospectors to the area, as well as large numbers of African-Americans after the Civil War. The discovery of oil in 1892 created a boom that was augmented with the development of the film industry in the early 20th century.

By the 1920s Hollywood was the centre of a fully fledged motion picture industry, a dream factory where fashionable glamour was kick-started and codified. The original blonde bombshell Jean Harlow seduced audiences in her tight white bias-cut satin dress and marabou mules; the beret and trench coat sported by Greta Garbo was widely copied; and the black veil and coq feathers of Marlene Dietrich (see image 1) framed her as an exotic hothouse flower in a smoke-filled Berlin cabaret.

Women revelled in such powerfully sexy imagery at a time of economic chaos and, as the Great Depression made every day a grim fight for economic survival, many took refuge in the aspirational fashion flickering across the silver screen. The media gave fans every opportunity to feast on the details of their favourite star's latest outfit, created by designers such as Gilbert Adrian and Edith Head.

Outside of mainstream fashion the city's original inhabitants clung to their cultural identity through significant street styles. The pachuco (see page 60) expressed pride in their Mexican identity with the use of the zoot suit and Los Angeles was the centre of the Zoot Suit riots

of 1943. The figure of the pachuco became a focus of the moral panic surrounding youth delinquency after the Sleepy Lagoon case of 1942, in which a young pachuco was killed in a gang-related incident.

Mexican-American gangs began to form in East Los Angeles during this decade as a form of protection against prejudice fuelled by sensationalist reports of gang activity in the press. One of the first, Cerca Blanca (White Fence), was set up expressly as protection for junior high school students from Boyle Heights who were being assaulted by kids from other neighbourhoods. Rivalries developed with other gangs, including Primera Flats, Varrio Nuevo Estrada and El Hoyo Maravilla, which became the cradle of the cholo/chola (see page 44) and the *vata loco* or 'crazy dude' of the barrios.

African-American gangs such as the Crips and Bloods in South Central Los Angeles followed a similar trajectory, formed in response to their alienation from mainstream society and as a means of protection for the community. By 1980, it was estimated that there were around fifteen thousand Crips and Bloods gang members in the Los Angeles area. Hip hop and gangsta rap provided the background music to life in the ghetto, with lyrics describing the constant threat of police brutality that exploded into the South Central Riots of 1992 after members of the LAPD were acquitted of the beating of Rodney King.

Musicians have always been drawn to Los Angeles. There was a thriving jazz scene in the 1930s; in the 1960s the surf sound of the Beach Boys and the production of Phil Spector challenged the dominance of New York. Clubs like Whisky a Go Go opened on Sunset Strip in West Hollywood, showcasing female disc jockey Rhonda Lane who spun vinyl from a suspended cage while dancing to the music, starting the worldwide craze of 'go-go' dancing. The West Coast folk scene emerged at the Troubadour, where Jackson Browne, Neil Young and Joni Mitchell performed. In the 1980s the nascent punk scene (see page 360) found a natural home on Melrose Avenue (see image 2) – a thoroughfare that stretched from Fairfax to La Brea, filled with vintage fashion at Flip and Aardvark's and vinyl at Aron's Records – which attracted swing kids (see page 40) and rockabillies (see page 50), punks (see image 3) and poseurs. Its reputation for avant-garde fashion increased after fashion designer Betsey Johnson opened a store in the early 1980s, supporting the street's growing global reputation as a prime indie shopping location. Today celebrities such as Kim Kardashian and Kanye West may be the dominant influence on mainstream Los Angeles style, but vernacular street fashion remains enmeshed with the counter-culture of the city, helping to create a sense of community and social adhesion in an increasingly fragmented world.

SWING KID

The 'summer of swing' in 1998 was the high point of the neo-swing revival that followed the release of *Swing Kids* (1993), a film about a group of jazz enthusiasts in Nazi Germany who thrived despite the restrictions set by a totalitarian regime, and *Swingers* (1996), a comedy directed by Doug Liman and set in the neo-swing 'cocktail culture' of Los Angeles. The latter movie featured a complex tracking shot filmed at The Derby, a swing bar on Los Feliz Boulevard in the former Brown Derby Restaurant building where enthusiasts danced to the sound of the Royal Crown Revue, Big Bad Voodoo Daddy and the Squirrel Nut Zippers while dressed to the nines in vintage threads.

At the height of grunge (see page 16), the ultimate in 'dressed-down' street styles, many young Los Angelites rejected its downbeat, informal, androgynous look and scoured the thrift stores of Melrose Place and suburban garage sales for high-waisted zoot suits, flip skirts, 1940s shirt-waisters, Bleyer shoes and Keds sneakers, anticipating the huge post-millennium trend for nostalgia. Labels were set up to cater to the swing enthusiast, including reVamp and Daddy-O's.

Swing or big band music, a popular derivation of jazz, was at its height from 1935 to 1946 and featured soloists accompanied by strong brass and rhythm sections under the leadership of musicians such as

3 Swing kids choose 1940s-inspired styles, either vintage or reproduction, worn with flat shoes for dancing.   4 Clothes are chosen for functionality as well as style.

Benny Goodman, Count Basie, Glenn Miller and Artie Shaw. Count Basie, in particular, was known for his sharp suits and spectator shoes by Stacy Adams – a company founded in 1875, who created the classic Dayton Spectator using combinations of shiny red or black patent leather on a white leather upper, which is still available today. The spectator shoe was perfect for pulling the focus in on dancing feet when worn on screen by Fred Astaire, and its long-standing relationship with dance made it the perfect shoe for the Lindy Hop. This spectacular style of dance evolved from Harlem in the 1920s as a mix of jazz, tap, hop and Charleston, becoming a partner dance in the early days of swing and incorporating acrobatic moves such as air steps in which the partner's feet leave the ground. In interwar Germany the officials of the National Socialist Party stared aghast at

hundreds of swing kids dancing up-tempo; one Hitler Youth description of 1940 read, 'the scenes that happened on the dance floor were fit for a lunatic asylum. Even the most hysterical and primitive Black jungle warrior war-dance would have paled in comparison to what happened here. Everyone jumped about like crazy while they mumbled English musical gibberish.'

Today at swing clubs such as Maxwell DeMille's Cicada Club, Rusty's Rhythm Club and the Lindy Loft, clothing is chosen for its revivalist aesthetic and fitness for dancing. Loose garments and practical footwear define the swing style, with baggy shirts, braces and trousers for men and puff-sleeved, shirred or printed dresses in synthetic rayon for women, plus 1940s-revival hairstyles such as the Victory Roll, where the hair is 'rolled' back from the face.

CHOLA

LOS ANGELES
COUNTRY USA
DECADE OF ORIGIN 1960s

The word 'chola' is popularly believed to be derived from Xolotl (pronounced 'cholotl'), an ancient Aztec god with a dog's head and reversed feet who guided the dead to the underworld. When Spain conquered the Aztec empire in the 1520s, all children born with mixed Spanish and Amerindian heritage were referred to by the insulting *xolo* ('cholo'), or 'dog'. In the early 20th century, the federal government of the United States, together with several railroad companies, encouraged the mass migration of Mexican workers to provide a source of cheap labour. The pejorative term 'cholo' began to be used to describe migrants who were forced to live in some of the poorest areas of Los Angeles, which were dubbed the 'cholo courts'.

1 Chola style has a tough urban glamour. 2 Tattoo artist Mike Giant documents chola street fashion and how the tattoo celebrates Latina pride. 3 Mexican girl gang members in East Los Angeles, 1983. 4 The cholo, or male equivalent of the chola, in trademark baggy Dickies and 'wifebeater' vests.

In the 1960s, the Chicano Movement, led by former zoot suiter (see page 60) and civil rights activist Cesar Chavez, reclaimed the word 'cholo' (and its female equivalent 'chola'), and gangs known as 'la vida loca' began to appropriate and distort traditional Ivy League style by wearing white vests under oversized Pendleton shirts and baggy Dickies chinos. A wave of Latino gangster movies set in Los Angeles, including *Walk Proud* (1979) and *Boulevard Nights* (1979), introduced a wider audience to Mexican-American street culture.

The chola finally took centre stage in *Mi Vida Loca* (1993), set in Echo Park, Los Angeles. It starred Seidy Lopez as Mousie and Angel Aviles as Sad Girl, and also featured Salma Hayek, in her big screen debut. The chola look combined finely arched, or 'Sharpie', eyebrows, dark lips and high hair with the cholo's oversized workwear, resulting in a hugely influential subcultural style. The chola's urban glamour – all hair-sprayed bangs, heavily defined eye and lip-liner, and huge gold hoop earrings – continues to make some of the most socially disadvantaged teens stand out from the crowd.

For both the chola and the cholo, tattoos play an important role in defining their style. The tattoos often celebrate the wearer's pride in their Mexican heritage, and designs can include the geographic shape of a home state, such as Michoacán, Oaxaca or Sonora, combined with a family name or crest and Roman Catholic iconography, including the sacred heart and the revered Virgin of Guadalupe.

LOS ANGELES
COUNTRY USA
DECADE OF ORIGIN 1980s

1 Compton's NWA present a more 'authentic' image.
2 Commuters in the oversized clothing of gangsta rap.
3 Public Enemy wear monochrome outfits to deride bling.

GANGSTA RAPPER

African-American music has a tradition of subversion. Sociologist Michael Brake describes how the migration of black people to cities in the north and west of the United States brought blues, jazz and gospel, adding that 'The music was never respectable, played as it was in bars, brothels and honky tonks, but it spoke of love, the battle of the sexes, gambling and the raw poverty of the big city.' Gangsta rap, formerly known as 'reality rap', forms part of this tradition, its lyrics and braggadocio stance a testament to life in the ghetto and the brutality of the powers that be. Eazy-E's Los Angeles-based group NWA (Niggaz With Attitude) reported with deadly accuracy on life and violent crime in the hood, and their song 'Gangsta Gangsta' (1988) gave rise to the genre's name. The cathartic rap of their double-platinum album *Straight Outta Compton* (1988) pushed the genre into the mainstream. As Ice Cube put it, '[we] deal with reality. Violence is reality; you're supposed to picture life as a bowl of cherries, but it's not. So we don't do nothin' fake.'

The style of the gangsta rapper followed the same path of authenticity, deliberately veering away from the conspicuous consumption of New York hip hop. Gangsta rappers believed that the B-Boys' obsession with materialism in the form of 'bling' and designer labels (see page 86) made black youth ignore the political nature of their oppression. Chuck D of Public Enemy made this clear, saying 'Man I work at McDonald's, but in order for me to feel good about myself I got to get a gold chain.' NWA's Dr Dre, Eazy-E, Ice Cube, MC Ren and DJ Yella wore all-black outfits, black shades and Starter script snapback hats with white Converse sneakers. The crew ignored designer labels in favour of logos denoting their local sports teams,

including the LA Raiders. Snoop Dogg, a former supermarket grocery bagger turned rapper, wore oversized LA Kings ice hockey gear. In 2010 Ice Cube described how 'we felt we needed to look like we belonged together. We decided we're not dressing alike but we'll at least wear the same colour. So we picked black.'

The oversizing of gangsta clothing had two origins. The style already had street credibility because of its associations with the neighbourhood cholo gangs who wore baggy Dickies chinos and 'wifebeater' vests (see page 44), a look that was worn by Snoop Dogg. Baggy low-slung jeans also made explicit reference to Californian prison dress at a time of so-called 'penitentiary culture', when huge numbers of young African-Americans were being incarcerated for drug offences in a police crackdown. Belts and shoelaces were banned from prison-issue uniforms because of their use as potential weapons or instruments of suicide, leading to the so-called 'sag' in the trousers. The oversized white T-shirt worn by gangsta rappers also refers to the prison-issue shirt of the penitentiary.

4 Rapper Roots Manuva wears the oversized style of gangsta rap that references penitentiary culture (1996). 5 Kanye West's athleisure label Yeezy plays with proportion in this look for S/S 2017. 6 Japanese streetwear brand A Bathing Ape has become synonymous with hip hop and gangsta rap style.

PSYCHOBILLY

Psychobilly mixes rockabilly (see page 54) with punk (see page 360) and is generally credited to have emerged in the early 1980s with two bands: The Cramps and The Meteors. US musicians Lux Interior and Poison Ivy created The Cramps out of their love of B-movie voodoo and garage rock, taking the name for their mutated musical style from the lyrics of Johnny Cash's song 'One Piece at a Time' (1976), in which he narrates the tale of a factory worker who steals parts of a car 'one piece at a time' to build a 'psychobilly Cadillac'. In London, The Meteors and the Guana Batz headed a rockabilly revival that was taking place at Klub Foot, a club night held at The Clarendon public house in Hammersmith. The Meteors' 1981 album *In Heaven* featured many of the stylistic elements that feature in psychobilly today, including the distinctive 'slapped' bass and macabre lyrics and imagery.

Psychobilly style morphs rockabilly and punk most obviously in the towering and vividly coloured pompadour/Mohican hybrid hairstyle, which is teamed with biker jackets, cuffed jeans and 1950s-style brothel creepers. Female aficionados make reference to a hardcore version of the pin-up, most notably 1950s 'cheesecake' turned fetish model Bettie Page, whose coal-black hair with high fringe is much copied.

Los Angeles has an important psychobilly subculture, with bands Nekromantix and HorrorPops heading up the scene. Psychobillies tap into the city's history of low-budget movies and Tiki, a 'lowbrow' visual style that originated in 1934 when the Polynesian-themed bar and restaurant Don the Beachcomber was opened in Hollywood by former bootlegger Ernest Raymond Beaumont Gantt. In the years following World War II, returning GIs brought back souvenirs of the South Pacific, cheaper foreign travel opened up the islands to US tourists and Hawaii became the fiftieth state in 1959, allowing a fantasy version of Polynesian culture known as Tiki Pop to become an important element of America's popular culture. Tiki imagery features heavily in psychobilly style in the form of tattoos, T-shirt designs and graphic art that can be seen at the Psyclone Psychobilly and Rockabilly Weekender held every year in Long Beach, California, during the first week of September.

1 Psychobilly girls toughen up vintage 1950s fashion with the use of tattoos.   2 The Cramps were one of the first bands to combine punk, psychobilly and low-budget schlock horror movies.   3 A 1950s greased pompadour is worn with a black shirt.

LAS VEGAS

The small township of Las Vegas was transformed into the neon-lit desert city of today by the arrival of the railroad in 1905. Las Vegas was the last stop on the way to Goldfield, the centre of the gold strike of 1902 and at the time the largest settlement in Nevada. After the gold ran out the settlement was abandoned and the workers and miners moved from the Goldfield ghost town to Las Vegas. The first saloon bars began to open up in the designated area of Block 16 and included the Arizona Club, famed for its luxurious Western casino and working girls. The State of Nevada forbade gambling in 1910, but it continued illicitly in Las Vegas's speakeasies and illegal casinos. With illegal gambling came organized crime; the Mob saw its infrastructure as the perfect way to launder money after crackdowns on other US cities such as Chicago. The word was out – it was an 'open city' with no one gang in charge of the turf. By the time gambling was legitimized in 1931, the Mob was in control. Bootleggers Benjamin 'Bugsy' Siegel, friend of movie stars and politicians, and Meyer Lansky opened one of the first resort hotels, The Flamingo Hotel and Casino, in 1946. A year later Siegel was dead, murdered by his own syndicate because of his alleged skimming of funds during the project.

The construction of the massive Hoover Dam in 1931 created a further influx of workers who were lured to the city's casinos (see image 1) on Fremont Street, and hydroelectricity was used to power what became known as Glitter Gulch, named for its rows of neon signage (see image 2). In 1941 the infamous Strip began to emerge on a section of Route 91, 3.2km (2 miles) north of downtown Las Vegas and outside the limits of the city's jurisdiction. The first casino-motel, the El Rancho, was built in 1940 to cater to the rise in car ownership and 'auto-vacations', while the construction of huge hotel-casinos such as The Last Frontier (1942) and The Golden Nugget (1946) continued apace. The Strip's first wedding chapel, the Little Church of the West, opened in 1942 advertising quickie marriages with no blood tests, helping to add to the city's fast and loose reputation.

Casino owners knew that they needed to draw customers to the isolated desert location of Las Vegas and the lure was excess – 'whatever happens in Vegas stays in Vegas'. Casino architecture became larger than life, as opulent and excessive as a Hollywood

stage set. When The Last Frontier was remodelled as The New Frontier in 1955, it was described as having 'a lobby of black and white Italian marble, a casino carpeted in French lilac weaving so deep that sparks flew when the mauve-tinted slot machines were touched. Chandeliers in the shape of men from outer space, flying saucers and spinning planets hung from raspberry glace and daphne pink ceilings. Walls of diadem lilac and Ruby Lake magenta displayed three-dimensional amethyst murals depicting the twelve signs of the zodiac.' By the end of the decade over eight million people were visiting Las Vegas to wine, dine, gamble and listen to Rat Pack stars Frank Sinatra and Dean Martin. Marlene Dietrich made her debut at the Sahara Hotel's Congo Room in 1953 in a famed 'nude' dress by Jean Louis, made out of flesh-coloured chiffon with strategically placed beads at a cost of $8,000. The Las Vegas New Bureau publicized such star-studded events and from 1945 consolidated the city's reputation as the Entertainment Capital of the World by syndicating stories and photographs.

Glamour pervaded Las Vegas from its themed architecture to its staff tuxedos. Couples dressed for dinner to go to a supper club and

some casinos even had their own dress stores, including Fanny Soss at The Last Frontier, which sold the latest gowns from Schiaparelli and millinery by Lilly Dache, and Hazel Gay's boutique at the first racially integrated hotel-casino The Moulin Rouge. Many stores initiated the custom of all-night opening in case a wedding outfit was needed at 3am. The most famous counter-cultural boutique was Suzy Creamcheese, named after the fictional writer of a letter on the back cover of the album *Freak Out* (1966) by Frank Zappa and the Mothers of Invention, which began 'These Mothers are crazy. You can tell by their clothes. One guy wears beads and they all smell bad.' Owner Leslie Fearon, former waitress at LA's Whisky a Go Go, adopted the name for her brand of one-off show-stopping outfits worn by singers Cher and Dionne Warwick; Elvis's wife Priscilla Presley and girlfriend Linda Thompson (see image 3); and the casinos' showgirls (see image 4 and strippers. The shop had tiger-striped wallpaper and a disco ball and was so popular on Saturdays that customers queued round the block to buy hand-painted tuxedo shirts, coats of peacock feathers, crocheted minidresses and Spandex jumpsuits.

ROCKABILLY

Rockabilly began to evolve immediately after World War II as a mixture of the country-boogie of acts such as The Delmore Brothers, the hillbilly sound of Hank Williams and the over-amplified rhythm and blues of recordings by artists such as Bobby Bland and Howlin' Wolf from Sam Phillips's Memphis Recording Service. The distinctive slapped bass sound of rockabilly can be heard in the early work of the Maddox Brothers & Rose, and Bill Haley.

The term 'rockabilly' describes rock 'n' roll music with a distinctive 'jumping' beat, played by Southern 'hillbillies' – particularly the Sun Studio recordings of Carl Perkins, son of a sharecropper, and Elvis Presley. The towering giant of the idiom, Presley mixed black rhythm and blues with country and western in his first hits 'That's All Right (Mama)' and 'Blue Moon of Kentucky' (both 1954), and was an enormous influence on Buddy Holly, Jerry Lee Lewis and Gene Vincent, among others. The singer frequented a Memphis outlet called Lansky Bros, whose flashy mohair and sharkskin suits – or 'cat clothes' – were worn by an exclusively black clientele that included jazz musicians Count Basie and Duke Ellington. Presley favoured hi-boy collared shirts, peg-top trousers and black suits with pink piping, and by doing so flouted the unspoken dress codes of segregation. As he told one reporter, 'My favourite hobby is collecting these real cool outfits. I'd almost rather wear them than eat.' The Lansky style was worn by other stars, including Carl Perkins, Jerry Lee Lewis and Johnny Cash, and became synonymous with the rebellion of rock 'n' roll.

1 The Lansky Brothers clothes store at the Peabody Hotel in Memphis, Tennessee. 2 Elvis Presley was drawn to the flashy, colourful clothing at Lansky's. 3 A fan in an authentic 1950s dress at the Viva Las Vegas Rockabilly Weekend.

4 The brash glamour of female rockabilly style.
5 A rockabilly girl in a powder blue vintage car at Viva Las Vegas.   6 A sweater girl-inspired rockabilly look.

The 1970s was a decade rife with nostalgia – the hippy project was over, its dreams of peace and love shattered at the 1969 Altamont Festival with the violent death of Meredith Hunter, and many young people began to look back at a decade they had never known: the 1950s. Movies such as *American Graffiti* (1973) and the TV show *Happy Days* (1974–84) introduced a new generation to the sounds and styles of the decade, all augmented by the death of Elvis in 1977. A nascent rockabilly revival emerged in the UK, and Long Island band Stray Cats, formed in 1979, achieved mainstream success on both sides of the Atlantic before breaking up in 1983. The group's look was exaggerated – the trio wore suits in searing colours with oversized silhouettes and extreme versions of Elvis's pompadour.

Today rockabilly fashion has returned to its authentic 1950s origins. The Lansky look remains a staple among men, together with a rocker style incorporating leather jackets, rolled jeans and biker boots. Female fans favour burlesque-inspired pin-up or sweater-girl style, with peroxide or black-tinted hair, fire engine red lips and doe eyeliner paired with pencil skirts, print dresses, full-circle skirts, seamed stockings and stiletto heels. An important centre of rockabilly activity is Las Vegas – an apt location, as the city inspired a popular Presley film and hit of 1964 and was the backdrop to the singer's final concerts. The Viva Las Vegas festival, dubbed 'the world's greatest rockabilly event', is held every April and attracts over twenty thousand fans with its mix of live music, vintage fashion and classic cars.

NEW
RAVE

LAS VEGAS
COUNTRY USA
DECADE OF ORIGIN 2000s

EDM (Electronic Dance Music) – the raver's music of choice, using synthesizer sequencing, sampling and multi-track recording – had marginal appeal in the United States until the early 2000s, when the style was hijacked by mainstream artists. By 2011 *Spin* magazine was referring to 'the new rave generation' and the city of Las Vegas became one of the key places associated with the trend. Its infamous Strip is home to huge DJ-driven clubs (Calvin Harris signed a three-year residency in 2015 for a reputed $400,000 per show) and the Las Vegas Motor Speedway holds an Electric Daisy Carnival (EDC) Week every June. Dubbed the 'American Ibiza', the Electric Daisy Carnival is a huge rave that was the brainchild of Gary

1 & 3 New rave style at the Anti-Social, East London (2007).
2 New rave camouflage shows the extreme styling of the street fashion akin to performance art.   4 Editor of *SuperSuper!* magazine on the London Underground (2006).

Richards and Stephen Enos (aka DJ Steve Kool-Aid) in the early 1990s and was originally held in Los Angeles. Today its home is Las Vegas, but the concept is taking hold all over the world with EDC events being held in a range of countries including Puerto Rico and the UK.

The origins of new rave are not entirely clear but many believe that the birth of the term dates to 2005, when Joe Daniel, founder of the Angular Recording Corporation, featured the words 'New Rave' on a flyer advertising the first gig by British band the Klaxons. The band later described the movement as a 'joke that's got out of hand. The whole idea of new rave was to take the piss out of the media by making them talk about something that didn't exist, just for our own

amusement.' That being said, an influential, if niche, scene was spawned in the !WOWOW! squat parties of East London and clubs BoomBox, Kashpoint, Anti-Social and All You Can Eat. Silver hi-tops, fake fur and cartoon hoodies were documented in the pages of *SuperSuper!* magazine and on dirtydirtydancing.com. Carri Munden (aka CassettePlaya), Henry Holland and Gareth Pugh provided the catwalk version of the look.

New rave style makes overt reference to early Californian rave. Apparel includes phat pants with reflective strips and 'stash' pockets made by Los Angeles-based underground rave label Kikwear, founded in 1992, accessorized with a pacifier and the ubiquitous glowstick.

EL PASO
COUNTRY USA
DECADE OF ORIGIN 1930s

PACHUCO

The pachuco was originally an inhabitant of El Paso, Texas – aka Chucotown – a city located on the border between the United States and Mexico. 'Pachuco' is a word from Mexican Spanish Caló dialect that refers to Pachuca, a Mexican city where some of the original pachucos originated. Many moved to El Paso in the 1910s to work the mines, but later became involved in the smuggling of liquor across the border during Prohibition. One infamous gang of El Paso bootleggers developed their own secret language known as Caló, a mix of Spanish gypsy *zincaló*, Hispanicized English, Anglicized Spanish and indigenous Nahuatl that was later used as an expression of pride in a Mexican-American or Chicano identity.

The pachuco took care with his appearance and wore a tacuche, or zoot suit. Its wide, padded shoulders and longline jacket gave an exaggeratedly macho silhouette and was combined with high-waisted, wide-legged trousers that tapered at the ankle, a conspicuous key chain and a pomaded duck-tailed hairstyle. Although usually presumed to be an exclusively male style, the zoot's longline jacket and peg-topped trousers were also worn by *las pachucas*. The pachucas feminized the look with knee-length gabardine skirts and huaraches (traditional Yucatán leather sandals), teased bouffants (rumoured by the press to hide switchblades) and heavy cosmetics – a glamorous challenge to the sugar-sweet bobbysoxer.

In the 1930s and 1940s, many El Paso pachucos migrated to Los Angeles in search of employment, introducing the style into different communities. These included the 38th Street Gang, who remained marginalized and invisible to the general population until the Sleepy Lagoon Murder in 1942. The Sleepy Lagoon, a bathing hole

1 The exaggerated silhouette of the zoot suit was viewed as mocking the wartime restrictions on material.   2 Police ignored white servicemen during the Zoot Suit riots in favour of arresting those wearing zoot suits.   3 A pachuco wears his zoot suit in 2014 as a protest against the treatment of Mexican immigrants north of the border.

4 A pachuco poses in a handmade zoot suit and two-tone shoes. 5 A trio of pachucos in 2014.

in a gravel pit in the rural east of the city, was a popular meeting place for Mexicans segregated from public pools. On the evening of 1 August, the 38th Street had a face-off with a gang from Downey, after which the body of José Díaz was discovered. The ensuing police investigation implicated the gang and they were detained until they appeared in court. During the trial the Mexican-Americans were derided by the press, who used their distinctive appearance as evidence of guilt. Many were given lengthy sentences in prison and reform school until the verdict was reversed at the Court of Appeal in 1944.

The Zoot Suit riots occurred in Los Angeles in June 1943, after the pachucos defiantly resisted the austerity measures implemented by the War Production Board in 1942, which limited the use of fabric – an act that was read as a deliberate attack on the pachucos' zoot suits. They refused to cooperate and continued to have bootleg suits tailor-made, an act of defiance that was regarded as unpatriotic in a time of war. The ensuing clashes between servicemen and pachucos brought national notoriety to the latter group, not least because they were determined to look sharp not servile.

The modern pachuco and pachuca wear their suits as a symbol of pride in their national identity at important formal occasions such as proms, weddings and festivals, and as a means of protesting the treatment of Mexican immigrants. Some say the long length of the chain fob that holds their pocket watches highlights the length of time that Mexican migrants have suffered discrimination in the United States.

HOUSTON
COUNTRY USA
DECADE OF ORIGIN 1960s

1 A rally celebrates the 50th anniversary of the Hollister incident.   2 & 5 A member of the Bandidos Motorcycle Club.   3 The Ed Hardy brand is inspired by biker culture.   4 The biker's leather jacket as a street fashion staple.

BANDIDOS

The image of the rebellious biker can be traced to one significant film – *The Wild One* (1953), starring Marlon Brando as Johnny Strabler and based on a real event of 1947 when three thousand bikers held a meet in Hollister, California, and took over the town. Brando's counter-cultural uniform of rolled Levi's 501s, black leather Perfecto jacket and heavy, oil-tanned cowhide, Goodyear-welted Chippewa boots became the garb of the nonconformist. The American Motorcycle Association, keen to distance itself from the events at Hollister, declared that 'Ninety-nine per cent of motorcyclists are law-abiding citizens,' describing the remaining one per cent as 'outlaws'. Almost immediately the more rebellious bikers dubbed themselves the 'one per centers', including the Bandidos Motorcycle Club founded in 1966 by Houston docker Donald Chambers. The name came from the tough

Mexican *bandidos*, or bandits, and the club's motto ran 'We are the people our parents warned us about'. Chambers's club originally recruited members from local bars, eventually growing into a global gang of over three thousand bikers with chapters in Europe and Australia. One of the original recruits, Royce Showalter, remembers how 'Don wasn't looking for people who fit into what he called "polite society". He wanted the badass bikers who cared about nothing except riding full time on their Harley-Davidsons.' After Chambers was given a life sentence for the murder of two drug dealers who were forced to dig their own graves, the Bandidos' renegade image was complete.

Bandidos wear distinctive black leather vests customized with red-and-gold rockers (patches) that are visible from 45m (150ft). Designs include 'The Fat Mexican' worn in the centre back of the vest, a top rocker reading 'Bandidos', and a bottom rocker denoting the chapter's location. The patches are of sacred importance to a bandidos member and the loss of them is considered a disgrace. Texas is considered to be their exclusive turf, and if any club other than the bandidos wears a Texas bottom rocker they are declaring a turf war.

CHICAGO

A drought began in July 1871. By October, small fires were starting among the dry foliage, causing an understaffed fire service to worry about the fate of their wooden-framed city. The Great Fire struck Chicago on 8 October and raged for two days, silhouetting the city in a bright orange glow. Ten square kilometres (4 square miles) were razed, three hundred lives were lost and ninety thousand people were left homeless. One of Chicago's first department stores, Marshall Field's (see image 1), founded in 1852, was completely destroyed. It had been a huge success the year before when its retail and wholesale income had hit $15 million and the owners began the rebuild almost immediately. Fashion in the city started to grow alongside the new storefronts; the Carson Pirie Scott building by architect Louis Sullivan was a masterpiece of stripped-back neo-classicism, prefiguring modernism by decades and providing a landmark on State Street at the intersection of the streetcar lines.

The city's moneyed residents looked to Europe for their fashion but added the modifications necessary for Chicago's high winds and extreme winters. Chicago was a major distributor of fur and local seamstresses incorporated utilitarian touches and used tougher material when copying the latest French and English modes using patterns from *Godey's Lady's Book* and *Chicago Magazine*. Hart, Schaffner & Marx opened in 1887, starting a tradition in men's suiting (see image 2) that still exists today, and Lady Duff Gordon opened a Lucile salon selling her exquisite chiffon 'personality dresses' in the 1910s. The city also had an indigenous film industry and in 1915 actor-director Charlie Chaplin was lured to work for the Essanay Film Manufacturing Company owned by George K Spoor and Gilbert M 'Broncho Billy' Anderson. The attendant publicity helped to create Chicago's reputation as a fashionable 20th-century metropolis.

In 1928 Cole Haan, named after its founders Trafton Cole and Eddie Haan, set up in Chicago manufacturing men's footwear. Like New York's Brooks Brothers, the brand infiltrated university shops and preppies (see page 78) loved their hand-sewn penny loafers and saddle shoes. These College Joe 'sheiks', in racoon coats and slicked back hair in emulation of their idol film star Rudolph Valentino, slummed it at the Savoy Ballroom and the Regal Theater, treating their 'shebas' to an illicit flask of hooch while dancing the shimmy and the black bottom. Chicago jazz was implicit in reflecting

the excitement of the so-called 'Roaring Twenties' and the youth rebellion against the moralism of Prohibition. The most innovative jazz advancements came from the African-American citizens based in the South Side, who had moved to Chicago from the South in the Great Migration to escape the Ku Klux Klan and the Jim Crow laws that limited their freedom. The Pekin Inn cabaret club was a 1,200-seat theatre on 2700 South State Street where 'Chicago style' jazz was created by stars Louis Armstrong, Jelly Roll Morton and Earl Hines. Musical innovation continued to emerge from Chicago. In the 1970s, the first electronic drum tracks were used in music production in the city and The Warehouse opened by Robert Williams in 1977 broke down the barriers of racial and sexual segregation in club-land with its inclusive audience and diverse playlist spun and mixed by DJ Frankie Knuckles. This was the spawning ground of 1980s house and deep house, heavily influenced by European electronica.

From 1919 the Prohibition in Chicago created a city of mobsters, including the notorious Al Capone, who became the primary source of illegal alcohol. The city's gangs became a subject of academic research with Frederic Thrasher's *The Gang: A Study of 1,313 Gangs in Chicago* (1927), in which he interviewed gang members and their retinues and, in a fold-out map within the book, mapped out Gangland by delineating their territories. Thrasher wrote that Chicago is a mosaic of foreign colonies with conflicting social heritages', with 'interstitial sites' or 'spaces that intervene between one space and another'. This was where Gangland resided, out of reach of social norms in the most deprived areas of the city.

Chicago was also a place of fashion innovation: in 1893 Whitcomb L. Judson invented the zip, a revolutionary way of opening and closing clothes and accessories that was to change apparel forever; cosmetics giant Maybelline was founded by Chicago chemist Thomas Williams in 1915; and Main Rousseau Bocher (image 3), a native of the city, launched his own fashion house in Paris in 1929, becoming the first American to find success as a Parisian couturier.

Today Chicago still has its own interstitial counter-culture existing in the cracks of the city's infrastructure. Street crews or 'drifters' re-enact scenes from the *Fast and Furious* movies on Lower Wacker Drive, while nomadic crust punks led by D J Pommerville invade Wicker Park every summer to the chagrin of local residents. A more mainstream voice of Chicago youth is former fashion blogger Tavi Gevinson (image 4), named as one of the most influential teens of 2014 by *Time* magazine, whose online magazine *Rookie* gets over three million hits per month.

RIVETHEAD

CHICAGO
COUNTRY USA
DECADE OF ORIGIN 1990s

The term 'rivethead' was originally used in the 1940s to describe industrial workers involved in steel construction and airplane and car assembly. Writer Ben Hamper revived the term in his 1991 book *Rivethead: Tales From the Assembly Line*, which exposed the working practices at the General Motors assembly plant in Michigan. By 1993 the rivethead had morphed into an aficionado of industrial music, an aggressive fusion of rock and electronic with sampled mechanical noises that reflected modern warfare — in particular the Gulf War — and the oppression of man by machine. Glenn Chase, founder of Re-Constriction Records, released a compilation of North American industrial music entitled *Rivet Head Culture* in 1993, the same year in which a track called 'Rivethead' featured on the Chemlab album *Burn Out at the Hydrogen Bar*. Trent Reznor of Nine Inch Nails and

  1 The rivethead look regularly features some form of face mask.   2 A rivethead-inspired street look.   3 Los Angeles DJ and model Perish Dingham.   4 Sascha Konietzko.

Sascha Konietzko of KMFDM are also acknowledged as significant influences on the scene.

Industrial music looked to the seminal work of Genesis P-Orridge's Throbbing Gristle (Yorkshire slang for an erect penis) in the 1970s and his experimental soundscapes released on Industrial Records. The rivethead's punk (see page 360) roots are also expressed in the wearing of the Mohawk and its derivatives, including the Mohican and death-hawk. The fetish (see page 102) elements such as multi-buckles, strapped Tripp NYC trousers and studs take inspiration from fashion designer Vivienne Westwood's Bondage Collection of 1976, with its innovative mix of sadomasochistic references and military detail. References to post-apocalyptic sci-fi films such as *Mad Max* (1979), *Escape from New York* (1981) and *The Matrix* (1999) can also be

seen in the rivethead's long leather coats, BDU (battle dress uniform) army surplus or paratrooper trousers, steel-capped 18-hole Dr Marten or Grinders boots, goggles and body armour. The male look is tough and masculine, while female rivetheads add a more overt sexuality into the mix with ripped, shredded and studded post-apocalyptic body-con clothing.

It is important to recognize that the rivethead's paramilitary references are there to draw attention to tyranny rather than to celebrate it, and are worn in anticipation of the destructive effects of political oppression. In contrast, a subgenre of goth (see page 164) dubbed military goth emphasizes the more fetishistic elements of the military uniform, particularly those worn by the totalitarian regimes of the 1930s.

SEAPUNK

CHICAGO
COUNTRY USA
DECADE OF ORIGIN 2010s

'Fads swept the youth of the Sprawl at the speed of light; entire subcultures could rise overnight, thrive for a dozen weeks, and then vanish utterly.' – William Gibson, *Neuromancer* (1984)

Chicago seapunk, a micro genre invented by music producer Albert Redwine (aka DJ Ultrademon) and musician Shan Beaste (aka Zombelle), began to be talked about on the Internet in 2011 after the duo held a number of themed nights in the city. The seapunk soundtrack is a mix of 1990s house music, electro and techno with a New Age ambiance, and its accompanying GIFs, memes and Tumblr

posts conjured a utopian marine underworld of turquoise-tinged intensity mixed with retro computer graphics. Redwine described how his Brooklyn-based friend DJ Julian Foxworth (aka Lil Internet) used the hashtag '#seapunk' on Twitter because 'he had this dream about a leather punk jacket that had barnacles on it. It kind of evolved from there and seapunk was a name and a way to unify everybody.'

In fact, fashion designer Alexander McQueen had already anticipated this digital marine theme with his final collection, Plato's Atlantis (Spring/Summer 2010). The first fashion show to be screened live over the Internet, its title referred to Atlantis, the island that disappeared

1 Nixi Killick's surreal designs envision a hybrid of man and creature. 2 Killick creates a modern interpretation of the mermaid using print and experimental cutting.

3 The street fashion trend for aqua-hued hair derives from seapunk, here teamed with Miu Miu glasses in Tokyo (2016).   4 Alexander McQueen's S/S 2010 Plato's Atlantis collection.   5 & 6 Seapunk-inspired designs by Nixi Killick (NXK), an independent label based in Melbourne with the intent to establish 'a global Colourtribe'.

beneath the sea. Models walked the runway slowly, morphing from land animals to sea creatures as they adapted to their new underwater environment, wearing sculptural shapes incorporating gills and jellyfish frills in a range of aqua colours digitally printed with marine life.

By September 2011 *SuperSuper!* magazine had published the first print article on seapunk, with an essential track-list that included 'putting your ear to a seashell'. In *The New York Times*, Ben Detrick reported on Williamsburg's first Seapunk Alien Disco Indie Rave held in a warehouse in February 2012, describing twenty-somethings wearing 'T-shirts plastered with pixilated sharks, raised neon glowsticks, several mops of hair dyed blue and green'. Beaste and Redwine's roommate, digital artist Molly Soda, had a look that was widely copied – especially her signature blue hair – and by late 2012 it had been co-opted into the mainstream by singers Azealia Banks, Rihanna and Katy Perry, who dubbed her hair shade 'perrywinkle'. Many aficionados claimed this was the moment that seapunk died,

but Redwine looked at it differently, saying 'it's better to be part of something that's inspiring people in that way'. In any case, seapunk, the spawn of the Internet, was already two steps ahead, mutating into the sampled muzak and public access TV graphics-based genre vaporwave. Tame Impala, the project of Australian musician Kevin Parker, has brought elements of vaporwave into the mainstream with the album *Currents* (2015) and its accompanying psychedelic vortex graphics. Melbourne-based artist-designer, 'mutant mermaid' and self-professed 'imagineer' Nixi Killick has a background in circus performance and the arts, and uses fashion as a platform for her own vision of an optimistic utopia. As she explains, 'I'm inspired by obscure art and music references, and this conversation between nature and technology. Look at sea creatures that are changing colours and their luminescence. If you look at technologies, they are mimicking this. In the animal kingdom the visual effect is so primal. As a skin-clad human, it's about figuring out where are my peacock feathers!'

OTHERKIN

KENTUCKY
COUNTRY USA
DECADE OF ORIGIN 1990s

'The Otherkin are making a Romantic appeal for a better world and a better life.' – Nick Mamatas, 'Elven Like Me' (2001)

The Otherkin community dates back to 1990, when R'ykandar Korra'ti, a student at the University of Kentucky, founded the *Elfinkind Digest*, a mailing list for people who identified as elves. Korra'ti expected the list would be confined to the elfish community, but instead 'found a large number of people with a large number of self-identifications'. The word 'Otherkin' was used to describe these non-elf 'others' who believed their soul or spirit had an animal or mythical non-human 'otherside', and in that year the first gathering of Otherkin took place in North Carolina. In 1992 the alt.horror.werewolves site appeared online, ostensibly to discuss the representation of the werewolf in

1 A golden wolf headdress by Lupagreenwolf. 2 Scale-mail armour gauntlets in bronze anodized aluminium. 3 Scale-mail top by Silmaril. 4 A winged top incorporates the features of a bird of prey into a knitted garment.

popular culture, but in actuality a place where werewolf identifiers could congregate. Similarly, the alt.dragons community was set up in 1994 for role players before evolving into an interactive environment for humans who identify as dragons. The growth of the Otherkin community has been made possible by the Internet, with Tumblr being an important vehicle for debate and support.

Otherkin are not role playing and believe their species dysphoria to be similar to transgenderism. Dusken, an Otherkin blogger, explained in her post 'Not Human: A Primer on Otherkin' (2012)

that: 'we have phantom tails and ears and snouts and wings that are energetically there. In extreme cases one can feel them hitting objects...Another common thing is feeling the instinctual need to do things normal humans don't. Like when confronted with an enemy, the urge to snarl and snap with teeth you don't have, or a feeling of wings making you look larger when you don't have any.' The human/animal nexus has a long history in culture, from Greek mythology through to the work of fashion designer Alexander McQueen, who featured hybridity in his 1997 collection 'It's a Jungle Out There'.

JUGGALO

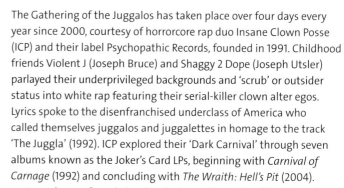

'We get one week of the year to be home.' – faygoluvers.net

The Gathering of the Juggalos has taken place over four days every year since 2000, courtesy of horrorcore rap duo Insane Clown Posse (ICP) and their label Psychopathic Records, founded in 1991. Childhood friends Violent J (Joseph Bruce) and Shaggy 2 Dope (Joseph Utsler) parlayed their underprivileged backgrounds and 'scrub' or outsider status into white rap featuring their serial-killer clown alter egos. Lyrics spoke to the disenfranchised underclass of America who called themselves juggalos and juggalettes in homage to the track 'The Juggla' (1992). ICP explored their 'Dark Carnival' through seven albums known as the Joker's Card LPs, beginning with *Carnival of Carnage* (1992) and concluding with *The Wraith: Hell's Pit* (2004).

Juggalos are fiercely loyal to their counter-cultural family and the Gathering is an alternative family reunion that first took place outdoors at Nelson Ledges Quarry Park near Garrettsville, Ohio, in 2003. Fans unite and resist mainstream culture by wearing the distinctive ICP clown face paint, using the same slang – including the characteristic 'whoop whoop' – and wearing T-shirts in black and Day-Glo green, many of which feature Hatchetman, the mascot of Psychopathic Records. His spiky plaited 'spider legs' hair is worn by both juggalos and juggalettes, as well as hardcore hip hop duo Twiztid.

Perhaps the most unusual tradition is drenching each other with Faygo, a discount soft drink. ICP throw gallons of the cheap, so-called 'ghetto pop' over the crowd when performing and the documentary *American Juggalo* (2011) opens with a shot of a juggalo with a clown face mask leering at the camera and pouring a bottle of Faygo over his head. This play with poverty – Faygo is regarded as the cheapest of brands bought only by trailer trash – allows the juggalo to wear his outsider status as a badge of pride. As Violent J explained, 'Run DMC always talked about Adidas and The Beastie Boys would mention White Castle Hamburgers in their songs. So we started mentioning Faygo, cause we always had some.'

1 Juggalos gather to see a performance by ICP at the Independent Powerhouse Tour (2016). 2 & 3 Juggalos and a juggalette with the distinctive ICP clown face paint. 4 Many juggalos plait their hair into 'spider legs' in homage to Hatchetman, the mascot of Psychopathic Records.

1 Preppy was one of the first street styles to take garments out of their usual sporting context and into fashion.   2 A classic example of the preppy look from 1953.
3 Ali MacGraw's take on preppy style was a key fashion influence in the 1970s after her appearance in the film *Love Story* (1970).

PREPPY

The term 'preppy' – originally pejorative when used to describe private preparatory school kids – was introduced in the opening exchange between Oliver and Jenny (played by Ryan O'Neal and Ali MacGraw) in the film *Love Story* (1970). The American prep school system was developed in New England in the 1880s and copied the traditional British model wherein sport – with its emphasis on fresh air and fair play – played a key part in a gentleman's education. A distinct prep school style emerged, including button-down shirts, popped-collar polos, chinos, Bass Weejuns penny loafers, boat shoes and Nantucket Reds (pink trousers), taking its cues from leisure activities such as fencing, yachting, golf and equestrianism. By wearing such garments the top-drawer students could recognize their old money WASP counterparts from the rest of the hoi polloi while manoeuvring through the upper echelons using family money and social connections.

It was a small step both socially and geographically from the Boston-based prep school to an elite Ivy League University such as Harvard, Yale or Princeton, where clothing became a clear indicator of class and social status. J. Press and Brooks Brothers became inextricably linked with preppy or collegiate style by opening outlets on East Coast campuses, and President John F Kennedy's studied casualness at the White House further popularized the look in the 1960s.

In 1949 a woman's shirt in pink was launched by Brooks Brothers as the firm realized how many female Ivy League students were wearing items of men's clothing. Pink was not a colour unknown to the company – a male shirt of the same hue had been introduced in 1900, but went largely unnoticed until women adopted it. By 1955 men had begun to wear pink Brooks Brothers shirts as a contrast with their charcoal grey sack suits, while women were now able to shop in Brooks Brothers at a counter discreetly set at the rear of the male floor. *Time* magazine described how, 'given this opening, more and more women have encroached upon the whole store, greedily discovering other items of male apparel that they can take over for themselves'.

4 Sarah Vickers wears a witty take
on preppy button-down in this white
cotton shirt dress.   5 The button-down
collar shirt and relaxed chinos are key
components of the male preppy look.
6 A chambray shirt and Gucci knit tank are
mixed with a Topshop leopard print mini
for a modern interpretation of preppy at
Milan Fashion Week 2016.

It was in 1980, however, that the preppy look became global with the publication of Lisa Birnbach's tongue-in-cheek style taxonomy, *The Official Preppy Handbook*. The book consolidated New England's sartorial aesthetic by listing its preferred clothing, including blazers, chinos, madras shorts, argyle sweaters and pastel-coloured polo shirts – cliches that were summarily dissected and democratized by fashion designers Ralph Lauren and Tommy Hilfiger. In that same decade, the notorious Lo-Life crew of Brooklyn, New York, hijacked the preppy look in a clever subversion of its signifiers of white power and conspicuous lack of marketing to minorities. As Kanye West put it in 2009, 'Ralph Lauren was borin' before I wore him.'

NEW YORK

The bright lights and economic prospects of New York City encouraged mass migration into the metropolis in the late 19th century. US farm labourers and European immigrants flocked to the increasingly overcrowded city and the miserable lives of its poorest inhabitants were described by reporter Jacob A Riis in *How the Other Half Lives: Studies Among the Tenements of New York* (1890). Riis wrote of 'dark and nameless alleys' where hordes of 'dirty children' play while 'the wolf knocks loudly at the gate'. He recognized the causal link between poverty and crime as large sections of the city came under the control of gangs, including Hell's Kitchen, home to the notorious Gophers, and Gotham Court, where the Swamp Angels operated in its sewers.

In 1920 the National Prohibition Act was passed, banning the export, import, transportation, selling and manufacture of alcohol

in an attempt to reduce crime and promote a 'moral' lifestyle. Illegal drinking went underground and speakeasies and saloon bars flourished Far from reducing crime, gangs prospered during Prohibition, bribing their way into the political system and the running of the city.

In the backstreet speakeasies, the music was jazz (see image 1) and the look was sharp. Pianist Earl Hines used his appearance as a form of showbiz advertising to get much needed work as the Great Depression loomed, while Jelly Roll Morton turned clothes into an integral part of his act – one observer noted that he would come on stage and 'take his overcoat off. It had a special lining that would catch everybody's eye. So he would turn it inside out and, instead of folding it, he would lay it lengthwise across the top of the upright piano. He would do this very slowly, very carefully and very solemnly as if the coat was worth

a fortune and had to be handled very tenderly.' Dress codes, class and ethnicity were subverted as many performers wore the clothes of the English gentleman, such as Morton's Norfolk jacket or Duke Ellington's snappy glen plaid-patterned tweed suit.

The city's sweatshops provided a cheap source of fashion for the young women who thronged the streets, described by writer Zelda Fitzgerald as 'hundreds of girls with Marcel waves, with coloured shoes and orchids, girls with pretty faces, dangling powder boxes and bracelets and lank young men from their wrists – all on their way to tea'. Zelda, wife of writer F Scott Fitzgerald, was one of the original flappers – those hard-boiled seductresses (see image 2) with a cigarette in one hand and a cocktail in the other – whose appearance on the city's streets seemed to embody fears of post-war women breaking away from their traditional domestic roles. New York journalist Brian Blixen wrote in 1923 that 'Women have resolved that they are just as good as men and intend to be treated so. They clearly mean that in the great game of sexual selection they shall no longer be forced to play the role, simulated or real, of helpless quarry.' Little did Blixen know that he was foreshadowing the attitude of more contemporary New York women, as depicted in *Sex and the City* (1998–2004; see image 3). Carrie Bradshaw *et al* negotiated the Manhattan dating scene with Manolo Blahnik heels and the Fendi Baguette bag brandished as fetish objects, conferring power and status through consumer spending.

But it was not always thus. The Greenwich Village beatniks of the 1960s (see image 4) – who rejected the conformity of the suburban 'rat race' in favour of a life lived without rules – expressed themselve with long, unkempt hair and casual clothing such as plaid shirts, jea and khakis. East Village art school hippies congregated around Andy Warhol's Exploding Plastic Inevitable wearing patched and shredded jeans, washed-out tees and sandals in a symbolic identification with poverty. The 'real' poor of the South Bronx in the 1970s did the opposite, following an African-American tradition that dated back to the Depression of always looking one's best despite hardship and displaying the symbols of affluence when no affluence was there. Fans of hip hop may have had little real economic clout, but their aspirations were writ large in thick gold chains with dollar signs, box-fresh sneakers and high-end branded sportswear.

Street fashion, art and club-life collide in the city. In 1975 fashion designer and artist Stephen Sprouse moved into the same building in the Bowery as Debbie Harry and Chris Stein, who gained fame at Max's Kansas City and CBGBs with their band Blondie. Sprouse found inspiration while wandering around the East Village or during heady drug-fuelled nights posing with the punks and provocateurs at the Mudd Club, the haunt of doomed supermodel Gia Carangi. From his silver showroom on 57th Street, Sprouse synthesized punk hip hop, the space age and Day-Glo pop into a series of inspired collections in the early 1980s, worked on the runway by transsexua model Teri Toye, the epitome of downtown cool.

FLY GIRL

Civil rights activist and poet Nikki Giovanni wrote rhymes in response to the racial politics of the United States and the assassinations of Martin Luther King Jr and Malcolm X. After the publication of *Black Feeling, Black Talk* in 1968 she became a prominent voice in the United States, using the notion of story-telling handed down from generation to generation to explore the experiences of marginalized African-American communities. Singer and poet Camille Yarbrough took a similar approach in the 1970s with her one-woman show 'Tales and Tunes of an African-American Griot' (in which she sang 'Take Yo' Praise', later sampled by Fatboy Slim in 1998 in 'Praise You'). The work of such poets influenced female rap and presaged the figure of the Fly Girl, the counterpart to hip hop's B-Boy (see page 86).

The first woman MC, Sha-Rock, emerged in 1979, the same year in which the all-female rap record 'Rhymin' and Rappin'' was released by sisters Tanya and Paulette Winley on their father's label, Paul Winley Records. The original Fly Girl look owed much to the 'fly' or chic stars of 1970s blaxploitation movies or the sportswear of the B-Boys, until rappers Salt-N-Pepa disrupted the phallocentricity of hip hop by injecting humour, colour and Afrocentricity into the style with their leather hats, asymmetrical bobs, dookie chains, Karl Kani trousers and distressed double denim designed by Christopher 'Play' Martin of Kid 'n Play. Salt-N-Pepa were also responsible for the short-lived craze of the eight-ball jacket. Originally designed by Michael Hoban for North Beach Leather *c.*1990, the jacket was fashioned from multi-coloured leather and had a distinctive cue or eight ball appliquéd on the back. Martin redesigned the eight-ball for the rappers, adding a Salt-N-Pepa logo on the sleeves, and the style took off. The shell suit was also taken up by Fly Girls, as its mix of cellulose triacetate and polyester allowed a brighter range of fabric colours than the traditional tracksuit. Salt-N-Pepa were ground-breaking for the representation of women in hip hop, while at the same time formed part of the lineage of black women blues performers who used sexually explicit and profane language to rebel against traditional codes of femininity.

1 Poet Nikki Giovanni in 1973.   2 Salt-N-Pepa in 1988.
3 Missy Elliott in androgynous logo-ed sportswear (2016).
4 & 5 Fly Girl style.

1 A teenager on 42nd Street, New York (1980).
2 A New York B-Boy in sportswear and a Kangol hat (1981).
3 Tokyo teenagers wear gang bandanas and the oversized
   sportswear of the New York B-Boy and Fly Girl.

B-BOY

The Bronx borough of New York City was once prime farming land, a bucolic backwater where New York's great families had their summer mansions away from the bustle of city life. In 1905 the subway reached the area and the borough became engulfed with streets of apartment houses filled with immigrant families from predominantly Irish, Italian and Eastern European Jewish backgrounds. During the 1950s the area was redeveloped; new highways cut through the borough and hundreds of houses were demolished to make way for public housing (known as 'the projects'). During this decade many of the original Jewish settlers moved out of the Bronx – a period known as the 'white flight' – while at the same time lower-income Puerto Rican and African-American families moved into the area's more affordable housing, creating what became stigmatized as a ghetto.

By the 1970s New York City was deep in debt; businesses in the Bronx closed and welfare cheques were frozen, leading to a rise in street crime. South Bronx became a no-go area, home to some of the most underprivileged people in the United States. This is where hip hop was born, a musical form that confronted poverty, racism and the isolation of a community, and provided a spectacular means of communication for the disenfranchised and ignored. At street parties DJs Kool Herc, Grandmaster Flash and Afrika Bambaataa hooked their sound systems up to the street lights, transforming turntables into instruments with breaks, backbeats, loops and scratches as B-Boys and Fly Girls (see page 84) breakdanced to the music. As Bambaataa declared, 'It's about survival, economics and keeping our people moving on.' B-Boy dress was functional – tracksuits liberated the body, trainers gave grip and support, and caps protected the head during spins. Yet the B-Boy was always aspirational, so designer labels conferring status entered into the mix with thick gold 'dookie ropes', as worn by Run DMC in their breakthrough hit 'My Adidas' in 1986.

1 Hood By Air's radical design concept has turned streetwear basics into luxury items.   2 Atelier MXDVS, Max Reynder's cutting-edge streetwear brand.   3 Venus X in gothic black and studded dog collar (2012).

GHETTO GOTH

Gothic tales are dark fantasies of cursed families and ruined castles, which at first glance may appear very different to hip hop's stories of life on the streets. However, academic Sean McCormick describes in his essay 'Gothic Hip Hop' the way in which 'the projects, or the immediate vicinity of the ghetto, have replaced the castle, and the reigning code of antiquity is not the barbarity of a specific family, but the prevailing social effects of slavery, discrimination and institutionalized racism'. He goes on to explain that 'Project buildings, which are only known to lower income residents who live in them, and government officials who visit them, thus become an occult location fertile for the imaginations of Gothic hip hop's poets to tell stories of murder, mayhem, and social injustice.'

The concepts of Gothic and the Fatal Man, as depicted in works such as Bram Stoker's horror novel *Dracula* (1897), were not far removed from the streets of the Bronx, and a similar link was made by New York-born DJ Venus X (Jazmin Venus Soto) when in 2009 she hosted the first GHE20G0TH1K night at a Halloween party in Brooklyn, New York. The event, initially called Deathwish, charged only a $2 entrance fee and turned into one of the city's most successful underground parties with its unusual mash-up of goth (see page 164) and industrial classics, including Siouxsie and the Banshees, alongside house, juke and reggaeton. Venus X explained that she was 'trying to redefine what goth is. If a rap song is about murder, that is pretty dark', describing her night as 'speak[ing] to the stories that people don't want to hear about – violence and struggle'.

The look, as Venus X described it, was 'morbid anime punk'. This was interpreted by her friend Shayne Oliver for his label Hood by Air, established in 2007 and funded through his DJ-ing at GHE20G0TH1K. Oliver used a monochrome mix of neoprene, nylon and leather to create a gender-fluid mix of sports, street and fetish (see page 102) fashion featuring baseball caps and oversized T-shirts bearing the company's HBA logo. Ghetto goths added occult symbols including heptagrams and third eyes, plus uncanny contact lenses in the style of those worn by South African rap-rave group Die Antwoord. Brooklyn-based designer Alyssa Thrall designed occult-inspired jewellery and clothing under the label Panda Eyes. After the style was appropriated by Rihanna (who had never attended GHE20G0TH1K) it moved underground, with Venus X tweeting in 2014 that 'if they will not accurately tell our story and let the brand grow into a worldwide alternative space for the weirdos of this generation, particularly minority youth, I [can] no longer pour all my money and time into this movement'. Today the once-cult brand Hood by Air is in the ascendant, gaining renown through the championing of Kanye West and its disruptive fashion shows-come-performance pieces designed to break down the barriers between catwalk and fashion cognoscenti.

1 A combination of baggy T-shirt and slouchy jeans at Milan Fashion Week (2014). 2 & 4 The anonymity of these looks is classic normcore. 3 Model Julia Hafstrom.

NEW YORK
COUNTRY USA
DECADE OF ORIGIN 2000s

NORMCORE

'Ardently ordinary clothes. Mall clothes. Blank clothes...[a] kind of dad-brand non-style.' — Fiona Duncan, *New York* magazine (2014)

In 2014 the debate raged over normcore, the ultimate anti-hipster street fashion. Was it a purely invented style, a satire on cool-hunting, or a spontaneous reaction to fashion's over-saturation? According to the Urban Dictionary the term was first used in 2005 in the webcomic *Templar, Arizona*, to describe a subculture 'based on conscious, artificial adoption of things that are in widespread use'. The character Cayce Pollard in William Gibson's novel *Pattern Recognition* (2003) could be another reference; she wears anonymous monochromatic clothes 'that seem to have come into the world without human intervention' because she is literally allergic to fashion. The movement began to take on a life of its own in 2013, after a report by trend-forecasters K-HOLE described normcore as 'moving away from a coolness that relies on difference to a post-authenticity coolness that opts into sameness'. After *New York Magazine*'s Fiona Duncan turned these conceptual musings into a fashion story in 2014, the look gained momentum and became a street fashion.

Whatever its roots, normcore appears to be a refreshing rejection of celebrity culture and the capitalist economics of fashion wherein clothes are thrown out for being outmoded rather than for being unfit to wear. Instead of designer duds, it's fleece, Gap cargo pants, turtleneck sweaters, tube socks, New Balance Classic 574s and baseball caps. Dressing in bland, 'boring' clothes like comedian Jerry Seinfeld — hailed as normcore's founding father — and buying own-brand clothes in multi-packs is a refusal to stand out from the crowd.

FURRY

PITTSBURGH
COUNTRY USA
DECADE OF ORIGIN 1980s

Pittsburgh is home to Anthrocon, 'the world's largest convention for those fascinated with anthropomorphics' (human-like animal characters). Five thousand members of the Furry Fandom – known as 'furries' – gather together every year at the David L. Lawrence Convention Center to celebrate their identification with animal characters from art, literature, cartoons, films and TV shows. Anthrocon's origins are in the Albany Anthrocon, a much smaller event first held in 1997, although the notion of anthropomorphics is embedded in popular culture through characters such as Br'er Rabbit and Disney animations like *The Lion King* (1994) – a film that has its own subgenre of furry fans. As chairman of Anthrocon Dr Samuel Conway (aka Uncle Kage) says, 'Cartoon characters are part of our culture; just look at advertising slogans. You've got tigers telling us what gas to buy, animals saying which cereal to eat and a talking gecko telling us what insurance to buy. It's what we're all about.'

1 Furries attend the Eurofurence Convention in Magdeburg, Germany. 2 A custom fursuit from Menagerie Workshop.
3 Furries at the screening of *Zoomania* (2016).

The first furry groups evolved out of science-fiction and comic book conventions in the 1980s before expanding online in the early 1990s with sites such as the newsgroup alt.fan.furry and the online role-playing environment FurryMUCK. There furries developed their own online animal alter egos or 'fursonas', ranging from foxes, cheetahs, rabbits and wolves to the Samurai cockroach of Uncle Kage.

At Anthrocon some participants go so far as to don full-body animal costumes or 'fursuits', custom made by designers such as Sarah Dee of Menagerie Workshop in Boulder, Colorado. Categories range from 'realistic' with moving jaws and airbrushed fur to the more cartoonish 'toony' complete with 3D 'Follow-Me' eyes. For many,

wearing a fursuit is a liberating experience, a disguise in which to explore the more playful aspects of their fursona through activities such as skritching or pseudo-grooming in a group or 'furpile'. Furry-speak is a language used by furries as a means of identification in the wider community. The New Furry's Dictionary describes how the language 'serves as a means of communication, complete with its own nuances, that more accurately relay ideas' and 'serves as a means of inclusion, and of exclusion'. It includes such terminology as 'graymuzzle', used to describe an older furry fan, and 'yiffy', used to describe the sexiness 'of either an anthropomorphic character, or the real-life attribute of a fellow fandom affiliate'.

STRAIGHT EDGE

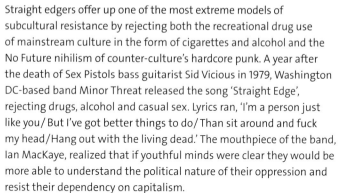

Straight edgers offer up one of the most extreme models of subcultural resistance by rejecting both the recreational drug use of mainstream culture in the form of cigarettes and alcohol and the No Future nihilism of counter-culture's hardcore punk. A year after the death of Sex Pistols bass guitarist Sid Vicious in 1979, Washington DC-based band Minor Threat released the song 'Straight Edge', rejecting drugs, alcohol and casual sex. Lyrics ran, 'I'm a person just like you / But I've got better things to do / Than sit around and fuck my head / Hang out with the living dead.' The mouthpiece of the band, Ian MacKaye, realized that if youthful minds were clear they would be more able to understand the political nature of their oppression and resist their dependency on capitalism.

Straight edgers follow a tradition of monk-like asceticism (one subgenre of the scene is Krishnacore). By the mid-1980s vegetarianism had been added to the list of their beliefs, followed later by veganism. This was in part inspired by the band Youth of Today, who helped shape straight edge into a youth movement with their anthems 'Can't Close my Eyes' (1985), 'Youth Crew' (1985) and 'No More' (1988). Devotees were clean-cut, rejecting the carnivalesque excesses of punk (see page 360) with crew cuts, Krishna beads, Champion hoodies, T-shirts and cargo shorts, and many began to sport a distinctive X tattoo. 'X-ing up' was originally used by bar staff to identify underage drinkers, allegedly as a result of an incident in 1980 when The Teen Idles were denied entry to their own gig at

1 2 3 4

1 Straight edge style in the 1990s.
2 A straight edger shows off his 'X' tattoos.
3 Fashion blogger Sofia Holmberg.
4 Straight edge street fashion is undergoing
a revival in the wake of recession and as a
rejection of celebrity culture.

Mabuhay Gardens in San Francisco because they were under 21. The management allowed the night to continue by putting a black X on the band's hands to stop staff from serving them alcohol, an act that was memorialized on the cover of their album *Minor Disturbance* (1980).

In the 1990s straight edge became more activist, particularly around the issue of animal rights with the work of band Earth Crisis. The style began to appropriate sartorial elements from metal, with camouflage pants, steel body jewellery and extensive tattoos. In 2000, the *More Than the X on Our Hands* compilation album showed the spread of straight edge across the world, with featured bands from locations including Colombia, Israel and the Philippines.

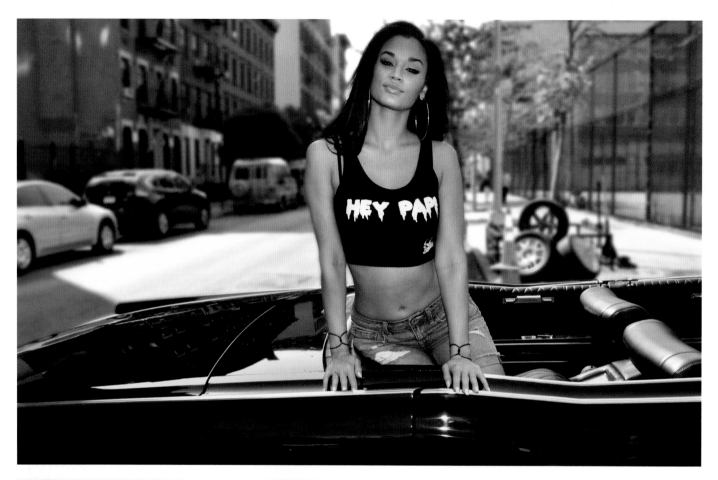

1 The aim of Bandida clothing is to use fashion and the Latina experience as a tool for female empowerment and self-expression.   2 'Flaca' or 'scrawny' can be used as a term of abuse or endearment depending on the tone of voice.   3 Snooki, star of reality TV series *Jersey Shore*, in an East Coast version of the chonga look.   4 Chonga style exaggerates glamour to extreme effect.

CHONGA

The word 'chonga' was originally used as an insult within Latino communities in Florida to differentiate privileged women from those considered trashy. Today in Miami and nearby Hialeah the term is being reclaimed by young working-class women of Cuban descent as a way of displaying their refusal to be assimilated into white American culture and as a means of asserting their Latina identity. The look may be read as 'slutty' by the mainstream, but the politicized chonga sees her hyper-feminine look as powerful. In the way that Girl Power changed attitudes to feminism and femininity in the 1990s, so the chonga uses an aggressively sexual appearance to reclaim her own body within her peer group, rather than dressing provocatively as a passive agent for male attention. Clothes are 'sexy' and body-conscious in the extreme, including crop-tops, tiny shorts and Brazilian stretch jeans designed to show off the 'booty'. Hair is gelled, nails are synthetic and huge hoop earrings are *de rigeur*. New York-based label Bandida was set up by Jamie Balbuena to appeal to the rebellious Latina chonga and her Los Angeles counterpart, the chola (see page 44). Balbuena describes her design philosophy as 'feminism through a bi-cultural, multi-ethnic lens. I incorporate feminism and Latinidad into my art by transmuting Spanish words which were once oppressive into terms of endearment and hopefully empowerment.'

In 2007 this little-known street fashion was introduced to global audiences after a spoof video for 'Chongalicious' by Laura DiLorenzo and Mimi Davila, a parody of singer Fergie's 'Fergalicious'(2006), went viral. The chonga has also engendered debate within US academe and the writing of Prisca Dorcas Mojica Rodriguez. In 'My Chonga Manifesto' (2015) and 'There's Beauty in My "Girl Culture"' (2016), Rodriguez describes how as a chonga she uses her appearance to disrupt assimilation within white culture by performing 'girl culture through an exaggerated lens'.

1 First Nations people at the entrance to a lodge (c.1866–70).
2 Canadian loggers fell trees (1911). 3 Dayton Boots of
Vancouver. 4 A view down Granville Street, one of the
city's main thoroughfares (1932).

VANCOUVER

The indigenous tribes of Canada lived off the land for thousands
of years until European settlers arrived. The Musqueam First Nation
(see image 1) of what is now Vancouver fished, hunted and trapped in
the fertile environment at the mouth of the Fraser River to provide for
large extended families living in settlements or 'bighouses'. However,
from the 1820s commercial logging began to change the landscape.
Trees were felled (see image 2) and transformed into masts for ships
in sawmills – a risky business, for hours were long, axes and handsaws
were sharp, and the hauling of timber over rough skid roads was
heavy on the feet. Canadian clothing had to be tough and built to
last, and the country developed a reputation for its workwear that
endures to this day. In 1946 Charlie Wohlford started one of the
country's iconic brands, Dayton Boots of Vancouver (see image 3),
and his rugged footwear went on to be worn by workers all over
North America. In 1965 the Dayton Black Beauty, a double-soled
motorcycle boot that eliminated the inside seam to reduce chafing
on the legs, became the boot of choice for Hells Angels (see page 24).

Vancouver's isolation changed with the gold rush of 1858, in
which an estimated thirty thousand American miners penetrated
the fur-trading territory of the Musqueam along the Fraser River.
They sifted or 'panned' beside its banks, washing through the grit
and gravel for any hint of gold. The settlement of Vancouver began
to grow as a commercial centre supplying equipment and provisions,
and the completion of the Canadian Pacific Railway helped transform
it into a bustling city by the early 20th century.

In the 1930s, African-Americans escaping the Dust Bowl wreaking
havoc in the Great Plains region settled in areas such as the notorious
Hogans Alley, a 2.4-m (8-ft) wide dirt track near the city's Pacific Central
Station. (It was later a temporary home to rock star Jimi Hendrix, who
stayed there as a child with his grandmother.) Jazz and the blues
could be heard in the unlicensed clubhouses and speakeasies of this
poverty-stricken area. By the 1950s, Vancouver had earned its place
as the last stop on the West Coast circuit or 'showbiz railway' that
moved seasoned US nightclub performers from Los Angeles, San
Francisco and Las Vegas, where many tried out new material at
discounted rates.

The city also had access to the latest European fashions from very early on in its history. Saba Brothers, a huge retail house and silk specialist, opened in 1903, and Albert O Koch established Vancouver's first garment manufacturing plant, the National Dress Company, in 1925, followed by the Lauries chain of dress stores in 1940. The work of Parisian couturiers and European fashion designers was imported and sold along Granville Street (see image 4) in Canadian boutiques and department stores including Eaton's, Simpson's and Hudson's Bay.

Post-war affluence drove the youth market and the collegiate (aka preppy; see page 78) look was imported from the United States. Alternative scenes such as beatnik coffee houses mirrored what was happening in other major cities. Vancouver's folk scene led to the founding of the Vancouver Folk Festival, still held today, and the city was an important centre of the hippy movement. Many young people seeking an alternative way of life in 1966–7 settled in the Kitsilano neighbourhood, known for its affordable rents, large Edwardian houses perfect for communal living and proximity to the universities and the beach. Head shops selling drug paraphernalia and independent boutiques opened on West Fourth Street (aka Rainbow Road),

including Doug Hawthorne's Psychedelic Shop at 2037 selling 'bright, groovy things', and the area gained a reputation as Canada's answer to San Francisco's Haight-Ashbury. A series of 'Human Be-Ins', visible expressions of Vancouver's counter-culture, were held at Stanley Park from 1967 to the mid-1970s, originally organized by concert promoter Jerry Kruz, who invited the flower children of Vancouver to dance, listen to music, fly kites and just be.

Punk music and style (see page 360) flourished in the city in the late 1970s with the Subhumans, Pointed Sticks and D.O.A. The latter's lead singer, Joe Keithley, described the city at the time as 'pretty much a backwater. There was no music industry or anything like that. At the same time, it fostered a really creative scene. There was no pressure like in Toronto or New York or LA, where a lot of bands conformed to what A&R people thought were successful formulas. But in Vancouver it was kind of like the Wild West and everybody just made everything up as they went.' In 1971 one of Vancouver's most notorious protests, the Gastown Smoke-In & Street Jamboree, was held in Gastown as a protest at Canada's drug laws. Today the city has many alternative communities with their own indigenous styles, including crust punk, folk punk, hardcore and steampunk (see page 384).

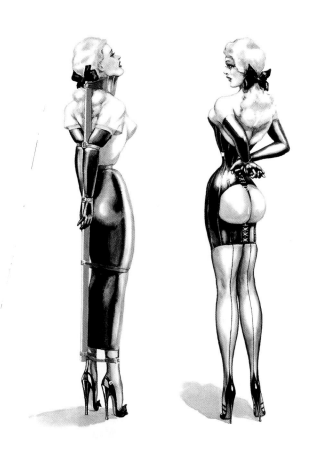

FETISH

VANCOUVER
COUNTRY Canada
DECADE OF ORIGIN 1890s

In the early 20th century, the psychoanalyst Sigmund Freud described how a fetish object could result when a male child recognized his mother's absence of penis during early sexual development. Fearing the possibility of his own castration – if it has happened to his mother it could happen to him – the child invents a surrogate that becomes the fetish object. Objects such as shoes can thus become the substitute for the corporeal presence of a lover. Fetishism also operates around the pleasure/pain axis inspired by the sexual fantasies of the notorious 18th-century French writer, the Marquis de Sade. Sexual role play can be given added frisson with clothing that constricts the body while exaggerating its sexual zones.

Vancouver's strong counter-cultural underground dates back to the heady, hippy days of the 1960s and has given the city a reputation for tolerance and inclusivity, as has the more experimental attitude to sexuality among its residents from Generations X and Y. Rascal's Club and Sin City in Vancouver have been holding fetish nights since the early 2000s and the city holds a well-attended annual fetish weekend run by DJ Pandemonium and alternative model and DJ Evilyn 13, billed as 'three days of pervy perfection'. Deadly Couture, run by fetish model Jenni Won Ton, is a well-established alternative boutique with its own latex label based in Gastown.

The origins of fetish clothing date back to the 1890s, when high-heeled 'staggerers' were worn for pleasure in the boudoir. In the 1940s the dominatrix became a popular figure in magazines such as *London Life* and *Bizarre*, the latter of which was helmed by fetish illustrator and photographer John Willie. Pulp artist Eric Stanton also

1 Fetish fashion exaggerates the body's sexual zones. 2 Bjork in couture latex by Atsuko Kudo and headpiece by James Merry, in 2016. 3 The boundaries between fetish and burlesque have been blurred, as seen in this latex outfit featuring fetish heels and a miniature top hat.

specialized in images of power-crazed women trampling over slave males. In the 1960s fashion began to flirt with fetishism and 'kinky' clothes such as knee-length leather boots and catsuits crept into the mainstream via the character of Emma Peel in *The Avengers* (1961–9), while in the 1970s overt references to sadomasochism were made by designer Vivienne Westwood. Her shop Sex, situated on London's King's Road, featured a blow-up pink rubber sign and sold fetishwear such as leather face masks, bondage trousers and rubber clothing by specialist labels including AtomAge, She-And-Me and London Leatherman. Westwood's adage was that 'sex is the thing that bugs English people more than anything else so that's where I attack'.

The fetish look was incorporated into punk (see page 360), the first of many street styles that integrated the look as a way of shocking mainstream society, and was followed by goth (see page 164), cybergoth (see page 116) and burlesque. Fetish-influenced fashion became socially acceptable by the mid-1980s after appearing in the work of designers such as Thierry Mugler, Jean Paul Gaultier, Gianni Versace and Pam Hogg. The fetish scene also continued to flourish in clubs such as London's Torture Garden and the magazine *Skin Two*. In the 21st century rubber and PVC have moved from the underground into street fashion and couture with the stunning designs of Atsuko Kudo, arguably making the fetish scene, alongside sportswear, one of the world's most popular street style influences.

	5			8
4		7		
	6			

4 An 'expression of freedom' by Lily Gatins.   5 Fetish fashion constricts the body.
6 Designer Christopher Shannon explores the relationship between materials and their cultural meanings in his designs.   7 Latex net skirt and top by Sashalouise.
8 Madonna wears a frame bra by Jean Paul Gaultier at the amFAR benefit show (1992).

1 A pegasister or female brony displays Hasbro merchandise on a store tour in 2013.   2 A pair of bronies attend the BuckCon My Little Pony convention in 2016.

BRONY

VANCOUVER
COUNTRY Canada
DECADE OF ORIGIN 2010s

The rise of the brony can be dated back to 10 October 2010, when the first episode of the animated series *My Little Pony: Friendship Is Magic* aired on The Hub, an offshoot of the Discovery Channel co-owned by Hasbro Toys. The company planned to create commercially lucrative toy tie-ins and to this end the original My Little Pony franchise of the 1980s was revamped by Lauren Faust, former writer and director of *The Powerpuff Girls* (1998–2005). Faust's character-based narratives, pop culture references and candy-coloured messages of love, friendship and tolerance had the unusual effect of attracting a new audience of white heterosexual males who became known as bronies ('bro' plus 'pony') and female fans known as pegasisters. They began to discuss the series in a thread on 4chan, an online image-based bulletin board, where they caught the attention of Internet trolls, whose ridiculing in the form of memes gave the movement huge online publicity.

3 My Little Pony has become popular as a visual source for cosplayers (see page 296) outside of the specialist brony convention circuit. 4 An attendee at BronyCon, the world's largest My Little Pony convention. 5 Cosplayers Lady Mella as Rainbow Dash and Shiya Wind as Twilight Sparkle.

The brony was something of a pioneer – a heterosexual man taking delight in feminized content and identifying with female characters as opposed to testosterone-fuelled point-and-shoot games. This blurring of gender hierarchy tended to pathologize the brony and the documentary *Bronies: The Extremely Unexpected Fans of My Little Pony* (2012) explored the heroism it took to 'come out' as a brony within a community. It also showed the huge global reach of the fandom, depicting the lives of bronies from the UK, Germany, Israel and the United States, and the importance of conventions such as BronyCon, an annual weekend event that attracts thousands of fans. Bronies also meet online at PonyChan, an image board for My Little Pony-related content, BronySquare, Equestria Daily and Ponyville Live!, and go so far as to create their own episodes, live-action shorts and fiction. In 2014, *The Globe and Mail* newspaper introduced Vancouver's bronies, who had decided to 'come out of the stable'. They included Mike Shay, or BronyMike, founder of the British Columbia bronies group, and Afion Ruki, aka Princess Afion, head of logistics for BronyCan, Canada's national brony convention.

The bronies' capacity for taking delight in the vestiges of childhood has been reflected in the rise of the kidult, a term used to describe an adult who fears the prospect of ageing within a worrying world. Global economic collapse, environmental concerns and terrorism make many fear the future, and comfort can be taken in a fantasy version of childhood. This has been expressed in the rise of the onesie (an adult version of a baby's romper suit), and in fashion brands such as Moschino, who reference cartoon characters in their clothing lines.

JUNGLIST

In the 1970s the crowded tenements of Arnett Gardens, a sprawling slum in West Kingston, Jamaica, were demolished and replaced by the Concrete Jungle. As described in Bob Marley's song of the same name on his album *Catch A Fire* (1973), this dense concentration of state-built, fortress-like apartments with narrow passageways was a place where the sun truly did not shine. It was also the spawning ground for gun-toting gangs and those who lived on the margins, known as the junglists. By the early 1990s the term was being used to describe avid followers of UK drum 'n' bass or 'jungle' music that incorporated shout-outs to 'junglist krus' amid its frantic breakbeat rhythms. The look took its cues from hip hop but incorporated a military feel with camouflage pants and MA-1 flight jackets; women were influenced by the body-con clothing of Jamaican dancehall, wearing stretch cut-out minidresses or high-cut batty riders (shorts).

In one of the most extreme dislocations of street style, the junglist has been thriving for the last decade in the former hippy mountain town of Whistler, British Columbia. On first opening in 1966, the ski resort had a double chairlift and two T bars, and the liberal sensibilities of the original hippy community could be found après-ski at Dusty's Bar and BBQ, named after a stuffed horse brought to the town in a pick-up truck and left in the bar. Today, Whistler is a year-round destination with 37 lifts able to move 70,000 skiers per hour, and is crowded with bars, dance clubs and lounges. The end-of-season celebrations have evolved into raves and monthly full moon parties held at Cougar Mountain and beneath the Cheakamus River suspension bridge, or at clubs such as Garfinkel's and Tommy Africa's, where DJ Phroh of the Whistler junglists plays drum 'n' bass and bass-heavy jungle. As he puts it, 'One thing that is unique about our scene is that people come to Whistler from all over the world. So we get Brits, Aussies, Kiwis and people from all over Europe and Asia – our tastes are more international than the rest of Canada's D'n'B scene.' The look is unique, too, in that it combines ski and snowboard wear, fluoro, and the ubiquitous hoodie, snapback and skate shoes.

MOD

In 1964 the mop-topped Beatles played at Maple Leaf Gardens, Toronto, inspiring a generation of Canadian teenagers to become devout Anglophiles. One fan remembers, 'I was nine years old [and] found the experience unforgettable. The constant flash of brownie cameras going off coupled with pandemonium and hysteria was a bit frightening. We couldn't hear the music at all. Just a wall of shrieking from beginning to end.'

The rugged masculinity of the Canadian logger was challenged by the suited mod, who used formal dress as a discreet form of rebellion. The mod look originated in the mid-1950s, a time when a rich fantasy of Continental life pervaded Europe and Italian style provided the sartorial foundation for a tribe of teenagers dubbed the mods, who arrived on the London Soho scene as the personification of 'modern'. Soho mods were obsessive about the cut of their clothes, priding themselves on their tailored elegance. Working-class boys wearing the clothes of their 'betters' was subversive, an ironic statement about the class divide. Country-style tailored tweed suits were mixed with elements of preppy (see page 78) for a lifestyle that revolved around the hedonism of consumption. Once the Beatles adopted the fashionable mod look, it spread across the world, and the word became shorthand for an international style.

Canadian teenage girls rejected domesticity in favour of a pre-adolescent coltish look inspired by Twiggy's much-publicized trip to the USA in 1967. Hippy style gradually replaced mod in Toronto until the look was revived in the late 1970s as an alternative to punk. Paul Weller of The Jam became a style icon and the film *Quadrophenia* (1979) gave its audience a series of visual clues on to how to dress like it was 1964, the year in which it was set. Bobby Tarlton, lead singer of

1 Twiggy made the mod look mainstream in the 1960s. Her Eton crop was cut by Leonard Lewis of Mayfair. 2 A contemporary mod look by Sassoon Academy. 3 Anglophile Mod girl in Yorkville, Toronto, 1969.

4 Russian editor and fashion icon Anya
Ziourova wears a mod-influenced look at
Paris Fashion Week in 2014, referencing
Mary Quant's Peter Pan collar and cuff
details from the 1960s. 5 French Boutik,
a 1960s-influenced band formed in 2010,
describe their music and styling as
'modernist pop'.

the mod-influenced band Dr Bird, remembers how The Jam 'changed
my life – three angry boys in sharp suits was something I could relate to'.

In the 2000s, Britpop – a musical genre in which bands such as
Pulp and Oasis referenced mod style – attracted a legion of fans in
Toronto. A club night called Mod Club became the hub of the city's
scene, hosted by British émigrés Mark Holmes and Bobbi Guy. Holmes
determined it should be a time capsule of all he loved, including
1960s mohair and iridescent tonic suits, Fred Perry polos and girls in
baby-doll dresses and Vidal Sassoon haircuts. It was a huge success
and led to a second Mod Club night complete with 1960s-style go-go
dancers. After the venue was closed for licence infringements, the
night moved into an old theatre housing a pool hall, complete with
balcony and stage. This became The Mod Club Theatre in 2004, a club
and live music venue with a capacity for six hundred. Bobby Tarlton
sees the mod look as ever-evolving because 'it's timeless and set the
rules I live my life by – look sharp, think smart and keep on movin''.

1 Cybergoth blurs the distinctions between the artificial and the human. Artificial hair known as cyberlox is created from a variety of man-made materials.   2 Cybergoth clothing borrows from punk, fetish and rave.
3 Shannon Chromegirl and Perish Dignam at the 'Warriors and Goddesses' party in Los Angeles (2013).

CYBERGOTH

In 1984, William Gibson's *Neuromancer*, a sci-fi novel of console cowboys and outlaw hackers, featured a dystopian future of designer drugs, body modification and cyberspace. Gibson's cyberpunk descriptions of the integration of humans and technology or the 'techno-colonization' of the human body in the form of circuitry implants and prosthetic limbs were mirrored in the cybernetic body art of Australian-based performance artist Stelarc, who used prosthetics, including laser eyes and industrial robot arms, to create a human–machine hybrid. A dystopian aesthetic also pervaded sci-fi movies: Ridley Scott's *Blade Runner* (1982) was set in a rain-soaked Los Angeles of 2019 inhabited by 'assumed humanoids' or replicants, and *The Terminator* (1984) featured a cyborg assassin sent back in time from a post-apocalyptic future. From these aesthetic roots rose the cybergoth, who changed the dark drama and desires of original goth (see page 164) culture into a neon-hued sci-fi fantasy set against a background of pulsing industrial music played at 140 beats per minute.

The look borrows from an array of sources: the neon, UV and glowsticks of rave culture; the vinyl, PVC, BDSM and uncanny of goth; and the post-apocalyptic goggles and boots of Tank Girl, the heroine of a British comic of the same name created by Jamie Hewlett and Alan Martin in 1988. Cybergoth also redraws the boundaries of the human body with the use of artificially coloured contact lenses and cyberlox made from neon extensions, crin, plastic tubing, rubber and foam strips. Key locations for the original cybergoth included London, in particular the club night Slimelight held at Electrowerkz, and the Cyberdog store, where founder Terry Davy still sells clothes complete with circuitry boards and electronic light T-shirts with sound-activated graphic equalizer displays that move in time to the music.

4
5

4 A cybergoth warrior woman dressed to survive in a post-apocalyptic future.   5 Princess Chaos, an industrial dancer from Montreal.

The French-speaking city of Montreal has been an important centre of experimental electronic music production since late 1970s disco and 1980s synthpop. In 1987 the first gothic-oriented bands began to emerge, including Disappointed a Few People and Voivod. Young musicians and their followers continue to be drawn to a city that has low rents, a boho lifestyle and, like Seattle, an inclement climate with long winters that encourages people to either stay in to rehearse/play or listen to bands. They also hang out at Igloofest, an innovative outdoor festival of electronic music held in the middle of winter. The MUTEK festival has been exploring and promoting the place of cutting-edge electronic music since 2000 and Component One is a thriving industrial music festival built on the backs of C.O.M.A., a weekend festival held in Montreal from 2004 to 2007, and Kinetik, which ran from 2008 to 2013. Today the cybergoth scene may be small compared to European cities, but as alternative model, cybergoth and industrial dancer, Princess Chaos says, 'French Canadians are often compared to Europeans. We have the same way of thinking, the way we treat our people and how we are open-minded. I've always loved everything that looks futuristic, industrial, cyborg – we look like a bunch of futuristic soldiers and I love it!'

LATIN AMERICA AND THE CARIBBEAN

MONTERREY HAVANA KINGSTON RIO DE JANEIRO
SÃO PAULO BUENOS AIRES

GUARACHERO SKATER RUDE BOY RAGGA FUNKEIRO EMO
LOWRIDER FLOGGER

A bloco or party in the Rio favela (previous page) is so called because it takes up a whole block. The chola of Bolivia (opposite) is a national figure marked out by her pollera or vividly coloured skirt.

Latin America comprises the continent of Central and South America, Mexico and the islands of the Caribbean. The entire area was variously colonized by Spain and Portugal from the late 15th through to the 18th century before the fight for independence in the 19th century. In 1492 Christopher Columbus began the long and bloody conquest of the indigenous population of this diverse region, many of whom were decimated by disease or forced into slavery. As in many geographical locations, dress became a marker of social status, caste and domination, as all were forced to conform to European standards. Clothing, such as the huipil of Guatemala, was also used as a regional marker to keep track of the continent's original inhabitants. This embroidered top, woven on a backstrap loom, originally provided information about the wearer's locale and was the clothing equivalent of cattle branding. Today, the huipil has evolved into an intensely personal garment that, if the symbolism of the intricate embroidery is read correctly, can provide details of its wearer such as their age, religion and social status. It is worn with an ankle-length wraparound skirt with a sash, or faja, around the waist.

The struggle for independence was also played out in dress; in Buenos Aires, under the totalitarian regime of Juan Manuel de Rosas, fashionable women in the 1830s began to wear a version of the traditional Spanish peineton, a tortoiseshell hair comb that had been imported into Argentina in the 18th century by Spanish colonialists. They took their dress cues from the headdresses of Marie Antoinette and the French court at Versailles, so as to display a superior fashion sense and thus independence from the customs and modes of Spain. Women are said to have worn such large headpieces that men used to walk to the left of the wearer to avoid being injured. Rosas had many rules regarding public conformity: men were required to sport huge moustaches and sideburns, and also to wear a red badge with the moniker 'Federation or Death', red waistcoats and red hat bands. Academic Regina A Root writes in *Couture and Consensus: Fashion and Politics in Postcolonial Argentina* (2010) of how fashion was used as a vehicle to promote revolutionary ideas through the pages of *La Moda* magazine: 'what better medium was there to import enlightened European ideas than to, quite literally, cloak them in a fashion magazine?' Enlightened European ideas were also expressed in the adoption of that continent's dress types, and the latest fashions were run up by seamstresses and tailors in the cities of Latin America.

Latin America has inspired global fashion trends such as the Panama, a hat made from toquilla palm fibre grown on plantations along the coast of Ecuador and imported to Europe by the Spanish conquistadors, who were supposedly so entranced by the delicacy of its material that they thought it had been fashioned from the skin of bats. By the 19th century, the Panama was an established summer hat, famously worn by Napoleon during his years of exile on Saint Helena, and in 1900 it gained fame in America after being worn by President Theodore Roosevelt when visiting the Panama Canal.

Every year the Mexican *vaquero*, a horseman revered for his prowess in cattle herding, drove huge flocks of sheep from the haciendas of New Mexico over a thousand miles to Chihuahua, a gruelling journey that needed expert skills. The cowboy boot was developed to cater to their needs, with a slim toe to slip easily into the stirrup and a low undercut heel to keep it there. Heavy leather protected the feet and the wide boot top and slick leather sole were safety features, enabling the cowboy to pull his foot out of the boot quickly or his boot out of the stirrup if he was thrown from the horse.

The wardrobe of Mexican artist Frida Kahlo is a touchstone for many who practise Advanced Style (see page 196) today. Her folkloric interpretation of the Mexican Indian outfits worn by women from the Isthmus of Tehuantepec was a political gesture, as this was a matriarchal district distinct from the 'machismo' of the rest of the nation. Women continue to trade in the markets wearing multi-coloured hand-woven dresses and gold jewellery, with orchids braided into their hair. Kahlo's long skirts and dresses were worn to disguise her right leg, which had been afflicted by childhood polio.

Latino and Caribbean style have been spread throughout the world by the diaspora, including the street fashions of rude boy (see page 130), a snappy Jamaican look that continues to inspire, and pachuco (see page 60), young Mexican-American men who developed their own distinctive identity by wearing the zoot suit. Although usually associated with male style, the suit's longline jacket and peg-topped trousers were also worn by the pachucas, girls with high bouffants and heavy make-up who were forerunners of the chola (see page 44). By the 19th century, the chola had become a recurring figure in the visual language of Peru, Ecuador and Bolivia as the countries became increasingly industrialized. She was a picturesque peasant woman who provided a cultural conduit between the country and the city, both literally and figuratively, by selling her fresh produce in the marketplace dressed in a tall Panama hat and pollera, or vividly coloured skirt. By the 1990s the meaning of the chola had shifted again, now a female gang member whose subversive style moved into the mainstream through celebrity appropriators such as singers Gwen Stefani and Christina Aguilera.

GUARACHERO

MONTERREY
COUNTRY Mexico
DECADE OF ORIGIN 2000s

The fashion for extending the toe of one's shoe or boot dates back to the 14th-century poulaine. This unusual shoe, also known as a crackowe (*poulaine* means 'Polish'), was popularized by Richard II of England's wife Anne of Bohemia, who was a major influence on court fashion. It had a long toe stuffed with horsehair and is thought to have been inspired by Middle Eastern footwear brought to Europe during the Crusades. The 20th-century successor to the poulaine, the winklepicker (named after the sharp pin used to prise winkles from their shells), inspired condemnation in the 1950s when worn by teddy boys (see page 184), in the 1960s when worn by mods (see page 112) and in the 1970s when worn by punks (see page 360). In 2009, a unique form of pointed footwear began to appear in the nightclubs

1 Aliados dance crew performs at Mesquit Rodeo nightclub in Matehuala, Mexico. 2 A guarachero wears pink pointy boots and matching shirt. 3 Comme des Garçons menswear collection S/S 2015.

of Monterrey — cowboy boots with exaggerated elongated toes known as *botas picudas mexicanas*, literally 'Mexican pointy boots'. Young Mexican dandies who belonged to rival dance crews danced intricately choreographed routines to tribal guarachero music, an innovative mix of indigenous South American folk music, the double-beat rhythms of cumbia and techno, complete with Aztec flutes. The most successful exponents of this unorthodox sound are 3BallMTY (pronounced 'tribal Monterrey'), whose album *Inténtalo* was a huge hit in 2011.

Cobblers trace the craze of the pointy boot back to the city of Matehuala in the Mexican state of San Luis Potosí, where men in neighbouring territories compete with each other to achieve the longest toe points — they can extend up to 1.5 m (5 ft) in length. The subverted cowboy boots are then accessorized with sequins, LED lights and mirrors by dance troupes such as Los Parranderos, in order to catch the light when dancing. Since 2010 the fashion has moved with Mexican migrants to the US border states, ending up in cities with a large Mexican community such as Dallas, Texas. The exaggerated size of the boots has links with the oversizing in important street fashions such as the pachuco (see page 60) and B-Boy (see page 86). Comme des Garçons launched its own version of the Mexican pointy boot for its Spring/Summer 2015 menswear collection, incorporating styling details from the traditional Chelsea boot such as elasticized side gussets and pull-on tabs.

SKATER

Cuba's skateboard scene started in the late 1970s when the offspring of Eastern bloc diplomats and the Soviet military introduced the first boards to the island. It remained impossible to source skate equipment in Cuba, however, particularly after the dissolution of the Soviet Union in 1991. The ensuing embargoes and trade restrictions, especially of petrol and its derivatives, created an economic depression known as the *período especial*, or Special Period. In those austere times, Cuban skaters such as Che Alejandro Pando Napoles and Alexander Gonzalez Borrego (aka El Negro) scavenged their environment and made rudimentary boards out of plywood with wheels taken from the bottom of old pairs of roller skates. Boards were precious as when they snapped it could take months to find the materials to make another, so skaters were restricted in their moves. Cuban skaters also faced hostility from the public and the police as a result of the anti-American feeling dating back to 1961, when the United States severed ties with the island after the US-supported Batista government was overthrown by Fidel Castro and his rebel army. Many women skaters also suffered a double bind for their refusal to be limited to the domestic in a machismo culture.

Today, it is still a struggle to source skateboarding equipment in Cuba. There are no skate shops, but US charities such as Amigo Skate and Cuba Skate (both founded in 2010) donate boards, pads and helmets, renovate parks and help link Cuban skaters with other skater communities around the world. In the early 2000s Red Bull began sponsoring events in Cuba and donated much-needed ramps that were used to create Havana's first and only skate park – El Patinodromo – in a disused drainage ditch. Today it is barely useable, especially when it floods during the rainy season, and skaters tend to congregate at the well-known intersection and downtown skate spot 23 y G. With the gradual strengthening of diplomatic ties between the United States and Cuba, as sanctioned by President Barack Obama in 2014, Cuban skaters are set to become stars outside the boundaries of their own capital city.

| 1 | | 3 | 4 |
| 2 | | 5 | |

1–5 The years of trade embargo means that Cuba's skateboard scene has not been commercialized. Branded clothing has yet to gain a foothold.

KINGSTON

Kingston rose from the ashes of Port Royal, a Spanish colony taken by the English in 1655 that became known as the 'London of Jamaica'. Port Royal was a garrison town and a centre of trade and commerce due to its situation at the centre of the Caribbean with a natural harbour of deep enough anchorage to accommodate the largest vessels. The Jamaican town was also an infamous haven for pirates such as Henry Morgan (see image 1), who sallied forth making raids on Spanish ports. Port Royal achieved a reputation across the Caribbean for its vice and debauchery. The slave traders, gambling dens, grog shops and brothels prospered, but it was, quite literally, built on sand. When an underwater earthquake hit on 7 June 1692, followed by a raging tsunami, the multistorey brick houses, stores and wharves on 21 hectares (53 acres) of sandy spit disappeared into the waves as their foundations liquefied. The Reverend Emmanuel Heath had just completed prayers and repaired to the local tavern, when the floor began shaking. He ran into the street to find that 'the earth opened and swallowed many people, before my face, and the sea I saw came mounting in over the wall, upon which I concluded it impossible to escape'. Heath believed divine retribution had destroyed the depravity at the heart of Port Royal.

The population was decimated; only 2,000 remained of the original 6,500 inhabitants after disaster was followed by disease. The survivors moved inland to Kingston, a plain spotted with pig farms and fishing shacks and the site of a newly planned colonial 'Kings Town', named after William of Orange. Kingston (see image 2) was built on a grid system of straight streets leading directly from the plantations to the wharves, where sugar, the island's lucrative export, was stored before being shipped all over the world. By 1716 this white, colonial, slave-trading town was the largest and most prosperous in the Caribbean. It was declared the official capital of the Colony of Jamaica in 1872. The geography of Kingston delineated the rich, who settled in large houses uptown, and the poor, who occupied the ramshackle shantytowns at the edges and suffered through

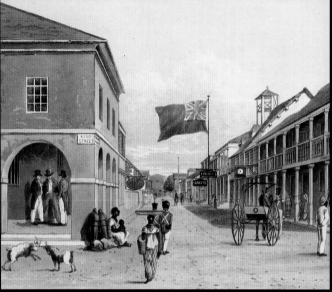

1   2
3   4

1 Pirate Henry Morgan, aka Blackbeard (1729).   2 The grid
system of Kingston.   3 Marcus Garvey, the leader of the Black
Nationalist movement.   4 Jamaican sound system.

and European music using banjo and bamboo flutes, with percussion provided by a rhumba box. The fast-paced jazz riffs of ska — favoured by rude boys (see page 130) — made their way via West Indian immigrants to the UK, where ska became the musical choice of the skinhead (see page 356). Rocksteady, a slowed-down version of ska with a syncopated bass rhythm, anticipated the heavy backbeat of reggae — a rege-rege or 'raggedy' mix of mento, ska, rocksteady and US R&B that was spread out of Jamaica with the success of committed Rastafarians Bob Marley and the Wailers. The 'skengay' guitar strum that kept reggae time was said to mimic the gunshots heard on the streets of Trench Town, which from the 1970s had become wracked by gang warfare and gun, or 'skeng', crime. Reggae music also gained international status after the success of the film *The Harder They Come* (1972) starring Jimmy Cliff, which documented how reggae was the voice of the rude boy rebels and dispossessed poor of Kingston.

Reggae was played on a sound system, one of Jamaica's unique contributions to street culture. In the 1950s speakers took over from orchestras in the dancehalls and streets, and home-grown record producers such as Prince Buster, Coxsone Dodd and Duke Reid used their own systems to test out and promote their recordings. Competition was fierce and had the potential for violence, so rude boys were used as protection. Sound-system culture has penetrated all corners of the world, including London's Notting Hill, where it is most visible during the yearly carnival (see image 4), and the Bronx in New York, where it was crucial in the development of hip hop through the breakbeats of Jamaican émigré DJ Kool Herc (Clive Campbell).

hurricanes, a cholera epidemic in 1850 and a second earthquake in 1907. Rebellion took many forms: the maroons — slaves who had escaped from their Spanish owners and taken refuge in the mountains — formed free communities and were allowed self-government in 1739; Rastafarians — spiritual warriors and devoted followers of Ethiopian emperor Haile Selassie — emerged from the slums in the 1930s after being inspired by civil rights activist and founding father of Black Pride, Marcus Garvey (see image 3). Garvey was born on the island, where he established the Universal Negro Improvement Association in 1914 for black self-determination. Workers also fought for their rights and formed the trades unions that underpinned the movement for Jamaican independence in the 1960s.

By the 1950s, unique forms of music could be heard in the community of Trench Town, a 1940s government housing project comprising four-storey apartment blocks with distinctive zinc-fenced yards — communal spaces where Yardies took control. Mento was one of the first vernacular sounds of Jamaica, an acoustic fusion of African

RUDE BOY

The swaggering rude boy conjures conflicting opinions in Kingston: some glorify him for his devil-may-care attitude; others condemn his criminal associations and reputation for mindless violence. The first ska song to rebuke the rude boy was Stranger Cole's 'Rough and Tough', recorded by Duke Reid in 1962, the year of Jamaica's independence after three centuries of British rule. Its lyrics warned, 'don't bite the hands that feed you'. Many others followed, including The Clarendonians' 'Rudie Bam Bam' (1966), Dandy Livingstone's 'A Message to You, Rudy' (1967) – later covered by The Specials in 1979 – and Desmond Dekker's '007 Shanty Town' (1966). *The Harder They Come* (1972), the first full-length feature film made in Jamaica, introduced global audiences to reggae as well as the deprivation of Kingston with its use of vérité footage. The desperado played by Jimmy Cliff was based on a real-life rude boy, Vincent 'Ivanhoe' Martin, aka 'Rhygin', who was gunned down by the police in 1948.

Many rude boys had migrated to Kingston in search of employment and when none was forthcoming had resisted marginalization by forming gangs known for carrying German ratchet knives and 'scuffling' or stealing to get by. By 1963 The Wailers' first bluebeat single on the Studio One label was calling them to 'Simmer Down' – singer Bob Marley, who was 18 at the time of recording and a habitué of the rude boy territory of Trench Town, used the message of the song to put his mother Cedella's mind at rest.

The rude boy looked sharp, styled after the modernist jazz musicians of the United States, but with a Kingston twist. Local tailors innovated the cropped slim trouser and bum freezer jacket – a suit silhouette that influenced the mods (see page 112) – and rendered it in iridescent two-tone or tonic material that shimmered in the dance hall. 'Stingy brim', or pork-pie, hats and shades helped create an intimidating gangster presence at sound-system dances, where many rude boys, including Prince Buster, were employed as protection or 'dance crashers' to break up rival bashes.

1 Clifford Fullerton, a tailor from Kingston, was one of many British immigrants who brought the snappy rude boy style to the United Kingdom in the post-war years.   2 Jamaican singer-songwriter and producer Prince Buster.   3 An early 1970s rude boy mixes fashionable knitwear with sharp tailoring and shades.

4 Fashion stylist and creative director Yinka Germaine takes the basic elements of rude boy style and fashions a slick, minimalist silhouette in monochrome. 5 The Specials were largely responsible for the rude boy revival that swept the United Kingdom in the early 1980s. 6 Fashion designer Bianca Saunders's 'London is the Place for Me' collection (2015) was inspired by the *Windrush* generation of immigrants and her own background as a third-generation British Caribbean.

The rude boy look was imported to the United Kingdom in 1948 with the first West Indian immigrants on the *Windrush*, and Jamaican stars such as Millie Small and Prince Buster found a new audience. Skinheads (see page 356) also adopted elements of the rude boy style, despite the movement's descent into racism by the 1970s. Its next incarnation, 2 Tone, was suitably inclusive at a time when membership of the far-right National Front was at an all-time high in the United Kingdom. Teenagers of all ethnicities skanked to the music of The Specials, a band from Coventry – a city decimated by the collapse of its car industry – who were signed to 2 Tone records by Jerry Dammers. Dammers created an iconic brand image for the label, taking inspiration from a Peter Tosh album cover to create the cartoon mascot Walt Jabsco, and fused punk and ska to create the Coventry Sound. Jamaican-born Neville Staple introduced The Specials to the rude boy style, insisting that 'there can be nothing worse than to look shabby in public', and the band kick-started a fashion for brogues, tonic suits, Ben Sherman shirts, trilbies and Harrington jackets.

RAGGA

Originally a pejorative term given to the disenfranchised ghetto youth of Jamaica, 'Raggamuffin' had become a mark of pride by the 1980s, used to describe renegades who refused to bow to convention. Raggamuffins set themselves against the traditional tropes of Caribbean respectability, as described by ethnographer Peter Wilson in his much debated work *Crab Antics: The Social Anthropology of English-speaking Negro Societies of the Caribbean* (1973), based on the results of fieldwork on the island of Providencia. Wilson posited that there was a 'dual value system' of 'reputation' and 'respectability' as a result of colonialism, which created cultural expectations among the island's inhabitants. Respectable citizens went to church, were monogamous and dressed neatly, and had formal manners and 'a restrained demeanour'.

Ragga music explicitly rails against respectability by positioning itself as deliberately 'slack', with brash drug- and gun-related lyrics (the Jamaican equivalent to gangsta rap; see page 46) and sexually explicit patois chanted over a digitally created staccato bass beat. Such a stance is the polar opposite to the Rastafarian spirituality and mutualism of Bob Marley's reggae, as expressed in songs such as 'One Love' (1977), which called for justice and encouraged the world to unite.

In the dance hall, the space where ragga music plays, a call and response is set up between the usually male DJ and his audience of female fans or 'queens', whose dress and dance are deliberately provocative and hyper-feminine. Clothes are body-con, attenuated

1 Ragga is deliberately provocative in its brash body-con clothing and sexually explicit lyrics.

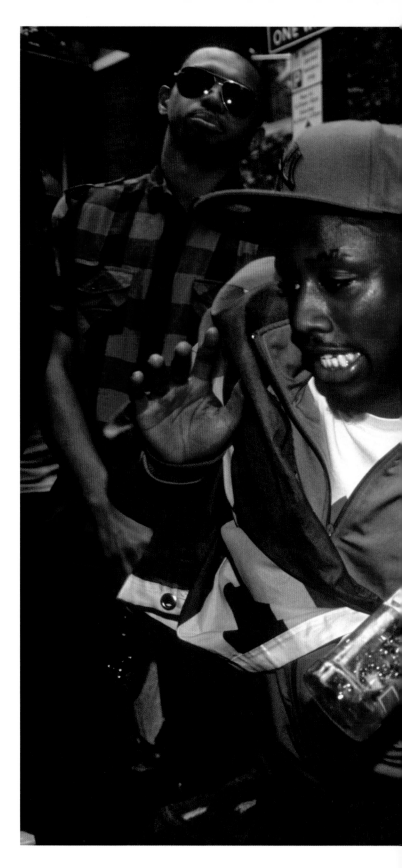

2 | 3

2 Clothes accentuate the body by showing off its curves and expose flesh through cut-outs and halter necks.
3 An all-night dancehall party on the streets of Kingston. The overt display of the body is about female sexual power and autonomy from men.

and transparent, and include fishnet tops over neon bras and extremely high-cut pum pum shorts – also known as batty riders because they expose the butt cheeks – g-string body suits and cut-out dresses. Hairstyles are elaborate, with the use of weaves, weft and wigs, and are complemented by gold door-knocker earrings; nails are exaggerated and expensively manicured – all of which deliberately rejects the idea of natural beauty and is indicative of wealth and social status. Academic Denise Noble, in her essay 'Ragga Music: Dis/Respecting Black Women and Dis/reputable Sexualities' (2000), argues that the queen's look is not about sexual objectification, but about women celebrating their own bodies. She writes that 'The

ragga Queen's "sexy" appearance increases her own value as an object of male consumption, but simultaneously her economic power and/or autonomy implied by her expensive clothing and hairstyles, may increase her power and autonomy from men in the dance hall.'

The first recognizable ragga song is believed to be 'Under Mi Sleng Teng' (1985) by Jamaican dancehall musician Wayne Smith, produced by King Jammy and featuring a Casio CZ-Series synthesizer. By the 1990s ragga had gone global, with artists such as Shabba Ranks garnering international audiences and more female performers gaining recognition, including Sister Charmaine, Ce'Cile, Lady G, Patra and Lady Saw from Kingston.

FUNKEIRO

RIO DE JANEIRO
COUNTRY Brazil
DECADE OF ORIGIN 1980s

'It's hard to explain what funk is because it's like a river. It's ever-flowing and ever-changing and every obstacle that it comes across, it will always adapt to continue in its course.' — MC Mano Teko

In 1977 German band Kraftwerk released *Trans-Europe Express*, an electronic, bass-heavy track that found its way into the favelas (shantytowns) of Rio de Janeiro via the Miami booty bass scene. Out of the mix came funk carioca, or favela funk, an innovative musical form that combined sampled electronic bass riffs and well-known melodies such as the theme from *Rocky* (1976) with African drumming, Brazilian singing and rapping that spoke of the raw life in the poverty-stricken favelas of the city. The lyrics of funk carioca, sung

1 Funkeiras wear Spandex skirts and dresses. 2 A dance competition held in the favela. 3 Revellers dance in the Cantagalo favela. 4 A participant shows off his dookie chain.

in Portuguese, veer from expressions of social injustice, criminality and police brutality to the sexually explicit 'putaria' and 'proibidao', a subgenre that includes lyrics allegedly composed by the local drug lords as a means of intimidation. Funk ostentação as performed by funkeiro MC Guimê, celebrates fast cars, money and drugs.

Dress is a mix of classic hip hop snapbacks and Brazilian beachwear, which for the funkeiro means board shorts and dookie chains and for the funkeira booty shorts and bikini tops. The violence of funk lyrics has been known to spill over into the 'baille funk' or funk balls held in the favelas or local dance halls where the music is played, giving funk carioca in Brazil a similar reputation to that of gangsta rap (see page 46) in the United States. From 2010 in Santos, a municipality in the state of São Paulo and a stronghold of the notorious PCC gang, eight MCs were killed within five years – including MC Daleste, who was assassinated mid-performance. In the favelas, the MC can find himself stuck between the protective embrace of the gang and the police, who see funk as glorifying violence and thus inciting crime. Allegiance to the PCC is occasionally displayed in the yin-yang symbol, whether in jewellery or the use of black and white in clothing, or in MC Bin Laden's bi-coloured hair. In the 2000s a new version of funk dubbed 'tamborzão' blasted the bailles of Rio, infused with percussive Brazilian offbeats and showcasing its own dance, the 'passinho' or little step. This dance is a mix of funk, breaking and traditional Brazilian styles such as capoeira, samba, pagode and frevo.

SÃO PAULO

São Paulo is one of the world's mega-cities, originally founded by Jesuit missionaries as São Paulo dos Campos de Piratininga in 1554 to convert the indigenous Guainás to Catholicism. The city was officially named São Paulo in 1711 and in the 1720s the fashion for coffee created a boom in the trade of coffee beans that accelerated the economy. In 1888 the Lei Áurea, or 'Golden Law', abolished slavery in Brazil, leading to an influx of Italian, German and later Japanese workers into the city, who colonized the areas of Brooklin, Bela Vista and Liberdade.

São Paulo has a history of anarchism dating back to the general strike of July 1917 after a young cobbler, Antonio Martinez, was murdered by the police. This tragic event culminated in a succession of riots that took place over four days. In the Brazilian capital of Rio de Janeiro, the Rio de Janeiro Workers' Federation held a series of rallies demonstrating against working conditions, pay and inflation, and after a crackdown by the police the organization was banned. The success of the Russian Revolution that year inspired militant action by workers all over Brazil, spearheaded by the propaganda machine of the Anarchist Alliance and the new General Workers Union (UGT), which urged strike action among its membership. All uprisings were violently suppressed by the army, as was the Constitutionalist Revolution of 1932 when São Paulo's population resisted an attempted coup d'état by the unelected president Getúlio Vargas.

São Paulo (see image 1), according to academic Frederico Freitas, 'has this tradition of being the place in Brazil where the cultural movements of the "First World" appear and are then re-shaped in our own image and reality'. In the early years of the 20th century the aesthetic of modernism influenced the work of São Paulo's poets and artists – including Anita Malfatti, Lasar Segall, and sculptor Victor Brecheret – and by the 1930s Brazilian culture had gained global attention through the international success of samba singer Carmen Miranda (see image 2), popularly known as the 'Brazilian Bombshell'. In 1946 Miranda was reportedly the highest-paid female entertainer in the United States, earning $200,000 that year (more than $2 million today), and struck a figure of Latina glamour in her famous tutti-frutti hat and huge platform shoes designed by Ted Saval. Her popularity was such that a 'South American fever' struck the United States as turbans, *baianas* (traditional Brazilian dresses) and tutti-frutti jewellery entered popular fashion.

In 1964 a military coup overthrew the democratically elected Brazilian government, initiating 21 years of ruthless military dictatorship and human rights violations. Avant-garde Brazilian writers, artists and musicians began experimenting with traditional culture, creating a movement known as the Tropicália as a subversive protest against the oppressive regime. They encountered much opposition from the authorities and members of the traditional music scene, who were appalled at musicians Caetano Veloso (see image 3), Gilberto Gil and the psychedelic band Os Mutantes for mixing Brazilian rhythms such as the bossa nova with the music of US and British rock bands such as The Jimi Hendrix Experience and The Beatles. The collaborative album *Tropicália: ou Panis et Circencis* (1968) was the mouthpiece of the movement. Veloso notably used costumes in his stage performances to play with the notion of sexual identity, blurring the lines between male and female dress. He described how by wearing, 'green and black plastic clothes, with beads around my neck and necklaces of electric wires and plugs'

and growing long, wild hair he was drawing attention to the notion of performance. Veloso's image constructions predate David Bowie's experiments with appearance in the 1970s and enraged the authorities. Both he and Gil were dubbed enemies of the state, imprisoned and then summarily ejected from the country.

São Paulo's politics of protest continue. Its first punk (see page 360) band, Restos de Nada, formed in 1978 and the city's credentials as the centre of Brazil's punk scene were firmly established in 1982 when the O Começou do Fim Do Mundo festival was staged, showcasing a number of local bands. Straight edge (see page 96), emo (see page 142), garage (see page 260) and metal scenes all exist in the city and still have the polemical edge that underpins São Paulo's history, with many young people involved in anti-government protests (see image 4) and anti-globalization pressure groups. In March 2016, 1.4 million people took to the city's streets to show their disapproval of president Dilma Rousseff's alleged tax violations and misuse of state funds in the midst of economic downturn.

EMO

In the mid-1980s emo, or 'emotional hardcore', emerged out of the hyper-masculine hardcore punk scene of Washington, DC, whose adherents realized that no political posturing could halt the rise of US president Ronald Reagan as he signed for a second term in 1985. Emo can be typified by its soul-searching, angst-ridden lyrics, exploring themes of dejection, rejection and alienation rather than the hard-hitting protest of hardcore. The Rites of Spring combined the speed of punk (see page 360) with an intensely personal vocal approach and their mix of punk aggression and soul-searching content created a safe place for young men, in particular, to explore their feelings. In the 1990s grunge (see page 16) stimulated interest in indie music in general and the band Sunny Day Real Estate, Nirvana's label-mates at Sub Pop, reaped the rewards after the launch of their album *Diary* in 1994. In 1997 Deep Elm Records launched *The Emo Diaries*, a series of compilations that helped to consolidate emo as an important subgenre of indie music. The first recognized idol of emo was Blake Schwarzenbach, lead singer of San Francisco band Jawbreaker, whose lyrics were taken directly from his journal – starting a subgenre of emo dubbed 'diary-rock' that included Alkaline Trio. São Paulo's emo scene emerged in the early 1990s out of its muscular straight-edge community and the city's Tatuapé Square became a regular meeting place. Emo evolved its own street fashion, with the 'darkness' of the lyrics inspiring a predominantly black wardrobe. Sartorial elements were appropriated from indie, punk – particularly in the use of tartan – and goth (see page 164) to create a bricolage of subcultural style. The rejection of the traditional tropes of masculinity was not only expressed in the music, but also in the androgyny of emo style, including the use of guyliner, hair straighteners and black nail polish. São Paulo teenagers raised in a conservative macho culture were attracted to the ambivalent gender fluidity of the emo look, but soon found themselves open to homophobic attack for looking *marecón* or 'gay'.

1 Classic Emo street fashion in basic black.

2 The characteristic emo hairstyle with asymmetrical side-swept fringe. 3 Andy Biersack of Black Veil Brides performs in 2011 at the Vans Warped Tour. 4 Original black lace-up Vans. 5 The potential girlishness of the fringed haircut is mitigated by the sleeve tattoos.

Today, jock culture, hip hop and its associated sportswear are still being rejected (apart from the black zip-up hoodie) in favour of black skinny 'girl' jeans and tight T-shirts or polo shirts with the collars turned up in an ironic take on the preppy (see page 78). Footwear includes low-top Converse and Vans. Geek-chic references can also be seen in the use of thick, black-rimmed Buddy Holly-style glasses and messenger bags. The key focal point of emo is the asymmetrical side-swept hairstyle – cut shorter in the back and graduating down to a heavy fringe covering one eye, usually tinted black with brightly coloured sectioning – and the distinctive 'snake-bite' or double lip-piercing. More recently a subgenre of the Brazilian emo scene, dubbed 'emo de luxo', has emerged, whose adherents enjoy brands including Hello Kitty and chain stores such as Hot Topic in North America and Dangerfield in Australia.

LOWRIDER

The car is the ultimate symbol of the American Dream and lies at the heart of lowrider culture. On Saturday nights in Los Angeles, Whittier Boulevard – a well-known hub for Mexican-Americans living in the Eastside of the city – undergoes a transformation as modified lowrider cars cruise down the wide strip that links the city's Latino communities. Chrome fenders are mirror-bright, rims are buffed, paintwork is elaborate Spanish baroque, windows are engraved and interiors are lined in plush velvet. Cars are *bajito y suavecito*, 'low and slow', with chassis riding a mere 8cm (3in) from the ground and hydraulic systems designed to make the front end 'hop' or bounce up and down. Nights like these are an important form of community cohesion and provide a courting ground, as social groups are drawn together to admire each others' handiwork and car clubs compete with one another for best in show. The highlight of the year for the committed customizer is the *Lowrider* magazine-sponsored car show in Las Vegas, the national championship of lowriding.

Lowriders have been pimping their rides in the cities of El Paso and Juárez on the US–Mexico border since the 1930s, and brought the culture into the barrios of East Los Angeles after World War II. Lowrider expert Dan Usner describes how the distinctive custom hydraulics 'evolved out of the necessity to evade police officers, who quickly targeted lowriders as troublemakers. You couldn't have a car whose chassis was lower than the wheels so people in the aviation industry working with hydraulic lifters for plane flaps realized they could adapt those so they could be legal when they needed to and when they could get out of sight, they could drop it down again.'

1–6 Lowrider cars form a key point of contact for the community, with owners cruising, competing and working on their cars together.

It is believed that Los Angeles lowrider culture found its way to São Paulo via Sergio Hideo Yoshinaga, a descendant of Japanese immigrants. After discovering the nascent lowrider movement in Japan, he returned to São Paulo and opened his own garage restoring and customizing vintage cars. As imported car parts can be expensive, customized bikes began to emerge with exaggerated handlebars and banana seats that referenced Harley-Davidsons.

Mooca is São Paulo's Eastside, where lowriders express their obsession with East Los Angeles not just in car customization but in clothes, too. They obsessively co-opt the cholo look (see page 44) wholesale by wearing oversized Dickies chinos or shorts, white tube socks, bright white Nike sneakers and flannel shirts with only the top button fastened, worn over a white T-shirt. The short sleeves of oversized LA Dodgers shirts reveal the traditional cholo black-on-gray tattoos. The home-grown label Otra Vida is also popular, started by José Américo Crippa (aka Tata) after he had been exposed to lowrider culture while living in Miami in the 1990s. 'It's a culture that adds so much to the city,' he explained in an interview with the *Los Angeles Times*. 'It helps the kids to forget a bit about drugs and crime, and instead they focus on art. It's art practiced on cars and bicycles.' Crippa's appearance on the Brazilian television show *Lowrider* inspired the São Paulo legislature in 2015 to establish and provide funding for the Lowrider Culture Week, held during the Cinco de Mayo holiday period.

FLOGGER

BUENOS AIRES
COUNTRY Argentina
DECADE OF ORIGIN 2000s

Flogger is a purely Latin American phenomenon that grew out of Argentina and revolves around a passion for electro music. Fans use the social networking site Fotolog, launched in May 2002 by Scott Heiferman and Adam Seifer, in which users set up photo diaries to record their lives and invite comment. The flogger (foto-logger) first emerged in Buenos Aires in 2007 after Agustina Vivero, known as Cumbio, began holding flogger parties in her parents' apartment in the barrio of San Cristóbal and documenting her antics on the site. Cumbio and her friends became the cool kids that everyone wanted to hang out with and the circle soon outgrew the apartment. They began to meet at the Abasto shopping mall, one of the largest in Buenos Aires, armed with camera-phones. There the group held matinee parties where an imaginary catwalk was strutted and photos were immediately uploaded to Fotolog. As the numbers swelled to over two thousand, the floggers were forced out onto the pavements where their atypical appearance and shuffle-step dance-offs caught

| 1 | | 2 | 3 |
| | | | 4 |

1 & 4 Floggers wearing an androgynous look, including Converse sneakers and asymmetrical haircuts.   2 The colour blocking and kitsch print of flogger style references the 1980s.   3 The louvred design of shutter shades requires no lens.

the attention of the local media. Vivero naturally assumed the position of flogger spokesperson and became a popular commentator on youth issues, and a refreshingly alternative representation of Argentinian femininity. Guillermo Tragant, president of marketing company Furia, spotted a potential star in Cumbio and invited her and her crew to front a nationwide advertising campaign for Nike.

Flogger style is androgynous, 1980s-inspired and bright. It includes slatted sunglasses or 'shutter shades', and deep V-necked T-shirts worn over primary-coloured cotton canvas skinny jeans with white sneakers or coloured Converse. Sneaker label Cover Your Bones also targets the flogger market with brashly patterned canvas footwear reminiscent of Vans. Hair is artfully tousled into an exaggerated emo-inspired style (see page 142). Floggers tend to come from relatively privileged backgrounds with smartphones and access to the Internet, and are consumers rather than political activists — lured by the potential fame offered by social media.

PEDESTRIANS
push button and wait
for signal opposite

wait   cross
with care

EUROPE

OSLO STOCKHOLM WHITBY WIGAN MANCHESTER LONDON
BRENTWOOD GLASTONBURY PARIS AMSTERDAM ROTTERDAM
BERLIN MADRID IBIZA MILAN ROME BELGRADE MOSCOW
AYIA NAPA

BLACK METAL RAGGARE GOTH NORTHERN SOUL CASUAL BAGGY TEDDY BOY CHAP HIPSTER
ADVANCED STYLE GRIME ESSEX GIRL NEW AGE TRAVELLER ZAZOU BOHO
LEATHERMAN PROVO GABBER ANARCHO-PUNK PERROFLAUTA RAVER PANINARO
ITALO-DISCO DIZELAŠI STILYAGI PUSSY RIOT GARAGE

The idiosyncratic hipster style of London's Shoreditch (previous page) mixes vintage and high street fashion. Actor Gina Lollobrigida (opposite) epitomizes Italian glamour in an elegant dress and stylish stilettos (1956).

In 1920s Europe, the modes and manners of the Edwardian drawing room were left behind. Women shed their heavy corsetry and abandoned their voluptuous curves. Men slicked down their hair and sales of Brilliantine soared. Arising like a phoenix from the ashes of the Great War, modernism offered a new aesthetic for the 20th century. Artists and architects, painters and poets believed that a culture in which the carnage of the trenches had been allowed to happen should be rejected outright and replaced, as design historian Penny Sparke described, by 'a different set of values from those which had underpinned Victorian society'.

Fashion underwent a transformation as the hedonistic Bright Young Things of Europe (an alliance of Bohemians), the upper classes and the underworld began to rail against convention, and the cities of London, Paris and Berlin became their playgrounds. Writer and photographer Cecil Beaton described how 'raucous, irritating and offensive as these young people were, they were undoubtedly the spearhead of those who broke down conventions'. Old sartorial rules became redundant, as expressed in the shortened hemlines and serpentine slimness of the flapper, a sportif woman on the move with her cloche hat and clutch bag. The libidinous figure of Iris Storm, the tortured anti-heroine of Michael Arlen's novel *The Green Hat* (1924), is one of the best-known examples of this radical 1920s femininity. Storm is a sexually emancipated outcast, rejected by polite society yet dazzlingly resplendent in her green hat, a woman out of male control and as disordered as the city of London itself when stalking its pavements in high heels and silk stockings. The sartorial distinctions between the classes were also being eroded; in 1934 one French commentator remarked, 'They all smoke, drink cocktails, loiter at dancing halls, drive cars…how can we place them?'

After the Depression, swing music moved across the Atlantic with US émigrés drawn to Europe's bars, cabarets and café culture. Swing found a fervent audience in the zazous (see page 212) of France, the Schlurfs of Austria and the Swingjugend, or swing kids, of Nazi Germany, where the music and Anglo-American tones of the style represented freedom from a repressive regime. In a report of 1940, the authorities described the swing kids as wearing 'long, often checked English sports jackets, shoes with thick light crepe soles, showy scarves, Anthony Eden hats, an umbrella on the arm whatever the weather, and, as an insignia, a dress-shirt button worn in the buttonhole, with a jewelled stone'. Girls rejected the Aryan folkloric stereotype favoured by Nazi ideology and wore their hair glamorously curled, rather than in blonde braids, and heavy make-up instead of

the bucolic 'natural' look. The swing kids' flouting of rules, including their refusal to join the Hitler Youth or to do military service, led to their oppression, criminalization and imprisonment in youth detention camps.

In post-war Europe, US movies and Italian design became dominant influences on street fashion; stars such as James Dean and Marlon Brando set the style for young men, and the Italian film industry based in the Cinecittà studios in Rome concocted a heady mix of sun, sea and film stars, juxtaposing Sophia Loren, Portofino and Pucci to invent a new kind of Italian glamour. It found expression in an emerging teenage culture, in which teenagers were inspired to create their own versions of Gina Lollobrigida's tight belts, frou-frou skirts and high stilettos, wearing glazed cotton dresses, hooped earrings and siren red lipstick, for example. Continental design had a chic modernity that appealed to teenagers with money in their pockets. The post-war economic boom allowed them to indulge in it, with the UK mods (see page 112) leading the way.

Taste was no longer the province of an educated elite but was predicated on the demands of a more populist consumer culture, which demanded design that was modern, deluxe, fashionable and, above all, glamorous. This feeling was exacerbated by the death of Christian Dior in 1957. The hold that haute couture had imposed over the changing styles and silhouettes of 1950s fashion was loosening; mass styles were beginning to emanate from the sidewalk and the cinema, rather than from the catwalk. For young women in Europe, film stars such as Marilyn Monroe, Jayne Mansfield and Ava Gardner transgressed the codes of respectable domestic femininity and made the lack of glamour to be found in motherhood plain to see. By consuming commodities associated with Hollywood stars, women embraced a new-found glamour and marked themselves out from the older generation. The stiletto heel exemplifies this transition: sleek, sharp and sexy, the shoe had an aura of elegant menace and was named after a Sicilian fighting switchblade associated in the public consciousness with the biker hoodlums of *The Wild One* (1953), the Puerto Rican gangs of *West Side Story* (1961) and the UK teddy boy (see page 184), whose Edwardian suits reputedly concealed razors, coshes and cutters. Teenagers had become the arbiters of style, 'absolute beginners' as novelist Colin MacInnes dubbed them in 1959: girls and boys who, in their casually elegant 'teenage drag', realized that 'for the first time since centuries of kingdom come, they'd money, which hitherto had always been denied…at the best time of life to use it, namely when you're young and strong'.

BLACK METAL

The story of Mayhem, Norway's most infamous black metal band, is as extreme as it gets in the history of rock music, with the suicide of lead singer Dead (Per Yngve Ohlin) in 1991 and the fatal stabbing of guitarist Euronymous (Øystein Aarseth) by fellow band member Count Grishnackh (Varg Vikernes) in 1993. Mayhem played as if possessed, Dead wearing clothes that he had buried several days beforehand and daubed with 'corpse paint' to resemble a cadaver, on a stage surrounded by pig heads on stakes. Dead's vocals were demonic and, as he sang in a high-pitched scream, he inhaled from a plastic bag containing a decaying raven to 'get the stench of death for every song'. The sound was raw, with abrupt tempo changes and a brooding rhythmic drive or drummed 'blast beat', and was recorded with deliberately low production values to differentiate 'real' black metal from the homogenized sound of its pretenders.

After Dead's death, the black metal movement gained momentum, with fans allegedly known as the 'Black Circle' drawn to the death cult surrounding the band. Euronymous's record shop Helvete (Hell) at Schweigaards gate 56 became their meeting place (and today is the site of the Black Metal Museum). According to rock journalist Darcey Steinke, 'Parties at Hell were legendary; huge, chaotic candle-lit affairs, where devotees wore corpse-paint, black capes, and replicas of Viking gear' and denounced Christianity in favour of ancient Viking religion or, following Euronymous's example, professed to worship the devil. Most notoriously, black metal

1 Norwegian Black Metal band Immortal plays at the yearly Copenhell heavy metal festival held in Copenhagen, Denmark. The guitarist wears a version of the scene's 'corpse paint'.

2 Taiwanese heavy metal band Chthonic mixes corpse paint with Taiwanese inscriptions that reputedly raise the dead. 3 Black metal band God Seed wears the ubiquitous black leather with extreme studs and spikes.

guerrillas would make nightly raids to desecrate graveyards. This sacrilegious behaviour escalated quickly to arson, and in a little more than four years (1992–96), 22 medieval wooden churches were burnt to the ground in an attack on the enforced Christianizing of the country by Olaf Tryggvason in 995–1000 and the destruction of the indigenous Norse paganism beloved by the original Vikings. (Many of the destroyed churches had been built on the original holy pagan sites.) Varg Vikernes, who was personally found guilty of burning down four churches in acts of pagan retribution, said, 'Christianity was created by some decadent and degenerated Romans as a tool of oppression, in the late Roman era, and it should be treated accordingly. It is like handcuffs to the mind and spirit and is nothing but destructive to mankind.'

In 1998 the publication of *Lords of Chaos: The Bloody Rise of the Satanic Metal Underground* by Michael Moynihan and Didrik Søderlind, containing interviews with many of black metal's key members, expanded the little-known scene and created a global fan base. Fans adopted the all-black look by wearing black jeans, black T-shirts, black leather jackets and motorcycle boots. They also sported Viking-inspired beards and braids, and used symbols such as the satanic pentagram and the Norse Mjöllnir – the hammer of Thor (god of thunder). Black Metal is still evolving, with many bands – aside from the notorious Gorgoroth – distancing themselves from the Satanist ideology. Subgenres include blackened death metal, which combines black metal and death metal, as played by Taiwanese band Chthonic, known as the 'Black Sabbath of Asia'.

RAGGARE

STOCKHOLM
COUNTRY Sweden
DECADE OF ORIGIN 1950s

Power Big Meet, the biggest American car show in the world, is not held in a US state but in the city of Västerås in Sweden. The raggares who attend are rock 'n' roll devotees and American car enthusiasts, and their numbers are huge – estimated at 500,000 at the last count. Raggare culture developed in the 1950s when teenagers across Europe looked longingly to the United States as an Aladdin's cave full of consumer durables. The traditional restraint of Swedish design seemed drab in relation to the exuberant futurism of US styling, particularly in relation to cars. The middle-aged middle classes may have found the gleaming chrome, candy-coloured paintwork and exaggerated tail fins of a 1959 Chevrolet Impala vulgar, but teenagers saw them as the ultimate expression of the American Dream. Many countries were suffering the effects of post-war rationing, austerity and rebuilding;

1 Raggare culture celebrates the down-home and shabby over the bourgeois values of suburban Stockholm. The Power Big Meet is the biggest US car show in the world, despite being held in Sweden. 2 Ola Billmont's Raggare series of photographs, exhibited in Stockholm in 2016, provides a fascinating insight into the region's subculture. 3 Raggare 'pilsner' cars are so called because their beaten-up exterior hides a brand new engine.

Sweden was in a different position, however, having remained neutral during World War II. The country's economy was up, there was plenty of employment and teenagers had money to burn on Elvis records, movie memorabilia and American fashion, as seen in films such as *Rebel Without a Cause* (1955) – the pompadour hairstyle, jeans and Varsity jacket of its star James Dean were widely copied. The American car became an important locus of teenage identity, customized with raccoon tails, bumper stickers and the Stars and Stripes.

In the 1950s, the fun-loving raggares inspired the same moral backlash as the British teddy boys (see page 184); the press viewed gangs such as the Road Devils, Road Stars and Car Angels as delinquent troublemakers cruising the roads around Stockholm, picking up girls and causing mayhem. The pulp film *Raggare!* (1959) followed the same theme, and British trade newspaper *Kinematograph Weekly* described the film as 'a sickening social document'.

The life of the raggare revolves around the American car. In the 1970s, when successive oil crises caused petrol prices to soar, many American families offloaded their gas-guzzlers and it became relatively cheap to buy one and ship it to Europe. It is down to the raggare that today there are more vintage American cars – known as Yankees – in Sweden than there are in the United States.

Within the raggare community there are differing attitudes to cars. The old guard tend to restore them lovingly over years at great expense, and the car is handed down through the generations and worked on as a family project. Then there are the so-called 'pilsner' cars – those that appear beaten up and rusty on the exterior but hide a brand-new engine inside. These raggare take on the identity of hard-drinking US 'trailer trash', wearing double denim and leather vests and using imagery that features the Confederate flag (in the main divorced from its political meanings). This is a stance of rebellion in a country known for its staid Volvos and Opels – in fact, any prospective raggare seen in one of these Swedish cars is referred to as a *blöjraggare* or 'diaper raggare'.

4 Raggare channel the spirit of US 'trailer trash' with their beaten-up cars and hard drinking. 5 James Dean, as the troubled Jim Stark in *Rebel Without a Cause* (1955), provided a touchstone for Swedish youth who copied his pompadour hairstyle, red Anti-Freeze jacket, white T-shirt and Lee 101 Riders jeans. 6 A raggare girl in a trashy ensemble of zebra top and cut-off denim poses against a 'pilsner' car.

GOTH

The goth subcultural tribe emerged in the early 1980s. It owes its epithet to music journalist Nick Kent, who used the term to describe the music of Siouxsie and the Banshees. Fans of 'dark' music with macabre themes congregated at the Batcave Club in Soho and listened to bands such as Bauhaus, whose ground-breaking single 'Bela Lugosi's Dead' (1979) helped to establish the goth aesthetic, as did the gender-fluid appearance of lead singer Peter Murphy. The Cure, Southern Death Cult and, later, The Sisters of Mercy, All About Eve and The Mission were important musical influences. Siouxsie Sioux of Siouxsie and the Banshees was the harbinger of goth femininity – particularly her black-tinted hair, which, like that of The Cure's Robert Smith, retained the verticality of punk but was backcombed to achieve extreme volume. The look of early goth women tended towards the hypersexual rather than androgynous, continuing punk's use of fetish-inspired attire such as dog collars, PVC clothing, ripped fishnets and studded leather. The key colour was basic black, from eyeliner, lipstick and fingernails through to drainpipe trousers and Blitz buckled boots. Ecclesiastical vestments and nuns' habits had been popularized by New Romantics including Boy George, and were incorporated into goth through the religious symbol of the crucifix. Macabre references to death in the form of skull accessories and print design (hugely influential on the later work of fashion designer Alexander McQueen in the 2000s), chalk-white foundation and heavily contoured gaunt cheekbones also distinguished the goths from their peers.

By the mid-1990s the scene was polymorphous and visually diverse. The popular vampire subgenre took inspiration from the Victorian England of Bram Stoker's *Dracula*, published in 1897 and remade as a film in 1992, as well as the 1994 film adaptation of Anne Rice's modern vampire novel *Interview with the Vampire* (1976). Count Dracula and Rice's Lestat were draws for young goth men, who liked

1 Bauhaus, one of the first gothic
rock groups, was formed in 1978 and
comprised Peter Murphy (vocals),
Daniel Ash (guitar), Kevin Haskins
(drums) and David J (bass).
2 Siouxsie Sioux, lead singer
of Siouxsie and the Banshees,
was responsible for many of the
elements of the original gothic
look, with her use of black clothing,
fetish references and Cleopatra
make-up.   3 Gothic style World
Zombie Day 2011 in London,
courtesy of Soulstealer.

4 A gender-fluid mix of influences, combining fetish, punk and biker with historical details.   5 Harajuku gothic, a quirky interpretation of the look that uses kawaii cuteness to soften the dark aesthetic, including a bat-shaped vinyl backpack.   6 At the Whitby Goth Weekend the streets are filled with black-clad goths who congregate to celebrate their community.

their heady mix of mesmerizing charm and savage blood lust, and who wore frilled, puffy-sleeved shirts, frockcoats and riding boots in emulation of the undead. Goth women took on the corsetry of the 19th-century vampiress, with garments fashioned from purple velvet, black lace and PVC. The Blitz boot gained a gigantic platform sole and a shiny patent leather surface, creating an imposing presence when mixed with goth's multiple facial piercings, tattoos and silver jewellery. As the 1990s progressed, goth began to lose its mainstream commercial appeal and its fans returned to the underground. Other musical influences and subgenres entered the mix, including

industrial music and its rivethead (see page 68) and cybergoth (see page 116) adherents. Today the goth community is extremely active online and has regular festivals where thousands gather together in an extended global community. One of the longest running is the Whitby Goth Weekend (WGW), founded by Jo Hampshire in 1994 and held biannually in the seaside town where Bram Stoker wrote *Dracula*. Key scenes in the book feature local Whitby landmarks such as the ruined abbey and St Mary's Churchyard, where Lucy Westenra is attacked by the sinister Count after he has run ashore after being shipwrecked in the form of a black hound.

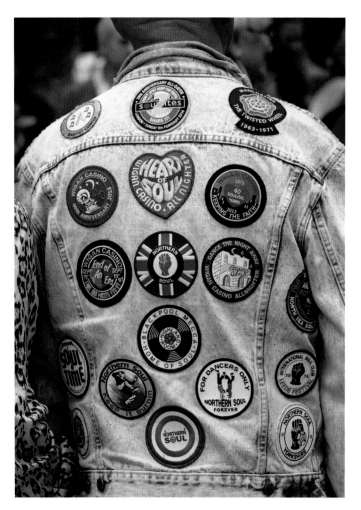

NORTHERN SOUL

In the 1970s, Wigan Casino was the Mecca for aficionados of Northern Soul. The cavernous club held up to two thousand partygoers, who gathered at all-nighters to dance to little-known soul imports from US record labels. In the wake of Berry Gordy's success at Motown in the 1960s, hundreds of small independent labels such as OKeh recorded songs in small studios. Their unsold reject records were left languishing in huge warehouses or thrift stores such as Goodwill until they were rediscovered by the few British soul music fans who could afford a trip to the United States. One such fan was budding DJ Ian Levine, who became one of the most important figures of the Northern Soul scene for his incredible record collection, encyclopedic knowledge of US soul music and legendary sets at Blackpool's Mecca ballroom. The term 'Northern Soul' was coined by Dave Godin, who owned the Soul City shop and record label in Covent Garden in London, as a means of differentiating between the type of fast-tempo soul played in the north of England at clubs such as the Twisted Wheel in Manchester and the Torch in Tunstall, Stoke-on-Trent, and the more funk-oriented music being played in southern clubs.

Northern Soul fans were fetishistic, obsessive even, in their quest for a rare groove — especially with the rise of despised commercial disco — and the DJs who could supply one attracted the biggest audiences. Competition was so fierce that it became commonplace to cover the labels of the latest floor-fillers, both as a way of ensuring that fans had to go to the club to hear them and as a means of preventing bootleggers from illegally pressing the rare records and selling them off cheaply. The movement attracted criticism for its drug use; amphetamine or 'speed' kept the night alive and the energy of the dancers up until dawn, as they whirled, back-dropped and did the splits. Clothing was practical and physically unrestricting, including high-waisted, 91cm (36in) wide Oxford bags — also known as Spencer's soul bags or Birmingham bags — with distinctive double

1 A Northern Soul music fan wears a jacket covered in embroidered patches, recording his attendance at events.   2 The KTF (Keep the Faith) clenched fist logo of Northern Soul was re-appropriated from the US Black Power movement of the 1960s.
3 The athleticism of Northern Soul dancing requires clothing that does not restrict the body.

4 A new generation of Northern Soul fans have created a demand for events
and music inspired, in part, by Elaine Constantine's film *Northern Soul* (2014).
5 The physical exertions of Northern Soul dancing require functionality in clothes
and footwear.   6 The Northern Soul scene remains vibrant with its original die-hards,
plus a new generation inspired by Youtube's Levanna Mclean (aka Northern Soul Girl).

crown back pockets with zip adjusters and a leg pocket. These were
worn with Dragonette T-shirts, Ben Sherman or Fred Perry shirts, or
vented bowling shirts, and brogues or tasselled loafers with leather
soles for spinning. Girls wore leotards, circle skirts with weighted
hems and Clarks Polyveldt shoes for dancing, then changed into
three-bar Kurt Geiger or Sasha wedges and full-length, half-belted
leather coats in black or ox-blood for the ride home. The Budgie jacket
was a short-lived fashion, a zip-up, pilot-style cotton jacket with large
round-ended lapels and collar in a contrasting colour, named after
the character played by Adam Faith in the 1970s TV series of the same
name. Faith's layered feather cut was also a popular hairstyle. Today
the Northern Soul scene remains vibrant, with all-nighters continuing
at venues such as the 100 Club in London and a generation of new
fans inspired by Elaine Constantine's film *Northern Soul* (2014).

MANCHESTER

The grand Victorian architecture of Manchester's Royal Exchange reveals the pivotal part the city known as Cottonopolis (see image 1) played in the textile trade of northern England. Industrialization made money for the mill owners but thousands of their workers lived in harsh conditions in the city's slums of Longsight, Hulme and Ancoats, home of the Forty Row Scuttlers (see image 2). Scuttlers – gangs famous for 'scuttling' or fighting – had a distinctive appearance as described by Charles Russell in 1908: 'a loose white scarf would adorn his throat; his hair was plastered down upon his forehead; he wore a peaked cap rather over one eye; his trousers were of fustian, and cut – like a sailor's – with "bell bottoms"'. The outfit was completed with brass-tipped clogs and a leather belt held with an ornamental pin, a useful weapon in any fight. In the 19th century social reformers began promoting football to the working man as a form of 'muscular Christianity' to instil the virtues of self-discipline through physical prowess, laying the foundations of the city's relationship with the so-called 'beautiful game'. Manchester United's George Best was the first footballer to have a crossover fashion appeal, due to his good looks and skills on the pitch and his champagne lifestyle after dark. Best had his own fashion label in the 1960s, financed by entrepreneur Harold Tillman, and three boutiques. Included among them was Edwardia in Deansgate, the meeting place of the Best Set, the fashionable movers and shakers of the city.

Music was and is at the heart of the Manchester scene. Mods (see page 112) and Northern Soul boys (see page 168) hung out at the Twisted Wheel, a legendary club that opened in 1963 in Brazennose Street, and the city's home-grown pop groups The Hollies, Herman's Hermits and the Bee Gees enjoyed huge success in the United States. The Reno and the Nile Club were important after-hours venues for the West Indian community from the 1960s to 1980s, located in the same building on the corner of Moss Lane and Princess Road. The city changed dramatically when recession hit, as factories and mills closed and slum housing was bulldozed to make way for huge high-rise

1 The Manchester Royal Exchange in 1890.
2 Manchester United footballer George Best, c. 1968.
3 David Bowie as Ziggy Stardust in 1973.
4 Ravers on the main stage of the Haçienda in 1989.

housing estates. The androgynous glam-rock styling of stars David Bowie (see image 3) and Bryan Ferry, whose devotees congregated at the Roxy Room at Pips discotheque, gave way to the confrontational style of punk. In the 1970s the Manchester punk scene rivalled that of London after Howard Devoto and Pete Shelley, founders of the Buzzcocks, booked the Sex Pistols to play a show at Manchester's Lesser Free Trade Hall on 4 June 1976. The gig is said to have been attended by just 42 people yet inspired several important bands, including Joy Division and The Smiths. Peter Hook, bassist with Joy Division and later New Order, recalls, 'I walked out of that gig as a musician. I came home with a guitar and told my dad, "I'm a punk musician now", and my father said, "You won't last a week." Here I am 40 years later.' The Ranch, a gay club owned by drag queen Foo Foo Lamarr, became the meeting place of the city's underground avant-garde including Mark E Smith and The Fall. Smith's paeans to the city included 'Industrial Estate' (1979) and 'City Hobgoblins' (1980) about punk's deadliest enemies the Perry Boys, the original casuals (see page 174) and the first style tribe to recognize the appeal of sportswear as street fashion.

Post-punk flourished in the city in the 1980s, a time of serious industrial decline and unemployment. Under the auspices of

Tony Wilson and Factory Records the movement made a name for itself in the UK and beyond, helped by the innovative writing of rock journalist Paul Morley. The Haçienda (see image 4), originally funded by Factory's New Order, opened in a disused yacht warehouse soon after the legendary Wigan Casino was bulldozed to make way for a civic centre that was never built. The nightclub became the centre of Manchester's burgeoning ecstasy-driven acid house scene and illegal after-hours raves were held in the disused industrial warehouses of the city now rechristened 'Madchester'. The Happy Mondays and The Stone Roses launched 'baggy' (see page 178) street fashion onto an unsuspecting nation, which was followed by the rise of the lad, as exemplified by Liam Gallagher of Oasis. In 1997 the Haçienda was forced to close after issues with drugs and gang violence. By the early 2000s, the Moss Side Gooch Gang's drug-related activities and shootings had contributed to the city's nickname of 'Gunchester', but a crackdown by police and mass arrests, plus investment, have transformed the city today. The Canal Street area developed from a dank and derelict quarter to a vibrant Gay Village. Manchester's strategic location at the centre of the UK has lured online retailers Boohoo and Missguided, and the Victorian cotton warehouses are now home to offices, studio spaces and luxury apartments.

CASUAL

The terrace of the football ground has been the scene of some of the most fashion-forward moments in the history of British menswear, courtesy of the casual street style that swept the UK in the 1980s. The Salford and Manchester Perry Boys, named after their penchant for Fred Perry polo shirts worn with straight jeans and sneakers, were forerunners of the movement and spread their style throughout the UK when travelling to Manchester United away games. As with many white working-class street styles, the difference was in the detail, and the labels most lusted after were the hardest to source. Casuals scoured specialist sportswear stores for ski jumpers, deck shoes and blizzard jackets, and subverted their meaning by wearing them on concrete terraces – for these 'ordinary boys' would never have set foot on the varnished deck of a super-yacht, the crisp snow of a ski slope or the manicured turf of a golf course. The functionality of sportswear and its associations with physical prowess also made it possible for casuals to wear bright colours and patterns without ridicule, anticipating the decade's brash clothing trends and hip hop's conversion of the tracksuit and trainers into fashion. The more adventurous football fan, or 'gaffer', would take a trip to Europe and come back with hard-to-get brands such as Giorgio Armani,

1 *The Firm* (2009), directed by Nick Love, was set in the world of the 1980s football-loving casual.   2 A casual wearing Ellesse and Fila in Wanstead, Essex, in 1983.

3 The Adidas Trimm Trab with polyurethane midsole was a classic footwear style for terrace casuals.   4 Paul Anderson in *The Firm* (2009), wearing the bright colours that were a feature of original casual street fashion.   5 Danny Dyer in *The Business* (2005), set in the 1980s. The original casual clothes were sourced and supplied by 80s Casual Classics.   6 A black-and-white Fila tracksuit.   7 A casual tracksuit finds its way onto the runway as part of Todd Snyder's menswear S/S 2017 collection.

Daniel Hechter and Sergio Tacchini. Away games in Europe provided the perfect opportunity for fans to check out European sportswear labels, and led to the popularization in the UK of brands such as Ellesse and Fila. At one point in the 1980s, Wade Smith in Liverpool sold more Adidas trainers than any other store in the world.

Every city's casuals (aka firms) had their own unique identity, and the first Manchester casuals took their cues from David Bowie – in particular, his image on the 1977 *Low* album cover, dressed in a duffle coat with a variation of the soulboy wedge haircut. The wedge, originally cut by Trevor Sorbie for Sassoon in 1974, was graduated from short through to long on top, tapering to a teardrop at the nape of the neck and coloured darker underneath with a lighter tone on top. (In Liverpool the flick haircut was preferred; it was shorter than the wedge at the back and sides with a long fringe that was 'flicked' out of the eye.) By 1982 the casual look had broken the surface of popular culture via an article in *The Face* magazine entitled 'The Ins and Outs of High Street Fashion'.

After the infamous 1985 Kenilworth Road clash between Millwall's notoriously violent firm the Bushwackers and Luton Town's MIGs, Prime Minister Margaret Thatcher called for a crackdown on football hooliganism. However, it was another youth phenomenon, rave (see page 238), that ultimately prompted the demise of the casuals, as nightclubs took over from matches and ecstasy-fuelled friendliness took over from fights. In 2005 a casual revival was kick-started by the film *The Business*, starring Danny Dyer, and many labels such as Fila opened up their back catalogues to a new generation of consumers.

BAGGY

'People have got to realize that you can't wear anything wider than 21-inch bottoms. Anything else looks ridiculous.' — Ian Brown

From 1983 to 1984 there was a 'scruff' backlash in Manchester against the neat and aspirational look of the casuals (see page 174). Non-branded, oversized clothing appeared on the football terraces, including cagoules, snorkel parkas and untucked shirts – all elements that would make their way into the 'baggy' style of the so-called 'Madchester' scene. Manchester casuals had adopted the flared tracksuit bottom of Continental sportswear and the silhouette began to naturally transition into jeans. Originals were hard to find, so casuals split the side seams of their straight jeans at the bottom so that they fell away from trainers. Phil Thornton, author of *Casuals* (2003), cites Phil Saxe, a Twisted Wheel DJ, jeans retailer and future manager of the Salford band the Happy Mondays, as responsible for the flared jeans craze. Saxe had a stall in the Arndale Market and recalls how in 1983, 'three girls came in and said, "Do you ever get any flares in?"' After going to a local warehouse he found a supply of deadstock Levis and 'within two months was buying one thousand pairs at a time. I was the granddad of baggy fashion.' As the baggy craze began to kick off, both girls and boys in Manchester wore Dickies corduroy bags with 50cm (20in) bottoms (later replaced with bags by Joe Bloggs, a label run by young entrepreneur Shami Ahmed) and snorkel parkas, and rejected the casuals' obsession with trainers in favour of Clarks shoes, anticipating the English heritage brand's revival with Britpop. Music was changing, too, as acid house took over from Northern Soul (see page 168); in 1986 the Haçienda became a dance-oriented club rather than a venue for live music, with DJs Mike Pickering, Graeme Park and 'Little' Martin Prendergast and sets from the legendary Frankie Knuckles who flew in from the United States. Bags had always been an important component of the soul dancer's uniform because the athletic steps incorporating flips and splits required ease

1		
2		3

1 The Stone Roses wearing deliberately oversized or baggy clothing in the 1990s as prime movers of the 'Madchester' scene. 2 Model Martin Lind wears a bucket hat during Paris Fashion Week 2016. 3 Baggy clothes disguise the body and can make the wearer appear diminutive. In New York a bucket hat is combined with an oversized coat and brogues in 2015.

4 Fashion editor Alex Badia creates a slouchy silhouette at New York Fashion Week, 2015.   5 Fendi S/S 2017, designed by Karl Lagerfeld and Silvia Venturini.   6 Bucket hat and tracksuit for agnès b, S/S 2017.

of movement. Tight-fitting tops were exchanged for cheap, oversized T-shirts from Fruit of the Loom, some of which were tie-dyed in reference to 1960s psychedelic drug culture and its modern equivalent MDMA (ecstasy). The counter-culture of the 1960s also influenced Manchester music, as bands including the Happy Mondays, The Stone Roses and the Inspiral Carpets fused 1960s garage rock and psychedelia with 1970s funk bass guitar and drum patterns, plus indie guitar, to create an innovative form of music at its most effective in The Stone Roses single 'Fool's Gold' (1989). It was The Stone Roses drummer, Alan 'Reni' Wren, who was responsible for the enduring Manchester trend of the fishing or bucket hat, later worn by Liam Gallagher of Oasis. Tracks were remixed for the city's acid house scene, creating a new dance/rock fusion. By 1989 the city had been renamed 'Madchester', a term originally coined by the Bailey Brothers, video directors for Tony Wilson's Factory Records, who floated it as a potential T-shirt slogan for the Happy Mondays.

LONDON

In 1953, the *Picture Post* magazine, a popular barometer of British opinion, published a series of photographs by Charles Hewitt of Colin Donellan, who was described in the article as 'a London boy from a good family background'. Donellan was of interest because he was a teddy boy (see image 1), who had 'been in trouble with the police since the age of eight' and had subsequently been incarcerated in a succession of approved schools, borstals and prison. The link between this particular street style – typically consisting of a long, dark drape jacket, drainpipe trousers, crepe-soled shoes and bootlace tie – and criminal delinquency was made clear, emphasized by the *Post*'s observation that 'these clothes are worn by many criminal gang members'.

Almost 20 years later, in 1971, fashion designer Vivienne Westwood (see image 2) and her partner Malcolm McLaren launched a series of anti-boutiques at 430 King's Road, an area of Chelsea dubbed 'The World's End' after an insalubrious gin palace that had opened in 1897. The first incarnation of the store, Let It Rock, took inspiration from the outlaw Teddy Boy by creating a space in which a jukebox blared Billy Fury, chairs were upholstered in kitsch leopard-skin and Formica display cabinets provided the backdrop to drape suits and brothel creepers (a thick crepe sole shoe originally designed by George Cox in 1949). The canny design duo knew the power of rebellious street style and began to harness it in the styling of their shops, moving smoothly through the outlaw biker of Too Fast to Live Too Young to Die in 1972 and the sado-masochistic fetishist of Sex in 1974 to Seditionaries in 1977, the now-iconic playground of the punk.

London has been a powerful spawning ground for many of the world's most subversive street movements: the teddy boys (see page 184) of Elephant and Castle, the punks (see page 360) of Camden, Croydon and the King's Road, and the Rastafarians and ragamuffins of Notting Hill. All still exist today, not just in the capital, but in pockets of street style all over the world. The most recent manifestation of this tradition is the ubiquitous hipster (see page 192) of Shoreditch. Once a gangland haunt of Teddy Boy heavies orbiting the infamous Kray twins, the area is now dominated by the Silicon Roundabout and is home to fashion tech brands including Farfetch, Thread and Wool and the Gang.

1 Teddy boys in 1955.　2 Sid Vicious and Vivienne Westwood in punk attire in 1976.　3 Carnaby Street dandy in 1968.　4 Carnaby Street in 1968.

The history of London's thoroughfares is inextricably linked to the development of sartorial style. The Strand, one of the grand thoroughfares of Victorian London, was once a muddy track running east along the River Thames, described by King Henry VIII as 'full of pits and sloughs, very perilous and noisome'. During the reign of Queen Elizabeth I, the route was improved to such an extent that the Engish nobility began to build grand mansions on both sides of the unpaved road. As the Strand connected two powerful institutions – the government at Whitehall and the finance industry in the City of London – it had by the end of the 19th century become a meeting place for gentlemen to discuss the affairs of the day over roast beef at Simpson's or a drink at the Savoy. This became the perfect location for a range of gentlemen's outfitters that still exist today and provide the gateway to London's prestigious Savile Row.

It was in this district that the dandy (see image 3) emerged: an embodiment of extreme fashion fetishism who was one of the earliest London figures to turn heads on the street. In 1825 an anonymous author wrote of how 'the most tyrannical uniformity is exacted in London... wearing a hat an inch too wide in the brim, a waistcoat too short, or a coat too long, subjects the unfortunate and unconscious foreigner to a suspicion of vulgarity quite sufficient to banish him from the elegant

For women, the flapper look of the 1920s encapsulated interwar London style and could be found in the West End, an area that had developed as a centre of haute couture and coiffure in the 17th century after the Great Plague of 1665 and the Fire of London in 1666 forced a general movement of the population away from the City and the River Thames. Empowered by gains made in political and legal reform, women embraced the physical freedom offered by the flapper's more tubular, androgynous look. Nightclubs, jazz clubs and cocktail bars were filled with society women wearing short skirts and bobbed haircuts, dancing the night away in defiance of sartorial and societal convention.

The dandy and the flapper are early manifestations of London street style, but it wasn't until the post-war years that subcultural or street style began to define the capital. Emerging youth markets combined with an economic boom to create what many have dubbed a 'youthquake'. A generation of young consumers gave rise to a new set of classless socia spaces centred around Carnaby Street (see image 4), the hotbed of the so-called Swinging Sixties, and Soho, home of the mod. And the arrival of the first wave of Caribbean immigrants on the SS *Windrush* in 1949 introduced new items into the vocabulary of London style that were channelled variously by mods (see page 112), skinheads (see page 356),

1 Young men in Edwardian suits in 1955. The name 'teddy boy' derives from the diminutive of Edward, 'Ted'.   2 Members of The Edwardian Drape Society (T.E.D.S.) meet in Clapham, London, in 1993. These teddy boy and girl revivalists strive for a truly authentic 1950s look.   3 A teddy boy at the Mecca Dance Hall, Tottenham, London, in 1954, with a greased pompadour or quiff. His ribbon tie references the cool saloon-bar gambler of the Hollywood Western.

TEDDY BOY

In North Africa and the Middle East during World War II, British soldiers found the standard army issue footwear unsuited to the blisteringly hot foreign climes. They coerced shoemakers in the local markets to custom make rough, lace-up suede boots with a rubber crepe sole for walking on hot sand that were dubbed 'brothel creepers' after they were spotted being worn in the Sharia Wag el Birket at the centre of Cairo's red-light district. By the end of the 1940s the shoemaker George Cox had exaggerated the sole into a thick wedge of crepe and made the uppers out of brightly coloured suede and they were being worn by one of the first post-war youth subcultures – the teddy boy.

Teddy boys hailed from some of the poorest districts of London such as Elephant and Castle, an area that had been severely damaged during the bombing of the Blitz. Down amid the bomb sites, as documented by young photographer Ken Russell, young men of the second Elizabethan Age began to assert their individuality through so-called Edwardian (shortened to teddy) dress, wearing drape suits consisting of narrow-lapelled, knee-length jackets with moleskin or satin collars, bootlace ties and skinny drainpipe trousers. Hair was a focal point, squared off at the back into a Boston neckline, the top grown long and styled with Brilliantine or Brylcreem into a greasy pompadour quiff. For teenagers with no real control over their education, work or economics, power came through personal appearance and clothes were used as a means of standing out from the crowd. The teddy boy soon gained notoriety as a territorial

4 & 5 A modern version of teddy boy street fashion by Saint Laurent for A/W 2014.   6 Fashion designer Pam Hogg in 2016.   7 Malcolm McLaren in teddy boy attire in 1972.

gang-minded juvenile delinquent obsessed with rock 'n' roll – one of the first examples of the teenage rebel in Europe, following the pattern set by James Dean in *Rebel Without a Cause* (1955). However, by the early 1960s the teddy boy look had been usurped by the fresh cosmopolitan feel that was entering fashion.

In the early 1970s the teddy boy look reappeared in a pop art form – a brightly coloured cartoon version that stood as an alternative to the glam rock movement and was worn by avant-garde artist Duggie Fields, fashion designer Antony Price and Andy Mackay of Roxy Music. Being a teddy boy was a way for men to dress up while retaining their masculinity in a sea of lurex and lip gloss as sported by stars such as David Bowie. Original and reproduction drape suits and brothel creepers could be found at Let It Rock on London's King's Road, a shop that opened in 1971 and was run by entrepreneur Malcolm McLaren and his partner, fashion designer Vivienne Westwood. The interior was pure 1950s kitsch, with Formica display cabinets, a jukebox blaring out Billy Fury and yards of fake leopard skin. At first, Let It Rock catered to both the old and new audience of teddy boys, but the premises soon morphed into other incarnations and became the meeting point of punk (see page 360) aficionados.

1 The Young Fogeys by Sassoon Academy in 2011, photographed by Colin Roy. 2 Female chap in moss green knitted suit at the Chap Olympiad, Bedford Square Gardens in Bloomsbury, London, in 2012. 3 London chap Stephen Myhill says, 'I don't have so many original items, so try to source things that look right even if they are more modern. I particularly like doing so without spending huge amounts of money – Chap on the Cheap is my approach.'

CHAP

In 1910 a manly fellow had to have a well-barbered and practical hairstyle that could be controlled without too much fuss. The popularity of the beard was at its height, with many a paterfamilias taking inspiration from the barbered hair and beard of King George V, shaped to be tighter at the sides and longer in the chin – a look that has enjoyed a revival in the 2010s as a global recession has caused a cultural shift in men's fashion. When set against a backdrop of economic chaos and environmental collapse, fashion tends to become retrospective as a fear of the future causes consumers to take refuge in the past. Heritage labels become lighthouses in a storm, worn by those reacting against cheap, ephemeral fashion in favour of well-constructed clothes designed to last a lifetime. *The Chap* magazine has been at the forefront of this reappraisal of traditional British menswear, launched by Gustav Temple and Vic Darkwood in 1999 in an attempt to convert the men of Great Britain to a more formal way of dressing as a reaction against the typical tracksuit and trainers combination. Sportswear had become ubiquitous on the streets and was completely divorced from the idea of physical activity after being re-branded as leisurewear. *The Chap* made its position clear from the outset, with a manifesto that included the tongue-in-cheek commandments 'Thou Shalt Always Wear Tweed', 'Thou Shalt Always Doff One's Hat' and 'Thou Shalt Never Fasten the Lowest Button on Thy Waistcoat'. Trousers had to have creases so sharp 'they will start a riot on the high street'. Chaps also were exhorted to cultivate interesting facial hair, which proved much in evidence at

4 A participant in the Chap Olympiad in 2016. 5 Stephen Myhill explains, 'Although I now dress in an ultra-conservative manner, I am actually pushing against the norm. I still go to punk gigs, and in a room full of people who dress to be different I tend to be the one who stands out. This is my punk.' 6 The retrospective fashions of the gentleman have proved popular during the recession of the 2010s and designers have taken inspiration from past styles, as in this shawl-collared Fendi suit.

their agit-prop stunts including the Chap Olympiad, held every July in Bloomsbury, London, since 1999, where events included cucumber sandwich discus and umbrella jousting.

In 2012 a selection of moustachioed chaps and chapesses in tweed demonstrated outside the Abercrombie & Fitch store at the corner of Savile Row, the historical tailoring district of London. They were protesting against the mooted opening of a children's store by the US brand at Number 3, thus destroying the bespoke traditions of the area. The editorial board of *The Chap* and its adherents wittily anticipated the reawakening of interest in traditional English brands such as John Lobb and Tricker's, as well as classic clothing such as the Norfolk jacket or waxed Barbour jacket teamed with Viyella shirts, skinny jeans and brogues. Facial hair also made a comeback in mainstream men's fashion, morphing from the chap-inspired waxed moustache to the full-faced hipster beard. In 2014, market researchers Mintel found that beards had become so ubiquitous that sales of razors and blades had fallen by 3.6 per cent.

1 2 3   4

1–3 The mix of vintage, high street and global fashion worn in an idiosyncratic way is the hallmark of hipster.
4 Hipster street fashion in London includes the Edwardian spade-shaped beard.

HIPSTER

Throughout most of the 20th century, Shoreditch remained an industrial slum, due in part to the heavy bombing suffered by the area during the Blitz of World War II. No real change in its reputation occurred until the recession of the 1990s, when its empty warehouses and industrial spaces became the cheap studio-dwellings of the Young British Artists (YBA). Damien Hirst's shark in formaldehyde or *The Physical Impossibility of Death in the Mind of Someone Living* (1991) and Tracey Emin's *My Bed* (1998) were the epitome of cool and transformed East London into a go-to destination for those in the know.

The Bricklayers Arms – a grungy Shoreditch pub – became a melting pot of many of London's most exciting creative talents. Propping up the bar were the first wave of hipsters: fashion designer Luella Bartley, fashion stylists Katie Grand and Fee Doran, and artists Hirst and Emin. Urban regeneration was followed by gentrification and brought the second wave of hipsters: apolitical cool hunters and early adopters of micro-trends that are then rapidly integrated into mainstream fashion via the Internet. The goal is to be the first to possess the most arcane of style knowledge and there are some very identifiable looks. Within the environs of Shoreditch, and more

5–9 East London hipster references include a nostalgia for childhood in the use of bright colours and graphic prints that often reference the 1980s, as well as the ubiquitous hipster cropped trouser and beard. The Americana influence on hipster style includes the heritage red-and-black Mackinaw check, usually worn by deer hunters.

latterly Bethnal Green, a wholesale identification with white working-class Americana prevails. Trucker hats and battered fedoras are mixed with vintage T-shirts and skinny jeans in a fashionable mélange that remains devoid of its original relationship with the working man. The red-and-black Mackinaw check is a case in point: originally a thick woollen cloth famed for its water-repellent qualities and worn by Canadian loggers in the 19th century, it became a badge of authentic working-class values, most notably when worn by Marlon Brando as ex-prize fighter turned longshoreman Terry Malloy in the film *On the Waterfront* (1954). Mackinaw check is now sported by the urban lumberjacks of Shoreditch in the form of shirts, vintage Woolrich jackets and original Filson Cruiser coats.

ADVANCED STYLE

'Don't wear beige – it could kill you!' — Sue Kreitzman

In 2008 photographer Ari Seth Cohen and filmmaker Lina Plioplyte started the blog Advanced Style to deliberately draw attention to the innovative clothing worn by older women, those usually considered 'invisible' by the fashion system. Participants wear the most glorious ensembles mixing print, colour, texture, era and found objects to become walking works of art. In a world that ignores the older woman, they insist on being seen. Forerunners of Advanced Style include the late Anna Piaggi, creative consultant for Italian *Vogue* in Milan, who collaborated for many years with fashion designer Karl Lagerfeld. His sketches of her were published in 1986 as *Karl Lagerfeld: A Fashion Journal: A Visual Record of Anna Piaggi's Creative Dressing and Self-Editing,* and in 2006 London's Victoria and Albert Museum held an exhibition of her outfits called 'Anna Piaggi: Fashion-ology'.

London's torchbearers of Advanced Style include fashion designer Zandra Rhodes, whose signature pink hair, bold make-up and Andrew Logan jewellery make her instantly recognizable, and writer and artist Molly Parkin, who wears handmade sequin turbans and flowing, ecclesiastical-inspired robes. Artist, curator and writer Sue Kreitzman is also instrumental in the scene. As she puts it, 'There is an old lady revolution happening now, and old men are starting to hang on to our coattails. We now live longer, look better, and keep on working long beyond what was traditionally retirement age. It really is a new world, and I feel that I, and those like me, are pioneers.' Many younger men and women are becoming involved, bored with the dominance of identikit fast fashion, and regular Colour Walks are held in the city in which participants walk the pavements as a joyful, inclusive tribe.

1 A guest at the Advanced Style book signing at Perrin Paris, New York, in 2016 rejects trends-based fashion for an idiosyncratic and individual look.   2 Two forerunners of Advanced Style, fashion designer Vivienne Westwood and Anna Piaggi, creative consultant for Italian *Vogue*.
3 Make-up artist Astrid Kearney on a Colour Walk, a regular meet-up in and around London for those who 'dress out of the box' according to organizer Galina Sherri.

4 Iris Apfel, interior designer, model and fashion icon, believes fashion designers are missing the mark. 'How can an older woman relate to a little kid running up and down the runway? You can't.' 5 Valerie and Jean, aka the Idiosyncratic Fashionistas, call themselves 'Style bloggers of a certain age, setting a bad example for older women everywhere.' 6 Judith Boyd, whose blog The Style Crone is dedicated to 'the older woman in her most creative, outrageous and proud era'.

The Advanced Style movement received a boost in 2014 with the release of the documentary *Iris*, about US interior designer turned model Iris Apfel, a nonagenarian known for her trademark round glasses and mix of antique, vintage and modern fashion and accessories. She became a poster girl for the style in 2005, when the Metropolitan Museum of Art in New York mounted its 'Rara Avis' exhibition of looks taken from her personal collection. It was a success through word of mouth as viewers were captivated by her sense of style and forthright views on fashion. As she puts it, after the age of 60 'you're supposed to fade away. The fashion industry has done itself in by neglecting the 60–80-year-old market. They have the time and the economic resources. They want to go shopping. Fashion has this youth mania. But 70-year-old ladies don't have 18-year-old bodies and 18-year-olds don't have a 70-year-old's dollars.'

GRIME

LONDON
COUNTRY UK
DECADE OF ORIGIN 2000s

By the early 2000s, hip hop was the voice of corporate music culture, the force of its messages drained by the champagne lifestyles of superstars such as Jay Z. The disenfranchised youth of East London's housing estates began to look to Jamaican toasting, dancehall, reggae, dub and ragga (see page 134) for musical influences, mixed with home-grown jungle (see page 110) and garage (see page 260). Created by crews such as Ruff Sqwad, formed in Bow in 2001, grime was made on home PCs using Fruity Loops software (also used in tribal guarachero, see page 124) and played on the underground massive of pirate radio stations such as Heat, Mystic, Deja Vu and Rinse FM.

Grime took many forms – eerie, aggressive, erratic, jittery – but was generally fast at 140 beats per minute, with dark synth-led tracks against which MCs clashed or battle-rapped using indigenous (rather than faux US) accents, London slang and site-specific references. (This

1 & 2 The grime scene rejects the ostentatious high fashion labels of garage street fashion in favour of black and a more authentic street look.   3 New Era 59Fifty baseball cap.   4 Nike Air Max trainer.   5 Break-out grime star Stormzy.

development was paralleled in indie music with the northern English accents of Oasis's Liam Gallagher, Alex Turner of the Arctic Monkeys and Paul Smith of Maximo Park.) The key event was Lord of the Mics, started up by Jammer, a member of Roll Deep (also the crew of MC Wiley, eskibeat innovator and a key figure in grime), Neckle Camp and Boy Better Know. It was the location of the now legendary clashes of Skepta versus Devilman and Wiley versus Kano. The lyrical flow of the battles, the remixing of each other's lyrics and general dissing was captured on a series of DVDs.

The insular network of radio, clubs and homemade promos and recording kept grime stars and labels underground and independent until 2003, when Dizzee Rascal's debut album *Boy in da Corner* created a short flurry of interest after winning the Mercury Music Prize for best album from the UK and Ireland. The second wave remains fiercely independent and includes Boy Better Know crew –

founded in 2005 and run by Tottenham-based MCs and brothers Skepta and JME, who signed Canadian superstar Drake (who has a Boy Better Know tattoo) in 2016 – as well as Stormzy, Little Simz, Novelist and Krept and Konan.

Grime style bears a similarity to the early style of gangsta rap (see page 46) in that it rejects the ghetto fabulous look of US hip hop and the ostentatious flashiness of UK garage in favour of the authentic everyday, such as Dizzee Rascal's shop-bought black Adidas tracksuits, oversized jeans and hoodies. The New Era 59Fifty baseball cap is worn straight with the peak low to cover the eyes and to show the Hologram sticker, while footwear is box-fresh Nike Air Max trainers, nicknamed '110s' after their £110 price tag. Garage clubs refused entry to those wearing such clothes, branding them 'trouble-makers', which has led grime stars to deliberately play with the 'bad boy' stereotype.

ESSEX GIRL

The mod revival (see page 112) and 2 Tone movement of the 1980s had an unexpected effect in the UK – a massive upsurge in the popularity of the white stiletto. In 1987 the British shoe manufacturer Dolcis sold 260,000 pairs, and they became associated with a stereotype of white working-class femininity known as the Essex girl. With permed blonde hair, an elasticated crop top or 'boob tube' and a Lycra miniskirt, she was known for dancing around her handbag at the local discos of Basildon and Brentwood. Basildon, a post-war New Town founded in 1949 for the burgeoning population of the East End of London, housed a majority of lifelong Labour voters resistant to the politics of Conservatism. In 1983, however, the East End migrant and Basildon voter switched allegiance to enthusiastically support the free market politics of Margaret Thatcher, spawning a disparaging stereotype – the flashy, shell-suited, aspirational working-class voter known as Basildon or Essex man, parodied by comedian Harry Enfield in 1988 as the character Loadsamoney. Television also made stars of three Essex girls, both fictional and fact: the character of Dorien played by Lesley Joseph in the comedy series *Birds of a Feather* (1989 – 98), who lived in Chigwell and was, in the popular British phrase, 'mutton dressed as lamb' (dressing too youthfully for her age), and the *Big Brother* reality game show contestants Jade Goody and Chantelle Houghton. After much condemnation, feminist Germaine Greer leapt to the Essex girl's defence in 2006, writing that she was 'a working-class heroine surviving in a post-proletarian world. She is

1 Gemma Collins found fame in the reality show *The Only Way is Essex* (TOWIE) set in Brentwood. Her blonde hair extensions, tan and body-con clothes created a glamorous image for plus-size women and spawned her own clothing range.   2 The Essex girl look is an exaggerated, almost parodic, version of female glamour, with artifice praised over 'natural' beauty.   3 Essex girl styling has become mainstream, with its adherents spending their cash on extreme grooming practices, including overly white teeth bleaching or veneers, hair extensions and obviously fake 'tango' tans.

4 Essex girl styling is highly polished and exuberant, a 2010s version of 1980s glamour. Clothes show off the body with particular emphasis on the legs, which are lengthened with sky-high heels and wedges by shoe designer Christian Louboutin or his copyists. **5** Joey Essex (left) is the break-out star of TOWIE and responsible for many UK menswear trends, including the revival of 1980s tennis shorts. **6** Glamour model turned reality star Katie Price spearheaded the Essex girl look and has cited her admiration for the hyper-glamorous style of drag artists.

descended from the mill girls who terrorized their neighbourhoods, raucous, defiant, pleasure-seeking.'

In 2010 a structured reality show called *The Only Way is Essex* (also known as 'TOWIE'), based on the same narrative format as the successful Los Angeles-based MTV show *The Hills* (2006–10), aired for the first time. This comedic, almost parodic version of life in Brentwood for a group of good-natured 'twenty-something' entrepreneurs struck a chord with the UK public, who enjoyed, and began to copy, the participants' patois, clothing choices and grooming habits. The look was maximalist and excessive, dependent on a retinue of cosmeticians, hairdressers, dentists and cosmetic surgeons, and derived in the main from the artificial look of glamour model Jordan turned reality star Katie Price, who herself took inspiration from the hyper-femininity of drag artists. The TOWIE look was expensive to maintain and included sculpted high-definition eyebrows, double rows of fake eyelashes, spray-on tan, expensive bright white tooth veneers and breast and buttock enhancement. The Essex girl supplemented the volume and length of her hair with hair extensions and wore body-con clothing and high-heeled shoes. The series introduced the 'vajazzle' (vagina plus bedazzle), a Hollywood wax followed by adornment of the pudenda with crystals, and the 'male cleavage', wherein the pectoral muscles are exposed in low-cut T-shirts. Unexpectedly, the series has had a huge effect on mainstream fashion, the high-maintenance look becoming an indicator of social status and regarded by many of its adherents as a way of transforming humdrum features into high glamour. The TOWIE cast who have opened their own boutiques and launched clothing lines include Amy Childs and Gemma Collins.

1 A New Age traveller wears a combination of layered clothing that references nature, world culture and the travelling minstrel or jester, while crossing gender and geography.   2 The white dreadlock references the spirituality of Rastafarianism while suggesting the wearer is without artifice, disinterested in mainstream grooming practices.   3 New Age Traveller Gathering at Stonehenge in 1984.

GLASTONBURY
COUNTRY UK
DECADE OF ORIGIN 1980s

NEW AGE TRAVELLER

The 1980s trappings of luxurious excess were anathema to those calling for a global change in consciousness. New Age adherents believed that spirituality, sensitivity and eco-awareness had to replace shopping for logo-laden designer labels if the world was to be saved, a pertinent stance on the back of environmental catastrophes such as the Bhopal industrial gas leak of 1984 and the Chernobyl nuclear explosion of 1986. These man-made disasters, where science had taken precedence over nature at the expense of humankind, inspired a generation to look back at the hippy movement with respect. The idea of 'dropping out' for a life on the road, travelling the free festival circuit rather than living a life of humdrum banality in 'straight' society, began to hold romantic appeal. By 1982 the press had heard about a fleet of battered and psychedelically painted buses, vans, trailers and decommissioned ambulances moving its way across the UK in a 'peace convoy' from the Glastonbury Festival to RAF Greenham Common, the site of a long-running protest against the stationing of cruise missiles in the UK (1981–2000). These were the New Age travellers, earnest defenders of the environment and comprising those who explicitly rejected the tenets of Thatcherism in favour of a more 'authentic' life. In a search for spiritual meaning they were drawn to ancient pagan sites such as Glastonbury Tor and the stone circle at Stonehenge, where they met up and celebrated their alternative community. Stonehenge, in particular, became a site of controversy

4 & 7 White dreadlocks require little grooming, so are suited to life on the road.   5 A travelling fortune teller at Stonehenge.   6 A graffitied vehicle fitted out for living accommodation in 2016.

during the first half of the 1980s, when attempts to block the yearly pagan celebration of the summer solstice were made by Wiltshire Council with the backing of English Heritage (who controlled access to the site). The Battle of the Beanfield in 1985 was a notorious incident near the ancient site in which 450 New Age travellers were ambushed by 1,300 police officers.

The Poll Tax introduced in 1990 and the concurrent crackdown on squatting in UK cities added an anarchist element to the New Age travelling scene. Photographer Iain McKell, who has documented the travellers for some years, describes them as a hybrid tribe of 'new gypsies' and 'present-day rural anarchists'. In terms of appearance, a punk style (see page 360) was combined with a ragbag hippy

aesthetic that mixed faded and patchwork layers of environmentally friendly organic materials, such as hemp, with thrift store finds and army surplus clothing. Both sexes wore heavy boots and garments with 'ethnic' accessories such as beads, Greek 'eye' talismans and Celtic or 'tribal' tattoos. The white dreadlock, originally created by Simon Forbes at Antenna, London, became a popular hairstyle for both men and women because it involved little grooming and was suited to a life on the road. Anti-Thatcher anarchists also introduced a post-apocalyptic look, comprising studded and battered leather clothing and facial piercings, inspired by films such as *Mad Max* (1979). This style was expressed most evocatively in the found object sculptures of the Mutoid Waste Company.

PARIS

'It was like a whole world – you had Paris and then you had "our" Paris – the music and the fashion, our own world inside the city.' — Elli Medeiros, Stinky Toys

The 1890s in Paris witnessed the birth of *la belle époque*, a decade as sparkling as champagne, but dubbed 'decadent' by those who disapproved. Paris appeared to be a glittering city of erotic pleasure, and the Italian writer Edmondo de Amicis was overwhelmed by its grand boulevards where 'windows, shops, advertisements, doors, facades, all rise, widen and become silvered, gilded and illumined. It s rivalry of magnificence...which borders on madness. The eye finds no place on which to rest.' For him it was 'a city of coquetry and pride, a great, opulent and sensual city, living only for pleasure and glory'. Paris's gaudy attractions were best expressed in its infamous, anarchic dance – the cancan – performed at the Moulin Rouge, where showgirls openly displayed their petticoats and drawers, private items of clothing normally kept hidden (see image 1). Women of the demi-monde became the acknowledged leaders of fashion, including La Belle Otero (see image 2), Liane de Pougy and Émilienne d'Alençon (see image 3), known as *les grandes horizontales*. These rebellious

women refused to obey the conventional rules of heterosexual love, remaining independent and in control in an era when women had little power outside of the domestic sphere. Otero had a list of lovers that spanned Europe, including Edward, Prince of Wales, who gave he a hunting lodge outside Paris in which to facilitate their assignations.

Paris was the centre of high fashion, having built its reputation from catering to the needs of the French court at Versailles in the 18th century. Charles Frederick Worth, an English émigré, helped establish haute couture in the 19th century. French poet and dandy Robert de Montesquiou, who was the inspiration behind Marcel Proust's fictional character Baron de Charlus, flew the flag for exquisite menswear. In 1834 the renowned Jockey-Club de Paris opened as the Société d'Encouragement pour l'Amélioration des Races de Chevaux en France (Society for the Encouragement of the Improvement of Horse Breeding in France) and became the meeting place for the social elite. By 1900 a notorious street gang known as the Apaches had emerged (see image 4), named after the indigenous tribe of America and reflecting the popularity of James Fenimore Cooper's novel *The Last of the Mohicans* (1826). According to writer Jon Savage, the Apache, a working-class dandy, wore 'a black jacket with a

1 The risque clothing of the cancan dancer.   2 Poster advertising dancer La Belle Otero.   3 *Grande horizontale* Émilienne d'Alençon.   4 The Apache street gang rioting with the police.   5 Paris cabaret Le Tabou in *c.* 1963.

coloured shirt underneath, sometimes worn with a foulard scarf. The most striking element of their garb was their "tummy-ache" pants... roughly made trousers with watch pockets that were baggy enough... to bunch them [up] from the pockets as if they all had serious stomach ailments. The whole ensemble was topped off with a flat cap, tattoos, and a sarcastic air of bourgeois hauteur.'

The zazous (see page 212) of the 1940s, the French equivalent of the Texan pachucos (see page 60), were more politically motivated in their defiance of the Vichy government, as noted by philosophers Jean-Paul Sartre and Simone de Beauvoir who wrote that they stood for 'a kind of opposition to the regime'. These two advocates of Existentialism discussed the human struggle to be free and how to make decisions in 'good faith' rather than through the constraints of culture, and the utter futility of human existence heralded an era of Parisian bohemianism that found expression in Le Tabou jazz club on the Rive Gauche (Left Bank), Café de Flore and Les Deux Magots, as well as in the 1960s cinema of La Nouvelle Vague. In 1968 left-wing students inspired by the spring pro-democracy riots in Prague began a series of demonstrations across France, demanding a reform of the university system and an end to the oppressive policing under Charles de Gaulle that had seen many of their cohort arrested. A general strike was called, and workers protesting against poor salaries, centralization and discrimination encountered much police brutality, which culminated in riots lasting ten days. They were joined by the Situationists intent on liberation through sabotage, a group of rebels inspired by the philosophy of Guy Debord who

attempted to transform the city into a spectacle through disruption and détournement, their mission to jolt the occupants out of their customary ways of thinking and believing. Their distinctive trench-coated figures were caught daubing the city with slogans such as 'Live Without Dead Time'. Malcolm McLaren, manager of the Sex Pistols, and Jamie Reid, the graphic designer responsible for the band's iconic album covers, drew their original inspiration from the Situationists. As McLaren put it, Situationism 'was bleeding from Paris into England', giving the British movement the political clout it needed. Parkour developed in Paris with the work of Raymond and David Belle, whose adherents, the free runners of today – together with Parisian skaters and street artists such as Kashink, Lek and Sowat (Urbex), and Seize – use the raw concrete of the post-war city as a platform for expression.

1 Zazous jitterbugging wearing hi-top sneakers in 1949.
2 A modern zazou wears clothing made from 1940s patterns. 3 A 1940s chignon with crocheted snood.

ZAZOU

PARIS
COUNTRY France
DECADE OF ORIGIN 1940s

The zazous of the 1940s were at large in the city of Paris during its military occupation by Nazi Germany. Originally, zazous were dubbed 'les petits Swings' for their love of jazz; the subsequent name change came from Cab Calloway, the African-American jazz singer and band leader whose song 'Zaz Zuh Zaz' (1933) introduced 'a phrase...with a very peculiar swing...zaz zuh zaz zuh zay'. Calloway's use of the zoot suit also struck a chord with young men wanting to thumb a nose at the oppressive and collaborating Vichy government who, under Marshal Pétain, ran France during the war years. The suit's long jacket and short, baggy trousers flouted the wartime rationing of materials and created a street style that remained independent of the couture industry and the fashion designers in Paris who were prepared to cater to the wives and mistresses of Nazi officials.

The zazous' hair was oiled into a pompadour with a ducktail back, in sharp contrast to the short back and sides of the military,

and crepe-soled shoes anticipated the brothel creeper of the London teddy boy (see page 184). Zazou girls styled their hair similarly high in the front with a chignon at the back or piled up on the front of their heads in a bun; they wore sharply silhouetted suits with padded shoulders or short pleated skirts that showed off their legs when jitterbugging in flat stacked shoes. The zazous were also the first street stylists to appear 'cool' by wearing sunglasses at night.

Christian Dior, employed by Lelong in Paris during the 1940s, wrote in his autobiography *Dior by Dior* (2015) how their 'hats were far too large, skirts far too short, jackets far too long, shoes far too heavy...I have no doubt that this zazou style originated in a desire to defy the forces of occupation and the austerity of Vichy. But as a fashion I found it repellent.' Zazous flaunted their 'repellent' fashion on the terrace of the Pam Pam café on the Champs-Elysées, at the dive bar Le Dupont-Latin, La Capoulade on Boulevard Saint-Michel and in the jazz clubs of Montmartre. Such flagrant displays enraged the authorities, who saw their clothes and attitude as a decadent Americanization of French national culture, and in 1942 a crackdown by police led to a series of arrests, with many zazous sent as forced labour into rural France or industrial Germany. The French equivalent of the Hitler Youth, the Jeunesse Populaire Française, promoted a *chasse aux zazous* (hunt for zazous) among their members who, interpreting the zazous' oiled pompadour as a tonsorial flag of defiance, made a point of shaving any quiff they encountered. Zazous remained defiant; after the ordnance of 1942 that required Jews to wear a yellow Star of David while in the occupied zone, they – like many other Parisians – wore a star substituting the word 'Jew' at the centre with an alternative: for them it was 'Swing'. By 1943 zazous were on the point of being wiped out by the regime and made their appearance more modest so as to melt into the background à La Résistance.

4 The late fashion designer L'Wren Scott was renowned for her sharp tailoring and 1940s-inspired aesthetic, seen here in her S/S 2010 show. 5 John Galliano ramps up the look of the zazou in his A/W 2003/2004 collection at Paris Fashion Week. 6 Zazou style during celebrations in 2004 to mark the sixtieth anniversary of Paris's liberation from Nazi Occupation during World War II.

BOHO

'Boho', from the French 'Bohémien', was a term originally used to describe travelling Romani people who were believed to have settled in Paris via Bohemia, today's Czech Republic. The term later gained popular usage as a way of describing those who chose to live a ramshackle life in the pursuit of art, love, life and liberty without due regard for financial hardship or the constraints of bourgeois society. Poverty thus gives rise to a casual scruffiness in dress; the artist Augustus John, for example, anticipated the lifestyle of the New Age traveller (see page 206) by jaunting down country lanes with his common-law wife Dorelia McNeill in a gypsy caravan in the 1910s. According to biographer Michael Holroyd, Dorelia wore brightly coloured Indian or Mediterranean print clothes including 'flowing dresses [that] reached the ground, with their high waistline and long sleeves topped by a broad-brimmed straw hat'.

In the late 19th century, Montmartre, Paris, became the city's bohemian meeting place. The area's rooms and studios were cheap to rent and a creative community, which included Vincent Van Gogh and Paul Verlaine, arose; by day, they frequented the Moulin de la Galette for a glass of wine and a hunk of bread and at night they sought entertainment at Le Chat Noir cabaret (1881) and the Moulin Rouge (1889). By the 1950s the idea of living a bohemian lifestyle had caught the popular imagination and was expressed in films such as *An American in Paris* (1951), starring Gene Kelly as an artist-émigré painting his masterpieces in a garret, high among the city's rooftops. In *Funny Face* (1957), Audrey Hepburn searches out a beatnik jazz club in the Rive Gauche, or Left Bank, district of Saint-Germain-des-Prés where she dances to free-form jazz and meets earnest, young, goateed beatnik followers of 'empathicalism', a skit on the Existentialist philosophy of Jean-Paul Sartre and Simone de Beauvoir. Her all-black ensemble of polo neck and cigarette-slim trousers was a nod to singer Juliette Gréco, whose style evolved out of financial constraint when only her male housemate's clothes were available.

1 *Dorelia McNeil* (1911) by Augustus John. Dorelia was the original boho, mixing bright ethnic prints and flowing, layered tunic tops and dresses.   2 Juliette Gréco set the trend for bohemian black in her monochromatic ensembles comprising black wool sweaters and capri pants.
3 Model Hailey Baldwin in West Village, New York, wearing a boho-style flowing print dress and high-heeled suede cowboy boots.

4 Yves Saint Laurent's muse and collaborator Loulou de la Falaise wears boho 'poverty de luxe' fashion and ethnic jewellery. 5 Jean Seberg, the consummate beatnik, in a striped Breton top, baggy jeans and bare feet, plus her trademark gamine cropped haircut. 6 Boho mixes global references to create a mélange of high-end hippy chic, such as this tasselled and embroidered leather waistcoat and black felt hat.

The short gamine haircut of Jean Seberg in Jean-Luc Godard's *A Bout de Souffle* (1960) was hugely influential, but as beatnik culture segued into hippy, the female boho now walked the streets of Paris barefoot with flowers in her waist-length hair. High fashion caught on and by the early 1970s the 'rich peasant' look appeared on Paris's catwalks courtesy of Yves Saint Laurent and was worn, most notably, by heiress Talitha Getty. From the 1990s onwards, boho style has become an established part of the fashion lexicon, entirely divorced from its counter-cultural origins and popularized by model Kate Moss and actor Sienna Miller. It comprises a dishabille of intent that takes its cues from hippy style, aka 'hippy-chic', in the use of floating Indian fabrics, length of hem and various forms of 'customization' usually created in-house by the brand rather than through the owner's creativity. A Pre-Raphaelite-influenced strain taken from the English originators of radical dress in the 1860s can be seen in the look of Florence Welch of Florence and the Machine.

AMSTERDAM

'The lawless youth live in a world which may be designated formless to a great extent. Their appearance is dictated by film fashion or is neglected entirely. They bellow, they yell, they chat endless drivel, they shriek and scream, they moan and whine.' — Martinus J Langeveld

This damning indictment of Netherland's teenagers was written in a report titled 'The Social Lawlessness of Dutch Youth', published in 1955 after a disturbance occurred at a jazz concert given by Lionel Hampton in Amsterdam's Apollohal the previous year. Jazz was the music of the rebels of Amsterdam and, according to reports, when confronted with the rhythmic intensity of Hampton's vibraphone the city's youth had jived so hard they broke up the wooden floor.

By the 1950s, different areas of Amsterdam had become associated with specific street cultures. The dijkers, also known as nozem (see image 1) after an article written in *Vrij Nederland* by journalist Jan Vrijman in 1955, were the consummate juvenile delinquents and could be found near the Central Station at Nieuwendijk and Haarlemmerdijk. Dijkers were immediately recognizable by their Brylcreem quiffs and black leather biker gear, and their girlfriends by their high lacquered beehives. Music was the requisite US rock 'n' roll, whereas their sworn enemies, the pleiners (see image 2), loved modern jazz. Pleiners were beatnik equivalents and avowedly anti-materialist, taking their inspiration from Jean-Paul Sartre and his coterie of Rive Gauche bohemians. Their home from home was Le Canard, a café-bar on Spuistraat that held jazz concerts, independent art exhibitions and poetry readings run by conscientious objector Hans Rooduijn. After Le Canard closed in 1957, the pleiner scene moved to Café Reijnders and Café Eijlders on Leidseplein, near the Stadsschouwburg (City Theatre), where followers filled the

1 Dijkers, Amsterdam's rebellious bikers in the 1950s.
2 Café 't Mandje, the city's first gay bar, opened in
1927. 3 Jan Cremer, author of *Ik Jan Cremer* (1964).
4 An Amsterdam coffee shop.

pavements – the boys with Caesar haircuts, the forerunner of The Beatles' mop top, wearing teddy boy (see page 184) brothel creepers with black corduroy drainpipe trousers, and the girls in versions of Christian Dior's New Look crinoline skirt, held out with a multitude of net petticoats, and high stiletto heels. The Parisian singers Françoise Hardy and the black-clad Juliette Gréco were also influential.

Marijuana began to enter youth culture as pleiners aped their hip heroes: musicians Miles Davis and Chet Baker, the latter a renowned jazz trumpeter who died in the city in 1988. Their seminal performances were photographed by Ed van der Elsken and published collectively in *Jazz* (1959). In 1964 the publication of the book *Ik Jan Cremer* (see image 3) by avant-garde artist Cremer caused a scandal, and went on to sell millions of copies, by detailing the life and times of a rebellious pleiner artist, womanizer and hash addict who brawled his way through the bars of post-war Netherlands. Amsterdam was beginning its popular association with drug culture and gaining its reputation as one of the world's most relaxed, secularized and liberal cities, an image boosted by the activities of the provos, hippy protesters and followers of absurdist performance artist Robert Jasper Grootveld. In the 1970s, the city opened its famous coffee shops (see image 4), where marijuana could be bought legally after the government decided to adopt a policy of tolerance on soft drugs.

Amsterdam's underground club scene is also significant: De Odeon Kring (DOK) was one of Europe's first gay clubs. The venue was a vaulted basement formerly used as a Nazi beer cellar during the Occupation, and in 1952 the doors opened, thus helping to establish

Amsterdam as the gay capital of Europe in the 1970s and 1980s. Guests included ballet star Rudolph Nureyev, drag artist Divine and singers Elton John and David Bowie. The Melkweg (Milky Way) was another important hang-out, home to European hippies after opening in an old milk factory in 1970. In the 1980s, hip hop and breakdancing began to appear in the city via the Afro-Surinamese community, which was the first to adopt the oversized sportswear and New Era baseball caps of the US scene. The label Karl Kani, founded in 1989, became the label of choice with its distinctive leather and metal plate affixed to the trademark baggy pants. The lammy coat was also popular: a three-quarter-length leather number lined with sheepskin, originally worn by sailors in the 19th century. In the early 2000s, fans of hardcore punk music in Amsterdam became known as Lonsdales because of their appropriation of the traditional boxing brand, founded in 1960 and originally worn by the first skinheads. However, due to the extreme right-wing attitudes and xenophobia of a minority, the brand became tainted and some schools called for it to be banned. In 2004 Lonsdale responded by launching a publicity offensive with the slogan: 'Lonsdale loves all colours.'

LEATHERMAN

'Symbolically, leather is equated with pain, power, "animalistic and predatory impulses" – and masculinity.' — Valerie Steele, *Fetish* (1996)

The leather biker look has become a mainstay of gay culture all over the world, from the illustrations of Tom of Finland to the Castro clone of San Francisco. The original black leather jacket derived, in part, from the German aviator jackets of World War I and it was originally worn for warmth when in the open cockpit. Bikers adopted leather outfits for protection, as the tough material prevented their bodies being scuffed on the asphalt in an accident. In Amsterdam, the adoption of the leather jacket and Levi jeans by the dijker gangs gave the look the requisite rebel appeal and, when worn on a motorbike, the frisson of the phallic. In 1927 motorbike enthusiast and lesbian Bet van Beeren became the proprietor of the first gay bar in the city, Café 't Mandje, and in 1955 the first European leather bar opened in a back room of the Hotel Tiemersma on Warmoesstraat, attracting gay men who were fans of the dijker style. It was later renamed the Argos and name-checked by Holly Johnson of Frankie Goes to Hollywood in the song 'Relax' (1984).

The leatherman look was tough, rebellious and overtly masculine, referencing sado-masochistic sexuality whether the wearer was an interested participant or not. By the 1970s, it was exaggerated into what became known as clone: leather jackets were strapped and buckled, Levi jeans were super-tight to draw attention to the crotch as an erogenous zone and white T-shirts were fitted closely to the body. The T-shirt, standard issue underwear for American GIs, moved to outerwear in 1942 when a buff soldier wore one on the cover of *Time* magazine. On the leatherman scene, it acted as a second skin, displaying the body's musculature, exposing the biceps and outlining

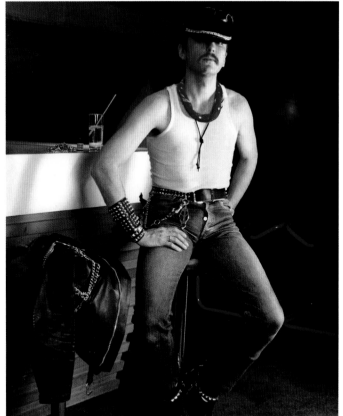

1 Two contemporary leathermen mix
steampunk references into the look.
2 Leather and fetish enthusiasts at a street
fair in San Francisco.   3 Marlon Brando in
A Streetcar Named Desire (1951).   4 Karl
Fox of Nottingham in a derivation of the
leatherman look, aka clone, in the 1980s.

the pecs. Marlon Brando appeared in a T-shirt as the menacing
Stanley Kowalski in *A Streetcar Named Desire*, directed by Elia Kazan in
1951, playing with the garment's blue-collar machismo.

By the 1970s, being a leatherman was to be upfront about gay
identity at a time when the movement for gay rights was increasingly
mobilized, plus it rejected the stereotypical camp effeminacy
associated with gay men in popular culture. The Sam Browne
harness belt and Master's hat were popular additions, as was the
full moustache, which became important expressions of group
identity and solidarity as well as sexuality. By the 1990s, Amsterdam's
leather bars openly displayed their credentials by flying leather
flags outside, and from 1996 onwards the Leather Pride weekend
has been held every year in October. Furthermore, the Amsterdam
leatherman has been able to buy specialist gear from Rob Meijer's
RoB Amsterdam leather shop since 1974. The city's liberal attitude to
the gay community has a long legacy: Amsterdam was the first city
to decriminalize homosexuality in 1811; the first gay magazine *Wij* was
published there in 1932; and in 2001 the Netherlands became the first
country in the world to legalize same-sex marriage.

PROVO

In 1962 W H Nagel, a professor of criminology in Leiden, wrote *From the Small Cold Front* under the pseudonym J B Charles, counselling the country to remain aware of and resist the threat posed by fascism during post-war recovery. Nagel understood that the Netherlands' youth were living with the legacy of Occupation and encouraged protest in the same manner as the Dutch Resistance during World War II – they should create their own 'small cold front'. The book was an unexpected hit, selling thousands of copies in a matter of weeks, and it created its own rhetoric of protest among Amsterdam's pleiners. From 1965 pleiner Robert Jasper Grootveld staged a series of playful 'happenings' in which he commented on the hypocrisy surrounding the city's stance on marijuana when a deadly alternative, the cigarette, was readily available. To the embarrassment of the city's authorities, Grootveld pointed out that after his fellow pleiners were arrested for possession they were taken to a police station lit up by a huge neon sign advertising a cigarette brand.

Grootveld's *antirooktempel,* or anti-smoking temple, became the site of his performances, during which young consumers were exhorted to rise up against their enslavement by capitalism to transform Amsterdam into a 'magic centre' of liberation. Such antics directly inspired the provos (from *provoceren,* 'to provoke'), a disparate group of protesters who staged sit-ins against the situating of a Mobil Oil refinery near the city; railed against Amsterdam's housing crisis, in which they promoted squatting by painting white the doors of empty houses; and created disturbances during the wedding of Princess Beatrix and Claus von Amsberg, the latter of whom had been a member of Hitler Youth, in 1966 by throwing smoke bombs at the procession.

4 & 5 White was the Provo's symbolic colour of protest. Fashion designers often use its blankness to create a vision of innocence or minimalist purity.   **6** Hippy street fashion remains a viable visual rejection of the mainstream.

While the provos were at large in Amsterdam, political forces were also at work in the United States, including the Civil Rights Movement and the hippies, young protesters taking a stance against the war in Vietnam and also their parent's straight and suburban way of life. Not for them a stultifying existence in a split-level ranch house; there was an alternative – the commune where all work and childcare were shared. Resistance could come through clothing, too, and hippies in Haight-Ashbury, California, deliberately referenced cultures that had been decimated by colonization. Native American fringing was mixed with Indian prints and Tibetan embroidery; ripped and patched jeans displayed an identification with the poorest members of the richest country in the world. Hair was grown long and natural, as opposed to the uber-grooming of the American matron and the brutish crew cuts of the military police. As Germaine Greer put it, 'Everybody had hair and lots of it. Floating around their head like smoke.' The hippy influence spread to Amsterdam, a city steeped in dissent and political activism, and figureheads of the movement spread the word by visiting the city, including original member of the Beat Generation Allen Ginsberg in 1957 and John Lennon and Yoko Ono, who held a week-long Bed-in for Peace at the city's Hilton Hotel in 1969.

ROTTERDAM
COUNTRY Netherlands
DECADE OF ORIGIN 1990s

GABBER

The animosity between the picturesque city of Amsterdam and the industrial port of Rotterdam runs deep; it is culture versus commerce, art instead of industry. Amsterdam may have a deep house and trance scene, but Rotterdam has gabber, an indigenous subgenre that went international in the 1990s. In Rotterdam, dance music aficionados wanted music that was harder, more industrial and better suited to their own city than that played in Amsterdam's clubs, an attitude summed up by Amsterdam DJ KC The Funkaholic who described them as 'just a bunch of gabbers having fun'.

Derived from Bargoens – a secret language used among the criminal classes in 19th-century Netherlands – the term 'gabber' means 'buddy' or today's 'bro'. In the 1990s, it was introduced to describe an aggressive variant of house music with a distinctive distorted bass drum sample and repetitive sampled vocals. The fast pace of the music created the hakken (hacking), an athletic scissor-kicking dance performed with the elbows held closely to the torso. Commonly seen at Rotterdam's Parkzicht club and the huge Thunderdome raves, which attracted up to forty thousand gabbers, the physicality of the dance called for a functional appearance that included loose, brightly coloured tracksuits from the favoured Italian label Australian, part of the L'Alpina family of brands founded by

1 Contemporary designers such as Nasir Mazhar are taking inspiration from street fashion's appropriation of sportswear.

Leardo Gabrielli in 1946. The Nike Air Max Classic, aka Air Max BW or Big Window, was launched in 1991 at the same time as gabber began to emerge, resulting in the shoe becoming inextricably linked with the subculture. Its air-bubble technology gave comfort and support, although gabbers began to add their own touches such as bursting the air bubbles in the window of the shoe and tucking in the tips of the laces instead of tying them. Hair was equally as distinctive and a clear marker of gender in what is essentially an androgynous style; the male gabber clippered his hair very close to the head in the same manner as the skinhead (see page 356), whereas female gabbers wore their hair slicked back tightly in a short ponytail to reveal a high undercut. A variant was the so-called Rotterdam cut, in which the sides were clippered and a long strip left to run from the forehead back to below the nape, held in place with gel. As the style evolved, the skinhead connection continued with the adoption of the MK1 flight jacket in black, customized with a Dutch flag on the back.

The Lonsdales grew out of gabber in the 2000s and a minority became associated with the politics of the far right, thereby unfairly damning the gabber scene with the same belief system. Today Dutch designer Tom Nijhuis creates collections inspired by the original gabber scene and uses gabber models from the rave site Party Flock.

2	3		
		4	5

2 The Gabber hairstyle features an exaggerated undercut.   3 Gabbers punctured the bubbles in the window of their Nike Air Max.   4 & 5 The aesthetic of menswear designer Nasir Mazhar is derived in part from gabber.

BERLIN
COUNTRY Germany
DECADE OF ORIGIN 1980s

ANARCHO-PUNK

From 1976 to 1979, David Bowie retreated to West Berlin to assuage his drug demons and to rejuvenate his music while hanging out with fellow musician Iggy Pop at the SO36 club, named after its postal code. Later, Bowie provided the soundtrack for the seminal film *Wir Kinder vom Bahnhof Zoo,* aka *Christiane F* (1981), directed by Uli Edel, a vivid depiction of heroin addiction among the city's teenage punks. The west of the city was a notorious bohemian enclave, an island set afloat in a sea of communism and a lure to young refuseniks who were dodging Germany's enforced military service and who found freedom in the communal squats of Kreuzberg. This was the spawning ground of the Berlin anarcho-punk, a member of the second wave of the movement that arrived when the stylish nihilism of its original British form developed into a more concrete political action under Thatcherism.

The band and collective Crass, formed in 1977 by performance artists Penny Rimbaud and Steve Ignorant, advocated anarchy as a personal philosophy and the politics of direct action. Their militant approach was expressed sartorially with the adoption of black army surplus clothing that was both cheap and functional, as well as a rejection of the 'pantomime' punk of studded leather, tartan bondage trousers and crazy-coloured vertically spiked hair. The DIY ethos of punk, most evocatively captured in Mark Perry's instruction in the fanzine *Sniffin' Glue* – 'here's three chords, now form a band' –

1 Christiane Felscherinow, author of the book that inspired the film *Wir Kinder vom Bahnhof Zoo*, in 1986.
2 A second-wave punk with Mohawk in 1984. 3 Anarcho-punks in sober second-hand clothes in London in 1984.

4–6 The downbeat look of the Anarcho-Punk led to micro communities such as the crust-punk and gutter-punk, whose functional clothes and Mohicans became an outward show of anti-capitalist protest.

became an important connection to an underground counter-culture of self-empowerment and resistance in some of the world's most oppressed countries, including the Eastern Bloc, Iran and Indonesia. Crass recorded and released tracks on their own record label, refusing to sell out like the original punk bands.

The fall of the Berlin Wall in 1989, a literal embodiment of the Iron Curtain that delineated the cultural boundaries between communism and capitalism in Europe, united the Ossis of East Berlin and the Wessis of the affluent West. The east of the city was ripe for gentrification, and the renovation and rebuilding of the formerly 'hidden' part of the city caused a substantial rise in property values. The anarcho-punks played a key part in the organization of street protests against the gentrification of the Eastern areas of the city and protesters were recognizable by the all-black anti-uniform approach, originally derived from Crass and including hoodies and cargo pants. Importantly, the anonymity of this street dress made it more difficult for the authorities to identify individuals. Hoods and balaclavas were used to hide conspicuous hair for the most potentially violent street protests.

MADRID
COUNTRY Spain
DECADE OF ORIGIN 1990s

PERROFLAUTA

The perroflauta emerged in late 1997 on the back of the New Age movement's advocacy of peace and love and the general anti-consumerist stance taken by a number of the decade's street tribes, including grunge (see page 16) and the New Age travellers (see page 206), the latter of whose white dreadlock hairstyles were an important component of the Spanish look. The word 'perroflauta' was coined originally as a pejorative to describe a modern-day minstrel or raggle-taggle gypsy who survived on the streets, with his dog (*perro*) on a string, by playing the flute (*flauta*). In contrast to the conformist

pijo, or 'rich kid', the perroflauta supplemented their peripatetic existence by selling craft and by performing tricks with the diabolo. *Pijos* power-dressed in designer labels; perroflauta made their anti-capitalist stance clear by wearing shabby but colourful layered clothes with ethnic references, such as harem pants. T-shirts declared their political affiliations, and at demonstrations many perroflauta used their bodies as canvases for sloganeering.

By 2011 Spain had entered an age of austerity; government cuts and record levels of unemployment made life hard for Spanish

1 A perroflauta clashes with police.　2 Protestors with slogans in Madrid in 2011.　3 Protest camp at the Puerta de Sol, Madrid.　4 'I think therefore I am'.

families, and mortgage defaulting left many without homes. Thousands were mobilized through the Internet platform Democracia Real YA (Real Democracy NOW) and took to the streets of Madrid on 15 May in order to protest against the harsh government sanctions that were making life intolerable.

The brutal police response brought back unpleasant memories of life under General Franco, whose military dictatorship kept the population in check from 1939 to 1975 by controlling 'undesirables' using heavy-handed policing and fines. There was a difference,

however, as social media, and YouTube in particular, was able to show the world evidence of the unfolding events. Despite the protesters emerging from all walks of life, they were stigmatized as perroflauta by the Spanish press, which conjured an image of filthy Blackfoot (due to walking barefoot on the city's grimy pavement), squatters and rabid gutter-punks tearing up Madrid for their own anarchic ends. Older demonstrators refused this blatant attempt at misinformation by referring to themselves as perro-yayas (dog grandparents).

RAVER

'Everyone was on acid or opiated hash from North Africa. Ibiza seemed ultra-laid-back: flutes, mysterious Californian drug smugglers, stylish black Americans dressed in white with white poodles, most people adept at meditation and trip-meistering, all sowing the seeds of hedonism.' — Richard Neville

Ibiza's metamorphosis from an isolated rural backwater to international party island began in the early 20th century when it became a destination for those wanting to establish alternative communities. They included artists Rigoberto Soler and Mary Hoover and writer Elliot Paul, who settled in Santa Eulalia and described how he had 'never seen a better life anywhere, a life more suited to human limitations and capabilities, a rhythm more in accord with beneficent natural surroundings, a verdant sub-tropical landscape and the sea'.

Beatniks arrived in the 1950s to be followed by hippies, known on the island as *peluts* or hairies, who stopped off in Ibiza on their alternative Grand Tour before continuing on to Goa and Kathmandu. Others escaped the draft for the Vietnam War by holding out in remote fincas. An alternative infrastructure of communes, drug dealing, full-moon parties and spiritualist practices created an oasis on the island, including the first clubs: Pacha (1973), Amnesia (1978) and Ku (1978). Amnesia, in particular, began to establish a reputation for ecstasy-fuelled hedonism with its 3am to 12pm opening times, alfresco dance floors and an international jet-setting clientele that included Grace Jones, George Michael and Mick Jagger. Here, a new form of music was invented by DJ Geraldo and DJ Massimo — Balearic beat, a combination of Synpop, New Wave and New Romantic — and it was taken back to London by DJ Paul Oakenfold after he had been exposed to it during his 24th birthday celebrations

1 The legendary Amnesia nightclub in the 1980s. 2 Dancers at Pacha in 1989. 3 Geena Matuson, aka the Girl Mirage, creates a modern version of rave with a range of fluorescent clubwear, Fluorotoxin by Shane Maxwell. 4 An original raver at The Trip at Astoria, London, in 1988.

with friends Nicky Holloway, Johnny Walker and Danny Rampling, the last of whom opened the Shoom club night as a result (named after the euphoric feeling induced by liquid ecstasy).

As the venues grew too small for the amount of clubbers, illegal unlicensed parties or raves sprang up in secret locations all over the UK during the second summer of love in 1988. The Ibiza hippy look was the basis for international rave fashion, in which clubbers tried to hang on to that holiday feeling by wearing oversized sweatshirts, dungarees, ponchos and the tie-dyed T-shirts that could be found in Ibiza's Las Dalias market. Such casual clothing made the Yuppie and his/her designer threads look staid and old-fashioned almost overnight. The use of acid-bright colours and the smiley face logo was also a rejection of the cool black minimalism that had dominated avant-garde fashion in the 1980s as a result of the innovative designs of Comme des Garçons and Yohji Yamamoto. The clubbing uniform had been minimal: black MK1 jackets, worn with jeans or leggings and classic Dr Marten boots. Rave was child-like, spawning a 1990s US-based subgenre of glowstick waving, face-painted kandi ravers who danced to happy hardcore.

PANINARO

MILAN
COUNTRY Italy
DECADE OF ORIGIN 1980s

In Italy the period of 1945 to 1965, known as the Ricostruzione, was one of unparalleled economic and cultural change, a time of social and material revolution after years of fascism. After World War II, Italy underwent reconstruction, abetted by economic aid from the United States, with the aim of boosting post-war trade and regenerating large areas of the Continent. This was also a rebranding exercise to help the country redefine itself as a centre of design innovation in the global marketplace, rather than a hotbed of fascism under Mussolini. This process of disassociation was a success, and Italy became known as the land of *la dolce vita* and stylish living.

By the 1970s the country was in disarray; the so-called Years of Lead were marked by the activities of the Brigate Rosse (Red Brigades), a group of extreme left-wing domestic terrorists who rioted and bombed their way across the country before kidnapping and killing the former prime minister, Aldo Moro, in 1978. The country's universities were the breeding ground of political extremism, and the

1 The paninaro look spawned its own fanzine.
2 Online vintage store Too Hot Limited's paninaro-inspired
editorial, 2016.   3 A group of paninaro in Milan, in 1987.
4 A paninaro wears a Moncler jacket and Timberland boots.

Indiani Metropolitani (Metropolitan Indians) took to the streets with painted faces and hippy-inspired clothing. By 1979 the youth of Milan began to distance themselves from such politics of protest by espousing a completely opposing set of values and lifestyles. Their meeting place was an American-style café-bar, the Al Panino on Via Agnello from which they took their name: paninaro. They later moved to the first branch of Burghy, an Italian fast food chain in imitation of McDonald's, and the area around San Babila where they posed with their Zündapp 175 motorbikes and primary-coloured Invicta rucksacks.

The paninaro look was sharp, colourful and label-oriented, as well as, most importantly, an apolitical celebration of consumerism, fashion labels, pop music and fun, as seen in the fanzine *Paninaro*. The conspicuous consumption of bands such as Duran Duran and Wham! – all blond, flicked, blow-dried hair and sunbed tans, as seen on Berlusconi's youth channels – created an Italian alternative of the Yuppie that had a huge effect both within and outside of Italy. Youth

identity was constructed through a strict taxonomy of clothing brands rather than politics, with Italian labels such as Giorgio Armani – which went on to dominate the 1980s – taking precedence. Paninaro were also early adopters of Levi 501s, worn rolled up at the ankle to display Burlington socks and Sebago deck shoes or Timberland boots (worn by Ferrari pit crews from 1980), and Alpha Industries MA-1 or Schott flying jackets. Americanino and Rifle corduroy trousers were worn in the same way as the Levis, accessorized with El Charro belts.

The Best Company is the home-grown brand most associated with paninaro street fashion. Italian ski-wear brand Moncler contributed down-filled puffa gilets and jackets that were also worn by the UK casuals (see page 174) and name-checked on the Pet Shop Boys song devoted to the look, 'Paninaro' (1986). In addition, the paninaro were responsible for popularizing the Henri Lloyd Consort sailing jacket in the United Kingdom.

1 Mokka were Italo-disco favourites and wore its sexy meets futuristic style. 2 Donna Summer. 3 Disco fashions of 1979 mix leopard print, sequins and body-con Spandex.

ITALO-DISCO

In the 1970s the angst and introspection of the singer-songwriter and the drone of middle-of-the-road rock were supplanted by the vital force of disco. This innovative form of R&B dance music could be heard in clubs all over the world, from Régine's in Paris, Annabel's in London and David Mancuso's The Loft in New York to Alibi in Rome. As the idealism of the 1960s was supplanted by the liberalism of the 1970s, DJs playing records back to back, including Larry Levan at Paradise Garage and Daniele Baldelli at the Cosmic Club, replaced live bands. In 1975 music journalist Mark Jacobson wrote, 'The new scene is all kinky eight-inch platforms, luminous make-up and outrageous sexuality.' It soon became clear that these discos were for, as the Jackson 5 sang, 'dance, dance, dance, dance, dancing machines'.

In 1975 Gloria Gaynor's *Never Can Say Goodbye* was the first album to have songs seamlessly segueing into one another, thereby creating the first extended dance mix, followed in the same year by Donna Summer's iconic *Love to Love You Baby*. Studio 54 was launched in New York in 1977 and became the place to be seen, with guests such as Andy Warhol, Cher and Liza Minnelli. The high-octane glamour of metal shimmering under the strobe lights led to a vogue for mesh fashioned into collars and faux bandanas that were worn on glistening bodies clad in Spandex and adorned with body glitter. Girls in shiny, satin cocktail dresses and Ultrasuede shirtwaisters by Halston hustled on the dance floor with peacock males in shirts slashed to the waist, crotch-hugging trousers and Cuban heels.

4 Disco diva at Studio 54, New York.
5 A woman shows off silver shorts at a disco clothing store in New York City in 1976. 6 Gareth Pugh's disco-inspired collection for S/S 2016 mixes Afro wigs with jumpsuits of gold paillette sequins.

US disco was first heard in Italy on European pirate radio, but disco imports were hard to source and prohibitively expensive. Italian producers and DJs began recording their own tracks in a uniquely lo-fi style, using Prophet-5 synthesizers and Roland 808 drum machines to create a driving, if tinny, 4:4 rhythm and sound. The resulting tracks, described as 'a Mediterranean mélange of disco, new wave, hi-NRG, and ESL pop', provided the missing link between US disco and Chicago house. Italo-disco (aka spaghetti dance) is derived from an album of such classic tracks released in 1983 by German company ZYX. The pioneers of the genre were La Bionda — comprising brothers Carmelo and Michelangelo Bionda, who recorded as DD (Disco Delivery) Sound — and Klein + MBO, whose track 'Dirty Talk' (1982) was imported into the United States by Walter Kapp of Kapp Exports and sold at Vinyl Mania, a record store near the Paradise Garage. Its monophonic, single-note production was a huge influence on the early house scene and the discos of Italy, including Milan's Studio 54 and Rome's Notorious and the Easy Going, the latter a gay basement disco whose DJ Marco Trani played to the city's clientele. The glossy, erotic covers of Italo disco reflected the fashion; it was high glamour with a hint of futuristic and it is being reappraised today, providing inspiration for Gucci creative director Alessandro Michele.

DIZELAŠI

BELGRADE
COUNTRY Serbia
DECADE OF ORIGIN 1980s

At the end of World War II, the communist dictator Marshal Josip Broz Tito united the six war-torn republics of Bosnia-Herzegovina, Croatia, Macedonia, Montenegro, Serbia and Slovenia under the federation of Yugoslavia. After the death of Tito in 1980, nationalist factions began to emerge, including followers of Serbian politician Slobodan Milošević. When Slovenia broke away from Yugoslavia in 1991, a series of brutal conflicts shocked the world. An atmosphere of lawlessness and unease pervaded Belgrade as gangs of black marketeers gained control of a city suffering the effects of hyper-inflation. They revved their fast cars and flashed their dookie chains in emulation of US hip hop stars, and such exploits were documented in the music and imagery of turbo-folk.

Turbo-folk was an indigenous form of music in which traditional Serbian melodies were set against a driving techno beat, and it included the popular tracks '200 MPH' (1994) by Ivan Gavrilović and Dr Iggy's 'Rainbow Coloured Eyes' (1995). Fans were dubbed Dizelaši, or Diesel Boys, after the US brand and the smuggled fuel used to run the gangsters' expensive cars. Sportswear brands such as Fila, Kappa

1 A Dizelaši in sportswear taking his cues from UK hip hop and the Rotterdam gabber.   2 The blend of baseball cap and hoodie evolved from hip hop to Dizelaši and the 'chav' street fashion of the 2000s.

and Reebok dominated, as in hip hop, but for pointedly functional as well as aesthetic reasons. Alex Eror writes in a discourse on 'the international ubiquity of the tracksuit' (2016) how 'Dizelaši made a habit of tucking their jackets into their tracksuit bottoms, which were in turn tucked into their socks.' This local peculiarity was popularized by a legendary gangster Aleksandar 'Knele' Knežević, who was said to have adopted the tactic as a way of ensuring that his gun, which he concealed in his waistband, would slide into his socks rather than drop out onto the pavement should he ever be forced to run from police.

The Dizelaši also copied the 'hard' look of the skinhead (see page 356) by shaving their heads, and the gabber (see page 228) by the adoption of Nike Air Max trainers. Dizelašice or Diggers (Sponzoruše), the female members of the Dizel movement, dressed to impress in a look that was sexually provocative in emulation of turbo-folk stars such as Ceca Veličković, Mira Škorić and Snežana Babić (Sneki). The publicity surrounding the marriage of Veličković to the paramilitary commander and war criminal Željko Ražnatović-Arkan (murdered in 2000) in 1995 also gave the music Milošević's seal of approval after being broadcast on state TV. After Milošević was overthrown in 2000, the Dizelaši all but disappeared until 2006 when the look began to re-emerge in Belgrade clubs as a new generation started to listen to Serbian music and the country exhibited a resurgence of nationalism in the wake of Kosovo's declaration of independence in 2008. An 'I Love the Nineties' event held in Belgrade and Novi Sad in 2011 attracted 15,000 attendees and plenty of media criticism for looking back with nostalgia to a truly traumatic era in the country's history.

3 Gosha Rubchinskiy's S/S 2016 show referenced the Dizelaši practice of tucking track jackets into tracksuit bottoms, which were in turn tucked into socks.   4 The glamorous look of turbo-pop star Ceca is much copied.   5 Nike Air Max, the Dizelaši footwear of choice.

MOSCOW

'The first thing that the 1980s generation of anti-Soviet youth did, once they'd been given carte blanche in this new landscape, was to pile on the pleasure.' — Artemy Troitsky

On 30 December 1922, Moscow formally became ratified as the capital of the USSR (Union of Soviet Socialist Republics), with the towered Kremlin as its seat of power. The city had a thriving avant-garde, which included the Constructivist artists El Lissitzky, Alexander Rodchenko and Lyubov Popova as well as film director Dziga Vertov. Art was taken out of the galleries and into the streets to function as agit-prop or propaganda, including Rodchenko's visually arresting posters and the architectural fantasy of Vladimir Tatlin's *Monument to the Third International* (1919–20), a 400 m (1,312 ft) tower design of iron, glass and steel intended to house government offices and a cinema. Clothes were not exempt from communist zeal, and Rodchenko and his wife, Varvara Stepanova (see image 1), experimented with innovative forms of modernist clothing, including an engineer's outfit with multiple pockets that Rodchenko wore while teaching.

Industrialization in the 1930s had attracted workers into Moscow and the city became seriously overcrowded, a situation that remained unresolved until vast high-rise building schemes changed the look of the city during the regime of Nikita Khrushchev in the 1960s. Khrushchev also encouraged a more liberal approach to cultural life (see image 2) and a thawing of the Cold War. Change came as information filtered into the USSR and the Komsomol (Young Communist League) began to loosen its grip on the nation's youth. It had been set up in 1918 to 'organize and train young people in a communist manner, to build a communist society and to defend the Soviet Republic' and it dispersed the official version of youth culture through schools, newspapers, magazines and meetings.

During the Khrushchev years, unofficial 'non-approved' clubs began to flourish as young Russians tuned into radio stations in Europe and visitors to the USSR brought in records. In the 1960s, rudimentary flexidiscs began to circulate, described by Troitsky as 'X-ray plates (chest cavities, spinal cords, broken bones) rounded at the edges with scissors, with a small hole in the centre and grooves that were barely visible on the surface. People bought them by the hundreds from hospitals and clinics for kopeks, after which grooves were cut with the help of special machines.' It was difficult to achieve the same creativity in dress, however, as clothes could be obtained only through state-run department stores such as GUM (see image 3) or bought at exorbitant prices at hard currency chain stores such as Beriozka. Dzhins (jeans) achieved mythical status, a symbol of Western freedom name-checked in song lyrics and worn by Moscow's hippies. Russian 'Montana' jeans were made of unyielding material and would not fade unless boiled in a mix of bleach and water; they were joined in the late 1980s by the home-grown labels Tver and Vereya. Highly prized Levis were brought into the city by diplomats and tourists and bartered for fur, caviar and amber.

Bulat Okudzhava (see image 4) was the country's most popular singer-songwriter in the 1960s and the rock group Aquarium was formed by Boris Grebenshchikov in 1972. By the 1980s, distinct and 'unofficial' street fashions could be seen on the streets of Moscow, including those worn by punks (see page 360), goths (see page 164) and heavy metal fans who, because of their unusual appearance, came under fire from gangs such as the Lyubery, whose attacks were ignored by the police. All changed with Glasnost, an era of openness established by Mikhail Gorbachev at the end of the 1980s after the disillusionment engendered by the Brezhnev era. The lifting of the Iron Curtain and the subsequent perestroika, or restructuring, created great political change, eventually dissolving the Communist Party and the Soviet Union. As Moscow encountered the might of global capitalism, a hedonism inspired by the free market created new scenes, including hip hop, rave (see page 134), techno and gabber (see page 228), with nights held at venues such as Palace, a former official Soviet entertainment centre. Raving was potentially dangerous because dance floors in the city were marred by the occasional gangster shoot-out.

Today, the machismo of President Vladimir Putin has sparked a culture of militant patriotism and what has been described as 'combat chic'. As the designer and creator of a Putin-themed clothing line Anna Kreidenko puts it, 'In the '90s, we wore "I love New York" shirts and thought it was cool. Now it's cool to wear a shirt with Russian writing.'

STILYAGI

'On the central streets of Moscow, Leningrad, Tbilisi, Erevan and several other cities loiter young men with Tarzan haircuts dressed up like parrots, so-called stilyagi. They do not work anywhere. They do not study but spend their nights in restaurants and pester girls. What kind of people are they?' — Izvestia (6 January 1951)

The Russian equivalent of the hipster (see page 192), the stilyagi (stylish ones) emerged in the 1940s. They were Moscow dandies who preferred Western fashion to the stodginess of Soviet 'official' style as dictated by the Komosol. Theirs was not a political stance but a form of escapism, based on romantic ideals about life outside the USSR that managed to filter through the Iron Curtain according to the restrictions placed by each successive regime. The products of Hollywood that managed to slip through the censor's net included *Tarzan's New York Adventure* (1942). When the film eventually reached Moscow in 1951, lead actor Johnny Weissmuller's greasy ducktail hairstyle was adopted by the stilyagi and worn on Gorky Street, or Broadway as they preferred to call it. This idiosyncratic street fashion was a mish-mash of styles: boys wore zoot suits or bee-bop slimline black, primary-coloured shirts, hand-knitted slim Jim ties and thick-soled standard workers' shoes. Girls were described in one official newspaper as wearing 'dresses which cling to the point of indecency. Her skirts are slit. Her lips are brightly painted. She wears "Roman sandals" during the summer' and her hair 'à la garçonne', 'with its pitiful bristles of cropped hair' (presumably a Russian version of Audrey Hepburn's or Jean Seberg's gamine cut). Reading between the lines, this description shows the fascinating mix-and-match approach of the stilyagi: the pencil skirt lifted from Paris couture, the red lipstick from the sweater girls of Hollywood, such as Marilyn Monroe, and the Roman sandals from Italy's Ferragamo.

1 Moscow stilyagi at the World Festival of Youth and Students in 1957 wear a mish-mash of styles denoting cool, including trench coats, English tweed and Russian workers' shoes.

2 A Russian model references home-grown style with her headscarf and retro couture detailing. 3 The contemporary stilyagi wears an Elvis-inspired quiff and jeans for effortless cool. 4 Costumes from Valery Todorovsky's comedy-drama *Stilyagi* (2008) on display at a Moscow exhibition titled 'Music and Cinema' (2016).

These clothes were acquired from a variety of sources; so-called 'lend-lease' clothes were available through state-run second-hand shops; knitted sweaters and ties were made at home; and black market tailors were prepared to make anything if the price was right and the source kept secret. Elvis-inspired pompadours were kept in place with sugar and water, as the stilyagi styled it out with a cupped Lucky Strike or when twisting to their favourite tunes.

Choosing to declare a love for Western imagery was openly inflammatory; in fact, a popular phrase used in the late 1950s to deride the stilyagi was 'today he dances jazz, but tomorrow he sells his homeland'. Komosol patrols tracked the stilyagi, forcing haircuts and conformity, until Nikita Khrushchev took control and prised open the country's borders. The World Festival of Youth and Students held in Moscow in 1957 invited more than thirty thousand delegates from all over the world into the city. They brought tales of life in the West and also the latest fashions and music, including the formerly 'degenerate' rock 'n' roll. In 2008 director Valery Todorovsky's comedy-drama *Stilyagi* (*Hipsters*) introduced this little-known style to a modern audience with a wry nod to its unquestioning acceptance of Western capitalism.

1 2

1 Following Pussy Riot's example, anti-fashion clothes and coloured tights are used as visual signifiers of a new feminism of protest.   2 Pussy Riot's infamous performance at the Orthodox Cathedral of Christ the Saviour in 2012.

PUSSY RIOT

MOSCOW
COUNTRY Russia
DECADE OF ORIGIN 2010s

'Pussy Riot use different codes of beauty, opposite to the traditional feminine image, in Russia or anywhere. Our look is not meant to be about long legs and high heels.' — Pussy Riot

In the 1990s the Riot Grrrls of Washington State demonstrated against patriarchy by mobilizing women to address the everyday sexism they encountered in the music industry. Bands such as Bikini Kill, led by Kathleen Hanna, and Bratmobile performed with the words 'slut' and 'rape' scrawled on their arms in lipstick to draw attention to taboo subjects at a time when women's reproductive rights were under attack from the Christian Right. Clothes followed the grunge (see page 16) thrift store aesthetic, in itself a reaction against the glossy logo-laden image that dominated high fashion throughout the 1980s. Childlike accessories such as plastic hair clips were worn with Disney T-shirts, knee socks and work boots. Hanna

used stage costumes to play with cultural notions of femininity. In 1993 she wore a dress with 'Kill Me' printed on the front, responding to the death threats the band was receiving at the time. The Riot Grrrl look was hugely influential, especially after being toned down and sold to the mass market by the Spice Girls under the slogan 'Girl Power'.

This DIY model of female subversion took hold in Moscow in 2011 with the formation of all-girl punk band Pussy Riot. Their protest against the repressive policies of Vladimir Putin took the form of flash gigs in which the band played songs such as 'Kill the Sexist' wearing primary-coloured clothes and full-face balaclavas to hide their identity. Clothes were used as a form of counter-cultural protest following the Riot Grrrl mode by creating an alternative image of

femininity to the high glamour and conspicuous consumption that reigned among the super-rich oligarchs of Moscow. Primary-coloured thrift store finds were worn with flat footwear, and there was an abject refusal to reference the erotic at a time when blown-out hair, body-con dresses and expensive furs were considered the appropriate form of dress. After the now-notorious 2012 performance in Moscow's Orthodox Cathedral of Christ the Saviour, where they performed on the steps of the pulpit wearing dresses and tights in off-kilter colours – a significant act as only men are allowed to stand there – three members of Pussy Riot (Maria Alyokhina, Nadezhda Tolokonnikova and Yekaterina Samutsevich) were arrested for 'hooliganism'. Their imprisonment and subsequent trial sparked global protest.

3 Pam Hogg's Courage Collection A/W 2014 was dedicated to Pussy Riot and explored themes of gay rights and protest. She referenced their 'balaclavas and colour'. 4 Hogg challenged conventions and gender boundaries by using a mixture of male, female and transsexual models. 5 Kathleen Hanna wears a red dress with cut-out panels and the words 'Kill Me' across the front to protest against death threats and the notion that women who dress sexily are 'asking for it'.

1–6 The garage scene reintroduced glamour into clubbing after the sportswear street fashions of hip hop. Versace prints and the Moschino label dominated the early scene and have enjoyed a recent revival.

AYIA NAPA
COUNTRY Cyprus
DECADE OF ORIGIN 1990s

GARAGE

Ibiza was clubbing central in the early 2000s and young promoters found it difficult to gain a foothold. The resort of Ayia Napa, once a small fishing village of only one hundred inhabitants on the island of Cyprus, provided an alternative venue. As rave transformed Ibiza into the ultimate party island, so UK garage created the resort of Ayia Napa. Garage derived from Paradise Garage, a legendary New York club (1977–87) held in a converted parking garage in Manhattan. The club's draw was DJ Larry Levan, an obsessive artist with sound who created a narrative of love and loss with his choice of disco, R&B and funk music for a predominantly gay, black and Latino audience. Levan mixed and distorted the tracks into extended mixes that lit up the dance floor. In the 1990s UK garage producers such as Wookie took Levan's soulful mix, speeded it up and added the heavy bass lines and drums of reggae to create a smooth sound that was the antithesis of Jungle. It was played on pirate radio and at venues such as Vauxhall's Colosseum, where the TwiceasNice nights were one of the first to play in Ayia Napa at Pzazz, a club owned by the Melas brothers.

As the vibe changed, so did the look as hip hop's hoodies and trainers were ditched for smart suits, Versace silk shirts and Patrick Cox or Gucci loafers. Glamorous girls wore Moschino bustiers and cropped jeans or leopard-skin cocktail dresses, gold hoop earrings and killer heels. In 2000 journalist Miranda Sawyer wrote of girls in all shapes and sizes being 'united in their rejection of unnecessary clothing. The skimpiest of skirts and the hankiest of tops are uniform, as are glamour heels. Their hair is twisted into works of art.' Tags were often kept on the clothes to show that they were new and the real deal – anything 'snide' or counterfeit was looked on with disdain. The drinks were high end, too, including Laurent-Perrier champagne and Courvoisier brandy with Coke.

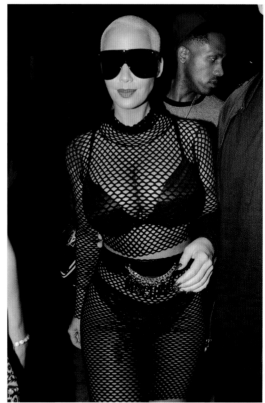

AFRICA

KINSHASA OKAHANDJA GABORONE
SOPHIATOWN JOAHNNESBURG SOWETO

BILL SAPEUR HERERO RENEGADE PANTSULA
ZEF IZIKHOTHANE SMARTEEZ

Africa is often mythologized as an 'exotic' continent, a construct that regularly inspires designers, from Yves Saint Laurent and his safari suits of 1973 to the much-debated Valentino S/S 2016 show influenced by 'wild tribal Africa'. Valentino's 'journey to the beginning of time and the essential of primitive nature' featured Kikuyu textiles, trade beads and feathers, with white models in cornrows walking the runway to the sound of bongo drums. Yet the continent of Africa is vast, and each of its countries has a distinctive cultural heritage, language and set of clothing references. Its rich tradition of hand-woven textiles dates back at least five thousand years and techniques are passed down through the generations. For example, bogolanfini originated in Mali in the 12th century and is dyed using fermented mud. Asoke is a silk weave sewn into strips by the Yoruba, and Cameroonian weavers use fibres from the bark of obom trees. Kente cloth, the national fabric of Ghana, is the best-known African fabric, woven by the Ashanti. According to legend, two weaving brothers stumbled across an exquisite spider's web while out hunting and tried to reproduce it in woven cloth, using strip looms to create contrasting colours and rhythmic patterns. Wax resist batiks are popular throughout the continent for daywear and the Ndebele of South Africa and Zimbabwe make quilts and blankets by hand for ceremonial occasions.

Fabric is worn in different ways throughout Africa, including the earliest practice of wrapping cloth around the body and the later one of sewing it into loose robes, shirts, skirts and trousers. The boubou is worn in Nigeria and Senegal, the agbada and riga in Nigeria, and the gandoura or leppi in Cameroon. Traditional African garments such as the dashiki have infiltrated global fashion. This is a patterned collarless shirt, worn with drawstring trousers or sokoto, and it became associated with the African-American radicals of the Civil Rights Movement in the 1960s. In 1967 Jason Benning, Milton Clarke, Howard Davis and William Smith launched New Breed – a company in Harlem, NY – to produce dashikis, which were popularly worn with the Afro, a black hairstyle that left the hair in its natural state rather than being pressed and ironed to conform to white beauty standards.

The wearing of Afrocentric fashions outside of Africa became an expression of black identity, but the Afro was rejected in some African countries, such as Tanzania, as being too American. The first Afrocentric ready-to-wear boutique in Africa was opened in Lagos, Nigeria, by Shade Thomas-Fahm, who created modern versions of traditional Nigerian dress. Young consumers combined garments such as ipele (shawls) and buba (cotton tops) with capri pants and ballet flats, mixing traditional and contemporary fashion. The sapeurs (see page 270) of Kinshasa in the Democratic Republic of Congo also looked to fashion influences and focused on European labels sourced in Paris, but as a political gesture and a form of sartorial resistance. After the death of one of the movement's leaders, Papa Wemba, in 2000, musician Manu Dibango said, 'His whole attitude about dressing well was part of the narrative that we Africans have been denied our humanity for so long. People have always had stereotypes about us, and he was saying dressing well is not just a matter of money, not just something for Westerners, but that we Africans also have elegance. It was all about defining ourselves and refusing to be stripped of our humanity.' The convention of the African dandy continues in Johannesburg with the Swenkas, Zulu migrant labourers who wear tailored suits, hats, gloves and polished Florsheim shoes to show pride in their appearance, despite being some of the poorest paid labourers in the city. The herero (see page 274) of Namibia also respond to their colonialist past. Their strategy is to inhabit the clothes of their former slave masters but give them a distinctly local flavour, with horn headdresses and brightly coloured fabrics. Herero men wear military uniform to psychologically 'take on' the power of their oppressors.

After the end of apartheid in South Africa and the transition to democracy, street and catwalk fashion responded in several ways. Afrocentric fashion took centre stage for many designers, and writer Adam Levin observed how 'we witnessed some very obvious declarations of patriotism on our catwalks. We had our fair share of "folklorish" garments and sequinned South African flag ballgowns.' Today collectives such as The Sartists, which comprises photographer Andile Buka, fashion designer Wanda Lephoto and journalist Kabelo Kungwane, challenge notions of 'blackness', black fashion and the cultural appropriation of African style. Cultural appropriation remains a hotly contested topic; in 2015 actor Amandla Stenberg described how 'appropriation occurs when a style leads to racist generalizations or stereotypes where it originated but is deemed as high-fashion, cool or funny when the privileged take it for themselves'. She criticized Kylie Jenner for wearing cornrows by tweeting under Jenner's photograph, 'When u appropriate black features and culture but fail to use ur position of power to help black Americans by directing attention towards ur wigs instead of police brutality or racism.'

Afropunk is growing as a global movement after James Spooner's documentary of the same name related what it was like to be the only black punk at a gig in America in 2003. His commentary on the absence of a black alternative scene created a DIY movement that has since gone global, with regular Afropunk festivals held all over the world.

1 King Leopold II. 2 Mobutu Sese Seko wearing an abacost. 3 Muhammad Ali versus George Foreman in 1974. 4 Papa Wendo in 2007. 5 A show by Marie-France Mumba, Kinshasa Fashion Week 2014.

KINSHASA

British explorer Henry Morton Stanley established the trading post of Léopoldville in 1883 and named it after the malevolent Belgian King Leopold II (see image 1), the monarch who used the Belgian Congo (now the Democratic Republic of the Congo or DRC) as his personal playground, squandering its rich resources and murdering its inhabitants. Léopoldville emerged as the seat of government, with French as its official language although the indigenous Lingala was still used in the streets, and the city began its sprawling growth along the south bank of the Congo River. After 75 years of oppressive Belgian rule, in which ten million Congolese are estimated to have died, the country gained independence. The metropolis of Léopoldville was renamed Kinshasa in 1966, after a small village that used to exist on the site, but the transition of power was traumatic: civil war, then a coup followed by the dictatorship of Mobutu Sese Seko (see image 2).

Despite the Congo being rich with resources, the corruption of officialdom left the majority of the population living in poverty, dependent on the churches for spiritual if not physical sustenance. Mobutu wanted to rebrand his country as a modern African utopia, banning any vestiges of colonialism with his 'authenticité' programme. Western fashion was prohibited and the abacost – a short-sleeved, fitted, lightweight suit, whose name derived from the French *à bas le costume* (down with the suit) – was mandatory for men, although difficult to enforce. It was worn without a shirt and with a silk cravat in place of a tie. Mobutu's abacosts were handmade by Alfons Mertens of Arzoni, based in Belgium, and he accessorized them with a leopard-skin hat and horn-rimmed spectacles. In 1974 the dictator spent $10 million to stage a boxing bout between Muhammad Ali and George Foreman in Kinshasa's Stade du 20 Mai (see image 3). Five thousand of the city's inhabitants flocked to see the so-called Rumble in the Jungle, in which Ali defeated Foreman to regain the Heavyweight title. Behind the scenes, Mobutu made sure

that the city was seen in the best light, by executing criminals to keep the streets crime-free and by designating the day a national holiday.

In the 1980s, the collapse of the copper market – the country's major export – began an economic decline that manifested itself in a shortage of basic foodstuffs and a sharp rise in unemployment. When the inflation rate hit 4,000 per cent in 1991, a series of riots decimated the city and destroyed its manufacturing infrastructure, events from which Kinshasa has never truly recovered. The period 1998 to 2003 continued to be cataclysmic for the country as war between six neighbouring countries backed by foreign powers left millions dead.

The people of Kinshasa have continued to be resourceful, living by their wits in the most straitened of circumstances and creating their own underground economies, plus a vibrant music, art and fashion culture (see image 5). Congolese music, aka soukous (from the French for 'shake') is celebrated the world over. One of the earliest stars was Papa Wendo (see image 4), a riverboat mechanic who sang songs with a rumba rhythm accompanied by acoustic guitar, including the

popular 'Marie-Louise' (1948). He was followed by the orchestras L'African Jazz in 1953 and OK Jazz in the 1960s, by Wenge Musica in the 1980s, and more recently by Fally Ipupa and Koffi Olomide, whose fast-paced soukous ndombolo music has its own risqué dance moves. International world music star Papa Wemba was also the leader of the sapeur movement (see page 270), Kinshasa's most celebrated sartorial contribution to global street fashion.

The documentary film *Kinshasa Symphony* (2010) shed light on the Kimbanguist Symphony Orchestra, one of the few classical orchestras in Africa that now tours worldwide. In 2014 journalist Katrina Manson described how the musicians scrape by with donated instruments and by using an empty warehouse or nearby car park as rehearsal space, repairing their instruments with whatever is to hand. Today Joseph Kabila, son of the assassinated Laurent Kabila who wrested power from Mobutu in 1997, continues to cling to nepotistic power, and his uneasy leadership has led to violent clashes with protesters and police throughout the autumn of 2016.

BILL

KINSHASA

COUNTRY Democratic Republic of the Congo
DECADE OF ORIGIN 1950s

The industrial growth of Kinshasa in the 1920s and its soaring population led to segregation or a 'colour bar', primarily targeting young African men who had to live in overcrowded tenements with little access to power and clean running water. The Depression affected European firms based in the city and the subsequent layoffs meant that many young men lost their jobs. They began to spend more time on the streets in search of work and also socializing, viewing movies shown in social clubs and, by the 1950s, in the few cinemas that began to open in African districts of the city. Some Hollywood movies passed the rigorous laws of colonial censorship, including the *Tarzan* franchise, which was deemed appropriate because of the racist assumption that it was set in the African

1 'The Bills', from the series *Day in Kinshasa* (*c.* 1955–65) by Jean Depara. 2 Musician Kwami Longange wears a tropical cowboy outfit in 2009. 3 Anna Sui S/S 2017.
4 Fashion consultant Desmond Lim Zhengs in 2016.

jungle. However, Western, or cowboy, films were by far the most popular, including *The Desperados* (1943) and *She Wore a Yellow Ribbon* (1949), as well as *Pony Express* (1953) starring Charlton Heston as Buffalo Bill.

Cowboy style and demeanour were taken out onto the streets of Kinshasa by the Bills (named after Buffalo Bill Cody), or 'tropical cowboys' (aka Yankees). These African teenagers were so inspired by US Westerns and the figure of the powerful gunslinger that they created a fantasy lifestyle in which they styled themselves wearing imported Stetsons, checked shirts and cowboy boots with fake guns in a holster. Bills renamed themselves after their cowboy heroes, including 'John Wayne' and 'Sheriff'. The Bills also incorporated

traditional customs into their culture, such as a ritual called kamon in which they prepared themselves for 'combat' by rubbing the ash of dead animals into a self-administered cut.

Bills were also at the forefront of the riots for independence that broke out in Kinshasa in January 1959. Didier Gondola, whose fascinating study *Tropical Cowboy : Westerns, Violence, and Masculinity in Kinshasa* (2016) documents the scene, says, 'It wasn't really the politicians or the trade unions that spearheaded the fall of the colonial regime. It was the young people...the young Bills and Yankees...they are the ones responsible for the first major insurrection in Kinshasa. The country owes a debt to them, but most people don't know that.'

1 Sapeur Papa Griffe.   2 Sapeurs at Parc de Prince in Kinshasa.   3 Little sapeur Prince Elvo.   4 Papa Wemba performing in 1991.   5 Young sapeurs at Gombe cemetery.

SAPEUR

In the 19th century, young African men living in some of the most impoverished townships of the Belgian Congo began to dress as gentlemen in order to belie their lowly social status. Their sartorial experimentation gained a more obvious political edge in 1922, when religious figure and politician André Matsoua returned from a sojourn in Paris dressed from head to toe in European tailoring. As Matsoua was an active critic of colonialist policies that refused the Congolese the vote, the rights to their own land and the ability to travel freely, the simple act of wearing the clothing of his oppressors was a visual expression of defiance against Belgian rule. By the 1960s, Matsoua's subversive gesture had been consolidated into an urban organization called La Sape, or the Société des Ambianceurs et des Personnes Élégantes (Society of Tastemakers and Elegant People). Its members, known as les sapeurs, amassed wardrobes of French and Italian designer labels, such as Pierre Cardin, Gucci and Yves Saint Laurent, as a form of cultural capital and as a metaphorical nose-thumbing at those in control.

In 1965 the Democratic Republic of the Congo came under the control of military dictator Mobutu Sese Seko. After the launch of his 'authenticité' campaign to rid the country of the vestiges of colonialism, any reference to Western culture was frowned upon, and practices

6 7

8

6 Mamitcho Kadithoza, one of the
few female sapeurs, in 2014.   7 A senior
sapeur shows the detailing on his designer
label clothes.   8 A well-groomed sapeur
establishes his identity in head-to-toe
tartan and designer shades.

such as hair straightening, skin bleaching and the wearing of ties
were all banned. Papa Wemba, a renowned exponent of soukous
music, took the helm of La Sape and began performing songs in
praise of Western fashion including 'La Firenze', a tribute to Italian
labels. Also known as Le Pape de la Sape (the Pope of the Sape),
Wemba blatantly disregarded the governmental dress codes, an act
of rebellion that was condemned by the press but loved by the people
of Zaire (modern-day Democratic Republic of the Congo).

As Didier Gondola explained, Wemba was utilizing his music and
appearance to 'blur social lines and make class status and social lines
illegible'. Following his cue, young men began using the soukous clubs
of Kinshasa and Brazzaville (Republic of the Congo) as their catwalks.
The vibrant street styles still exist today, with clothes sourced through
the Internet, via relatives based in Europe or from local markets where
fake designer goods are available to any budding sapeur.

HERERO

'A correctly worn long dress induces in the wearer a slow and majestic gait.' — Dr Lutz Marten

The city of Okahandja – 'the place where two rivers join' – in Namibia, Africa, holds its Maherero Day on 26 August in memory of the Herero chiefs who fell in battle during the country's troubled and bloody colonial past. Women in brightly coloured crinolines walk the streets alongside men in turn-of-the-century military dress, sporting caps adorned with bird's plumes and jackal fur. This picturesque presentation belies a brutal history and the importance that this form of dress holds for each participant.

In 1884 Germany laid claim to the country and renamed it German South-West Africa. Land was annexed, farms and cattle seized, and property plundered until the brave Herero, a peaceful farming nation, rebelled and fought back in 1904. Over three years, the Herero population was decimated by General Lothar von Trotha, under the command of the Kaiser, with more than sixty-five thousand tribespeople slaughtered in an act of genocide that prefigured the Holocaust. Those who survived became slaves forced to work on the colonized farms and for German-owned companies.

After the end of German rule in 1918, Namibia became a British protectorate administered by South Africa. The Herero began to copy the clothing of their oppressors in the 1920s, creating a form of national/ceremonial dress that parodies the clothing of the colonizers. Women wear African versions of the Victorian silhouette worn by Christian missionary women, consisting of a high-buttoned, long-sleeved blouse and ankle-length crinoline skirt held out by heavy petticoats. The outfit is topped by a hat of cloth rolled to resemble the horns of the cattle that are so important to the life of the Herero people. Women walk with a stately gait, imitating a Victorian 'lady' who has the time to stroll while her servants do the domestic work – thus a sign of social status. Men don military uniforms, including cardboard puttees and gaiters, symbolically transferring the power of the German army that was responsible for the tribe's traumatic past and subversively using Western dress as a form of African identity.

1 The original dress of the Herero. 2 A hybrid headpiece of leather and horn. 3 Crinoline skirt and rolled cloth hat. 4 Herero tribesmen in personalized versions of military uniforms. 5 Colonial dress that mixes African symbolism with European silhouettes of the 19th century.

RENEGADE

GABORONE
COUNTRY BOTSWANA
DECADE OF ORIGIN 1990s

Heavy metal music originated in the declining industrial city of Birmingham, UK, with the formation of rock band Black Sabbath in 1968, who mixed blues, rock 'n' roll and guitar to create a 'heavy metal' sound. Swathes of young, white, working-class men were witnessing their traditional apprenticeships in factories and steelworks being wiped out as recession set in. The hippy sentiments of peace, love and understanding seemed incompatible with life in a grey windswept city of Brutalist concrete architecture, built in a wave of post-war optimism. Black Sabbath's 'Paranoid' (1970) and 'Smoke on the Water' (1972) by Deep Purple introduced the sound; heavy guitar riffs were backed up by thundering bass lines and minimalist pounding drums.

Rob Halford, lead singer of Judas Priest, created the heavy metal look, taking his cues from the Amsterdam leatherman (see page 222) and the gay S&M scene in Soho, London. His black leather biker jackets and trousers by Ray Brown of London were accessorized

1 Rob Halford, lead singer of Judas Priest. 2 A Renegade in head-to-toe black leather. 3 The original line-up of Skinflint. 4 A Queen shows off her studded leather jacket.

with chains, spikes and studded wristbands. Fans wore traditional biker and Hells Angels-inspired clothing (see page 24), including flared jeans and Harley-Davidson logo T-shirts. By the 1980s, heavy metal had reached Gaborone, the capital of Botswana. The city became Botswana's administrative centre in the 1960s and rapid rural migration followed as a result not only of employment opportunity but also the continued droughts that were making farming difficult. Gaborone prospered not least because Botswana avoided the civil wars and dictatorships that blighted other African countries.

Botswana's first heavy metal band, Metal Orizon, was formed in the 1990s and released its first album *Ancestral Blessing* in 1998. Death metal band Wrust was founded in 2000, followed in 2006 by Crackdust and Skinflint, the latter of whose tracks mix lyrics about ancestral beliefs, tribal warfare and African mythology with classic heavy metal music. Fans enjoy the rebellious look and passionate lyrics

of metal and over time have evolved their own unique interpretation of the style that turns heads in a conservative country. Many of their metal clothes are handmade, using local leather mixed with the cowboy references traditionally used by the Bills (see page 268). Jackets are extended with studded leather wings and adorned with ancestral tokens such as animal skulls, thereby creating a link to their African heritage. Dressing in this outwardly aggressive street fashion gives symbolic power to the wearer, plus the respect of the community who regard the renegades as guardian angels keeping the streets safe at night. Heavy metal 'queens' dress in fringed leather jackets, skirts with bullet belts and bandanas, as well as cowboy boots, hats and spurs. Recently, the corpse paint of death metal has appeared on the scene. Vulture Thrust, lead singer of Overthrust, says, 'This is a scene that we have created ourselves...It's our own subculture that gives us identity, we feel happy and life goes on.'

PANTSULA

SOPHIATOWN
COUNTRY South Africa
DECADE OF ORIGIN 1960s

The township of Sophiatown was originally a farm on the outskirts of Johannesburg and it was designated a whites-only area after being purchased by speculator Hermann Tobiansky, who named it after his wife. His plans to make Sophiatown a pleasant white suburb suffered a setback when the city's sewage plant was located nearby, so he sold the plots to black workers who were able to live there without restrictions. The community expanded when Johannesburg's slum clearance programme removed the black population from the inner city areas, and many relocated to Sophiatown. Houses were built haphazardly and commonly owners paid their mortgages by letting out rooms and outbuildings to poorer tenants.

A vibrant community flourished and clothing became an important area of self-expression. Two distinct looks emerged:

1 Pantsula wearing Dickies chinos, Converse sneakers and spotties. 2 Pantsula Bhanzele Masango, member of the Real Action dance crew. 3 Chulaap show, A/W 2016. 4 Florsheim brogues with ankle-skimming cuffed trousers.

the clean-living Ivies followed the US Ivy League look (see page 78), wearing button-down shirts, ankle-bone-skimming trousers and loafers, whereas the pantsula looked sharp in their cuffed trousers and Florsheim or Crockett & Jones two-tone shoes. Often found in the local shebeens (illegal clubs run by female beer brewers), these gangster-dandies competed over who could be the snappiest dresser. The best dancers wore black Bata hi-top sneakers and Converse, or Black Cats, to perform the complicated steps of the pantsula or 'duck waddle' dance to the township's own indigenous kwaito music. Peaked caps or felt hats covered cropped hair, a prison reference prefiguring the baggy trousers of hip hop (see page 46). The mshoza, the female version of the pantsula, wore pleated skirts and berets over straightened hair. Academic David Coplan described how

the same style could still be seen in the 1980s in the bars of Lesotho, where women wore 'fresh light-coloured blouses, modest skirts falling below the knee, jaunty berets and caps'.

Today's pantsula crews are committed to the dance, with many of the troupes practising for several hours a day. 'The guys are trying to spread a message of better living through the dance,' explains photographer Chris Saunders. Pantsula style centres around cholo-inspired (see page 44) outfits of white sleeveless T-shirts, Dickies chinos, original Converse hi-tops and short-brimmed spotties, the South African equivalent of the bucket hat. African designers such as Shaldon Kopman of Naked Ape, Stoned Cherrie and the label Chulaap have appropriated the pantsula in a celebration of the culture of the townships within a modern South Africa.

JOHANNESBURG

In 1885 two itinerant gold prospectors, George Harrison and George Walker, discovered a seam of gold in an area of farmland known as Witwatersrand (the Rand). They sold their claims without realizing that they had stumbled on the largest gold field in the world. President Paul Kruger designated the area open for public digging in 1886, thereby starting a gold rush of miners from all over the world hoping to 'strike it rich'.

The process of segregation began in the 1890s when specific areas were mapped out for African, Indian, coloured and white residents. In 1910 the Union of South Africa created a single nation state and segregation, or apartheid (apartness), became an official policy. It included the Land Act (1913) and the Natives (Urban Areas) Act (1923), which forced non-whites to live in specific territories and introduced the need for passes in order to be permitted to work in white areas. The segregated city of Johannesburg emerged in 1926 with a 'whites

only' inner city and black residents pushed into townships at its extremities, including Soweto (South-Western Townships). Here, the communities who were barred from the city's places of entertainment conceived their own. Jazz was played in the shebeens of Sophiatown and Soweto (see image 1) and by the 1930s local records were being produced, including 'Izikhalo Zika Z-Boy' (1939) by the Jazz Maniacs.

In 1955 the Freedom Charter was signed, which stated that 'South Africa belongs to all who live in it, black and white', thus initiating the Anti-Apartheid Movement. By the 1960s, several different styles could be discerned within the townships: the swenkas dressed with exquisite taste to take part in competitions to see who looked the snappiest; the pantsula (see page 278) were sharply dressed jazz aficionados; the Ivies were obsessed by US Ivy League style (see page 78); and the hippies wore dashikis (originally from West Africa) and grew their hair into Afros inspired by Angela Davis and the Black

Power Movement. The city's white middle-class hippies hung out at pavement cafés and the underground flea market on Pretoria Street smoking dagga (marijuana); in 1969 Alan Alexander Telford wrote of part time "hippies" (who) loll about, the males in beards and purple shirts, the females in jeans. None of them are real "drop outs".'

American and European influences could be seen in the output of fashion designers who worked in the city, but their work had little global appeal because of apartheid, particularly after the Soweto Uprising of 1976 in which many protestors, including children, were killed by heavily armed police after protesting against Bantu Education's mandatory teaching of Afrikaans in every school. The global outcry at the photograph of the slain 12-year-old Herman Pieterson being carried in his brother's arms strengthened the resistance movement, eventually leading to the end of apartheid. In 1990 President de Klerk released a number of political prisoners, including Nelson Mandela, who became the first democratically elected president in 1994.

One prominent designer who did achieve success through her understanding of indigenous culture was Marianne Fassler, who wanted to 'create clothing that could only have been made in South Africa'. Her trademark use of leopard-skin print under the moniker 'Leopard Frock' played with both African and European sensibilities as a material associated with status and power in tribal groups and also with fashionability within the context of 1980s fashion designers such as Gianni Versace. Fassler's use of the indigo-dyed, printed, stiff cotton fabric shweshwe (see image 2) – traditionally worn by the Xhosa after it was introduced by French missionaries in the

19th century – is also significant. Shweshwe was imported from India, the Netherlands and Czechoslovakia, and also later from Wigan, UK, under the label Three Cats. The fabric's stiff texture is a result of the heavy starching used to prevent damage from damp when in sea transit and perhaps the reason for its name after the rustling noise it makes when the wearer is in motion. The first local production of the cloth was by Da Gama Textiles in Zwelitsha in 1982, when the firm slowly moved away from its traditional customers and ceremonial dress into the world of fashion through the work of Fassler and Stoned Cherrie.

Johannesburg street fashion has always been an intriguing assemblage of both indigenous forms of dress and Western influences, with items of clothing being reappropriated and reframed. These include the pantsula's love of the Converse hi-top, which continued to be part of their look after designer trainers had become ubiquitous in global street culture. The spottie or bucket hat had a different shape and brim make, confirming its township location, and when worn by kwaito performers Trompies and Alaska its cool credentials were reconfirmed. Butan (a rearrangement of the word Bantu, see image 3) is a brand in business since 2006 that fuses South African township heritage with contemporary streetwear, including a range of ispotties. The felt hat of the 1950s inspires the work of designers Simon and Mary who have built on the legacy of hat manufacturer Simon Pozniak, owner of Supreme Hat and Cap Manufacturers in operation in the city since 1935.

It is these fascinating identifiers that are inspiring young designers and stylists such as the creative collective The Sartists today.

ZEF

'Zef is South African underdog kind of style. Zef has been an insult for so long in South Africa. It means you're like a piece of shit.'
— Ninja, Die Antwoord

The Afrikaners are the descendants of Dutch settlers who arrived in South Africa in the 17th century and developed their own language and identity. The dream of establishing a land independent of British rule inspired a mass migration of farmers, known as Voortrekkers (Pioneers), on the Great Trek of 1835—36 into the interior of the country now known as South Africa. In 1910 the Union of South Africa created a single nation state and in 1948 the National Party representing the Afrikaners gained control, with apartheid as its official policy. Afrikaners were the empowered race. In 1971 the price of gold began to rise after US President Richard Nixon put an end to the direct convertibility of the US dollar to gold at $35 an ounce. Afrikaners working in the gold mining industry became cash rich, and their flashy lifestyle led to the term 'Zef' being used as a descriptor, based on their alleged love of the Ford Zephyr customized with fat tyres and rims. The stereotypical Zef had an oversized walrus moustache and a mullet hairstyle as worn by US 'trailer trash'. With the end of apartheid and legislated 'whiteness' in 1994, life for Afrikaners changed dramatically. They were now members of a taboo culture that was

1 Voortrekkers, or Afrikaners, in 1938.
2 Afrikaner rapper DJ Jack Parow.
3 Zef rap-ravers Die Antwoord.

being systematically dismantled; streets named after Afrikaner heroes were changed, as was the national flag. African National Congress members had been branded terrorists, but now they were praised internationally and domestically as freedom fighters, and some entered positions of power in the new democratic Parliament.

Today, as Anton Krueger writes, 'The inheritance of the present generation of Afrikaners is largely one of shame.' More recently, Zef is being re-appropriated, some say parodied, by young people in Johannesburg who have embraced this marginalized culture. The scene has grown up around Die Antwoord (the Answer), a Zef rap-rave trio comprising the tracksuit-wearing Ninja, Yolandi Visser who sports an outlandish platinum mullet and DJ Hi-Tek, who all rap in Afrikaans. Yolandi describes Zef as 'people who soup their cars up and rock gold and shit. Zef is, you're poor but you're fancy. You're poor but you're sexy, you've got style.'

1 An izikhothane wears shoes of different colours to show he can afford two pairs. 2 Izikhothane crews dress to the nines and arrange meet-ups to compete with other crews. As one explained, 'Showing off swag is what we love. We want attention.' 3 Crowds gather to cheer on their favourite izikhothane crew. 4 An izikhothane crew wear brightly coloured, coordinated outfits.

JOHANNESBURG

COUNTRY South Africa
DECADE OF ORIGIN 2000s

IZIKHOTHANE

*'The old people say that what we're doing is devil worshipping.
It's not that. Being izikhothane, people respect you, and there's
all that attraction and attention.'* — Mpho, izikhothane

The izikhothane (from the Zulu, 'those who lick') are the ultimate in conspicuous consumers mixed with a rebellious punk nihilism. Every izikhothane is a member of a township crew, with names such as the Commandos, Reflection Destructor Crew, the 18 Boys and the Material Boys. They dress in brightly coloured, coordinated outfits at events that are planned well in advance, with the date and venue spread by word of mouth. They arrive in taxis and proceed to dance while brandishing and pouring bottles of alcohol on the ground. Some wear their shoes with the left shoe a different colour to the right, to show that they can afford two pairs; others layer up three pairs of trousers for the same effect.

At one point crews destroyed high-priced and highly prized designer items and mobile phones and ripped up or burned bundles of R100 and R200 bank notes in front of hundreds of spectators. The winning crew was the one that was prepared to consign the most wealth to the flames and not get 'licked' or beaten by another crew. Crews did this to show that they had so much money that all items were meaningless and could be easily replaced. The South African press reacted with horror to such flagrantly ostentatious behaviour and began to clamp down on the meet-ups. Today the behaviour is more scaled down, with designer items flouted with price tags to prove they are not counterfeit. In addition, the izikhothane pour Ultramel, a brand of custard, over each other because it is considered a luxury among the black families of the townships. They are the 'born free', the generation who never lived under apartheid, so this revelling in consumerism is the ultimate rebellion against the hardships their parents endured in Johannesburg's townships. The pay-off for the izikhothane is fame, albeit fleeting, and the performance, if not the reality, of wealth and swag.

SMARTEEZ

'I was born into the free world. And some people accuse me of taking my freedom for granted. But to that I say fuck you! It's my freedom to take for granted.' — Sibu, The Smarteez

The Smarteez are a young generation of South Africans taking up the reins of the older sapeurs (see page 270). The 'first borns' or Rainbow Generation have no memories of apartheid and they experiment with their appearance by avoiding the literal expressions of African identity that dominated the early freedom years of Johannesburg fashion. The notion of 'Africa' generates its own set of ethnic or tribal clichés: Yves Saint Laurent's safari look of the 1970s, Roberto Cavalli's animal print in the 1990s and Burberry Prorsum's batik designs in the 2010s are all read generically as 'African' despite the fact that Africa is a huge landmass made up of different cultures and identities.

The Smarteez, originally a collective of four young Soweto designers – Kepi Mngomezulu, Thabo Tsatsinyane, Floyd Avenue and Sibu Sithole – refuse to work within the boundaries of race or location. From a small studio in Soweto in 2009, they began to challenge African stereotypes with DIY fashion that, unlike the sapeurs, ignores Western luxury labels in favour of sourced fabrics from Market Street

1 The collective group Smarteez, known for their township-inspired street style, in front of the Mandela murals in Soweto, South Africa.

2 A headdress fashioned from a cheap laundry bag turns low culture into high fashion.   3 A typical Smarteez mix of classic menswear and African heritage textiles.   4 Smarteez in 2013 in the Kliptown section of Soweto.   5 Designs by Apparel shown in Johannesburg. Designer Craig Native takes inspiration from the Nelson Mandela Foundation Centre of Memory's archives.   6 Smarteez ignore luxury labels in favour of African fabrics and second-hand clothes from thrift stores and markets.

and second-hand clothes from thrift stores and markets. Their aesthetic makes use of primary colours, after the sugar-coated sweets Smarties from which the Smarteez get their name. (Smarteez are also smart and dress smartly.) Colourful garments are deconstructed and redesigned and there is much play with meaning, including the use of the vestiges of colonialism such as khaki uniforms and pith helmets, traditionally the clothes of the white oppressors. Preppy (see page 78) and 'nerd' references are also used, including oversized horn-rimmed Buddy Holly-style glasses, braces and shortened trousers.

The increased access to the Internet makes Smarteez global, not local citizens who want to construct new post-apartheid identities. As Floyd Avenue puts it, 'It's not expected, from Sowetans, to think out of the box. This IS the box. Black culture is a very conservative culture. Now with the new age kids, we've been breaking that restriction.'

ASIA

BEIJING SEOUL TOKYO OSAKA LAHORE
BANGALORE KUALA LUMPUR JAKARTA BANDUNG

COSPLAY SHAMATE K-POP STARCRAFT BOSOZUKOL SUKEBAN FAIRY KEI DECORA
GANGURO GYARU-O KOGAL GOTHLOLI GENDERLESS KEI TAQWACORE DESI RAP
METALHEAD SKINHEAD PUNK SCOOTERIST

'Asia' is an entirely geographic term for the huge landmass that makes up the most culturally diverse continent in the world. It holds the mega-cities of Beijing, Tokyo, Seoul and Delhi, and because of its rich resources it has been colonized repeatedly. Colonization has had a significant effect on the history of Asian dress and traditional costume, such as the Chinese cheongsam, Japanese kimono, Korean hanbok and Indian sari, which have been variously modified, outlawed or rejected in favour of European and US-influenced fashion. European designers, in turn, have made fashion out of Asian clothing archetypes; the opening of Paul Poiret's atelier in Paris in 1903 saw a host of Asian-inspired designs, including shimmering kimono gowns and Indian turbans. Karl Lagerfeld's 2016 Cruise Collection for Chanel featured the Korean hanbok, and for his A/W 2008 Collection Alexander McQueen married British Victorian colonialism with Indian maharajas, using traditional sari silks and gold jewellery.

When certain garments enter a different culture, their meanings can change dramatically. For example, the Chinese cheongsam became shorthand for a decadent orientalism, associated with the city of Shanghai, an Art Deco paradise and the so-called 'Paris of the East'. The city's dance halls, brothels, clubs and restaurants indulged the tastes of the international set, but Shanghai's fortunes changed dramatically after World War II when communists took control of China after a three-year civil war and the city became isolated from the outside world. Partition and World War II transformed many Asian cities. The nuclear bombings of Hiroshima and Nagasaki in 1945 and the annihilation of many thousands of citizens brought a malaise upon the post-war generation. Academic David Goodman writes of how defeat 'discredited the institutions and values for which millions of Japanese had just given their lives, in particular the emperor system, its institutional expressions, and the philosophical and mythological systems of thought that informed it. Henceforth, what should the Japanese live and die for? It was a question not easily answered.' The ruined cities of Japan were under US occupation until 1952 and there was an uneasy ambivalence towards the forces who were helping to rebuild the same country they had devastated. This is reflected in the bosozoku (speed tribe; see page 312), who not only reference the kamikaze but also celebrate the rebellious rockabiri, or rockabilly, wearing pompadours and leather jackets.

In 1964, in an article titled 'The Young in Rebellion', a journalist for *Time* magazine described the post-war ennui felt by Japanese teenagers and how some spent their pay on 'movies, motorcycles, on all the latest clothing fads from Europe and the US, on the latest modern jazz records...going Western with a vengeance'. One group shut down entirely: the raritteru (sleeping pill kids) were a tribe of modern jazz fans in Shinjuku who spent their time intoxicated by sleeping pills so as to 'drowse through life, withdrawing into nothingness'. By the 1960s there was a huge Beatles fan base in Japan; they inked love messages to the band on their sweatpants in an early form of customization. The areas around the US compounds in Japan and Korea developed into black markets, selling cola, chewing gum, sweets and cigarettes. In Tokyo US troops were stationed around Harajuku, the area where the first distinctive groups of zoku (street tribes) emerged, including the taiyozoku (sun tribe).

In 1947 India and Pakistan won independence; the territories that made up British India were made into separate states in a process of partition and Britain withdrew from the process of ruling its overextended empire. Both countries suffered ethnic and religious unrest and oppressive military rule, with young people finding a focus for their dissent in street fashions such as punk (see page 360), heavy metal and hip hop (see page 46). Bollywood has been a huge popular force, too. The sumptuous costuming of Bollywood follows the traditions of royal dressing that hark back to the Mogul Empire, in which rich combinations of colour and gold jewellery were markers of high social status. Many of the most ostentatious Bollywood screen costumes are copied and worn at family weddings. A former Miss World, Aishwarya Rai, played a Rajput princess in *Jodhaa Akbar* (2008) and according to academic Angma Dey Jhala 'blazes onto the screen in a kaleidoscopic palette of colours. She wears heavy ornate red, orange, green, vermillion and yellow silk and chiffon gaghras and odanhis, while flashing strings of pearl and diamond necklaces, gold naths and jewelled toe rings and amulets.' This royal style continues to influence Indian fashion designers and global street fashion, including the Advanced Style trend that combines colours and patterns in an artistic celebration of the possibilities of fashion.

One of the most important emerging street fashions has its roots in Asia; many millennials are looking back to the heritage of their own countries and discovering traditional clothing, or what J C Flugel in *The Psychology of Clothes* (1930) refers to as 'fixed' dress as opposed to 'modish' or fashionable. Fixed clothing rarely changes and tends to be worn on ceremonial occasions; modish changes style regularly and is the product of capitalism. These designations have altered, and today the kimono, cheongsam, hanbok and sari are being worn as daywear, mixed with elements from a range of street and contemporary fashions, in many geographies.

BEIJING

'So vast, so rich and so beautiful, that no man on earth could design anything superior to it.' — Marco Polo

Beijing stands on the site of an ancient imperial city built more than three thousand years ago around a formation of lakes known as the 'six seas'. Its construction followed theories of city planning developed during the Shang dynasty and based on the cosmos. The Pole Star was believed to be a marker that defined the centre of heaven and it was used to calculate a series of meridian lines that, if channelled correctly, could distribute qi – a life-giving force – to the city's inhabitants. Architects used what became known as the Code of Zhou to map out a grid system of boulevards that depicted hierarchies of power, with the emperor and his imperial palace at its core. The court was known for its brightly coloured robes (see image 1), blouses and skirts, incorporating pure silks and brocades decorated with Beijing's famed palace embroidery. Silver and gold threads were stitched to depict dragons, phoenix, suns and butterflies.

The bound 'lotus' foot (see image 2) of the imperial court has become infamous for its injurious subjugation of women. Female children had their feet bound tightly from the back to the front, with the four smaller toes pushed down under the ball of the foot. The forefoot and heel were bound together securely until the bones ossified into place. The tiny lotus foot was considered the epitome of femininity and a symbol of social status, marking out the lady of leisure from the labouring peasant and her broad, unrestricted feet.

In 1912 the monarchy was overthrown by the Kuomintang, the Nationalist Party led by Chinese statesman Sun Yat-sen who founded the Republic of China. He introduced the zhongshan suit, based on the cadet uniform, as the Chinese equivalent of a Western business suit, with four pockets to the front for symmetry and a button front. The cheongsam, a derivative of the qipao, was worn by women.

Beijing's ritualistic structure remained relatively untouched until the 1920s. Industrialization increased the population of the city;

1 The brightly coloured robes of imperial dress.   2 Chinese lotus shoes made for bound feet.   3 Actor Nancy Kwan having her long hair cut.   4 Beijing Fashion Week 2015.

consequently, streets were widened, imperial gardens were turned into public parks and sanitation was improved. Beijing began to develop beyond its outer walls until they were demolished in the 1960s to make way for a ring road. In 1949 Beijing was declared the administrative centre and national capital of the People's Republic of China under Mao Tse-tung. Systematically, the city began to be stripped of the vestiges of its imperial past: Tiananmen Square was enlarged to make space for rallies; concrete high-rise buildings in the Socialist Realist style of the USSR began to appear; and factories were built in the suburbs. Mao Tse-tung was determined to create a productive socialist city and instituted policies such as collective farming, which wreaked havoc by inadvertently causing a famine that decimated the population in 1959.

The zhongshan suit became known as the Mao suit and it was worn by all men as a symbol of proletarian unity. In addition, the cheongsam – in a new, more form-fitting guise with a tapered waist and darts at the bust – became a popular Western fashion thanks to the popularity of the film *The World of Suzie Wong* (1960), in which Hong Kong-born actor Nancy Kwan (see image 3) played Mee Ling/Suzie Wong, a 'yum yum' girl or prostitute. Kwan went on to achieve fashion fame when Vidal Sassoon cut her long black hair into an A-line bob, photographed by Terence Donovan for British *Vogue*.

Little of this reached Beijing because of the state-imposed blackout on Western information, and when hippies were enjoying the Summer of Love, Chinese youth were upholding the tenets of communism as members of the Red Guard. After Mao's death in 1976, the country saw a period of reform, and under the leadership of Deng Xiaoping connections began to be made with the outside world. However, the events of May 1989 in Tiananmen Square – in which a peaceful student demonstration against political corruption and rising inflation was brutally quashed by soldiers firing randomly into the crowd from tanks – shocked the world.

Post-Mao reform had led China into the free market by the 1990s and young people began to revel in fashion (see image 4), beauty and celebrity culture. Some, such as the new 'educated' youth, turned their backs on city life, moving to the country and following the old Maoist principles of collectivism and communal living. Today the idea of a rebellious street fashion is still a relatively new concept, but the rise of the netizens, or the generation with access to the Internet, has created a curious mash-up of styles in the shamate subculture (see page 300).

COSPLAY

The first fan convention was staged in Leeds, UK, in 1937 by a group of British science fiction enthusiasts, followed by the first World Science Fiction Convention from 2 to 4 July 1939 in New York City as part of the World's Fair. The city was trying to recover from the depths of the Depression and the World's Fair, with its futuristic exhibits and dreams of Utopia, was an attempt to persuade citizens to look to the future with optimism.

There, one couple aroused curiosity, dressed to impress in 'futuristicostumes' based on the outfits worn in the movie *Things to Come* (1936) written by H G Wells. They were Myrtle R Jones (Morojo), who designed the costumes, and editor and literary agent Forrest J Ackerman, who went on to launch the first movie-monster magazine – *Famous Monsters of Filmland* – in 1958. Teenage fans of horror, including embryonic directors Steven Spielberg and John Landis, eagerly anticipated each edition, wanting to hear about the latest movies and to read interviews with stars such as Bela Lugosi, the hypnotic Count Dracula of 1931. Ackerman was a super-fan and amassed a legendary collection of memorabilia that was held in his Los Feliz mansion until 2002 when, due to his ill health, it was dispersed. He was also responsible for coining the phrase 'sci-fi' after hearing record players being called 'hi-fis' in the 1950s. By the time of the second Worldcon, as the event began to be called, held in Chicago the following year, the word was out and fans caroused in costume with prizes awarded for the best in show. By 1956 costuming had become an established tradition and Ackerman described

'Monsters, mutants, scientists, spacemen, aliens and assorted "Things" [who] thronged the ballroom floor as the flashbulbs popped.'

The term 'cosplay' (costume play) was first used by game designer Takahashi Nobuyuki after visiting the Worldcon held in Los Angeles in 1984 and seeing fans dressed as their favourite fictional characters. Today, China has a burgeoning cosplay scene in which young people take inspiration from film, television, fiction, gaming, anime and manga in order to create costumes for social events. Every year a competition is held in Haidian Theatre and Beijing Amusement Park in which participants stage dramatic performances imitating their characters. Images are then uploaded to social platforms for comment. Indeed, a huge online community has emerged, including sites such as cosplay.com, which encourages fans in their creation of a fantasy identity and offers advice on how to make outfits. Academic Li Shiqiao points out in *Understanding the Chinese City* (2014) that the notion of dressing as a fantasy character has a long lineage in Beijing, dating from Chinese theatre through to the modern marriage ceremony in which the young couple is encouraged to 'put on thematic costumes ... and engage in multiple reconstitutions of themselves appearing in several cultural and intellectual identities'. He adds, 'The ability to nimbly shift from one cultural setting to another, from one identity to another, is normal, accepted and regarded as a source of aesthetic pleasure.' There is some disapproval from the Chinese authorities, however, and in 2015 edicts were issued before ChinaJoy, Asia's biggest digital entertainment expo, stating that women who exposed more than 2cm (¾in) of cleavage would be fined $800.

| 4 | 5 | | 6 |

4 The term 'cosplay' was first used by game designer Takahashi Nobuyuki after visiting the WorldCon held in Los Angeles in 1984. Fans dress as their favourite fictional characters.
5 Hatsune Miku, a cosplayer at Comic World, Seoul, in 2013. **6** A cosplayer at Cosplay Carnival in Pasay City, Philippines, 2016.

SHAMATE

BEIJING
COUNTRY China
DECADE OF ORIGIN 1990s

Shamate (meaning 'smart') is an ironic name given to a Chinese street fashion that mixes goth (see page 164), glam rock, anime and visual kei to create a hyperbolic version of youth style. The term was used originally by Hong Kong-based Mai Rox in 1999 to describe a series of online posts that documented her changing hairstyles and outfits, influenced by visual kei, glam rock, cosplay (see page 296) and K-pop (see page 304). The Flowers, a similarly styled Chinese rock band, popularized the look. Initially, the shamate fashion was extremely popular but it was soon picked up by young migrant workers who had moved from rural areas to cities such as Beijing and who were looking for ways to stand out from the crowd. Shamate was seen to be downgraded by this association and it attracted a large number of disparagers in the press who regarded the style as anything but smart. For them, the shamate look was a cultural misreading of street fashion by the unworldly with a piecemeal understanding of style tribes and a hackneyed notion of 'teenage rebellion'.

1 Shamate in black leather.　2 A shamate version of US punk.
3 The shamate punk-emo hybrid look.　4 A specialist
hairdresser.　5 An extreme teased and coloured hairstyle.

However, the shamate can also be read as an exuberant and creative Chinese variant of street fashion that plays with the idea of 'formal' to break the rules in a culture that has suffered decades of sartorial constraint under communism. They loot the image banks of street fashion and tend to fix on the most overtly expressive of looks. Hair is a focal point, teased high and brightly coloured, mixing punk verticality (see page 360) and emo volume (see page 142) with a nod to the Saiya-jin warrior race in the Japanese anime series *Dragon Ball Z*. Aladdin Sane, David Bowie's 1973 incarnation, is the inspiration for the face painting. However, this interpretation is much parodied on the Internet on popular microblogging platforms such as Sina Weibo, where it is compared to the moneyed fuerdai (the second generation of the rich), whose parents have made their fortunes thanks to the free market economy and who express their identity through the purchase of designer-branded luxury goods. In addition, the shamate are linked to the emergence of 21st-century selfie culture. The staged self-portrait has been given new impetus by the selfie, a format that can be spread across a global network in an instant and that plays with fashion and identity. In 2010 the introduction of the front-facing camera on the iPhone 4 offered even more detailed self-scrutiny. It has become an important tool for self-promotion among the Chinese netizens, who create sub-communities on social networking sites, such as Qzone, within their vast country – not unlike the extended family kinship network of the juggalos (see page 76).

SEOUL

Situated by a natural basin of the Han River, Seoul (meaning 'capital' in Korean) has been the political, trading and cultural centre of South Korea since 1394 and it remained so when the peninsula of Korea was divided officially in 1948. Korea was known as the Hermit Kingdom for its limited contact with the outside world and it was only when the Chosŏn dynasty began to lose its hold at the end of the 19th century that Westernization began to affect the country. The annexation of Korea by Japan in 1905 started a long and uneasy relationship between the two countries. As the colonizer, Japan began an authoritarian rule that attempted to clear the country of Korean national identity, including the demolition of the Royal Palace in 1911. However, the distinctive Korean hanbok (see image 1) survived.

The hanbok ('dress of our race', as opposed to yangbok, meaning 'Western dress') is traditional Korean clothing that can be traced back to the Goguryeo Kingdom (37 BC–AD 668). The symmetrical upper garment (jeogori) is worn with trousers (baji) by men and with a bell-shaped wraparound skirt (chima) by women, with the waistband placed high and delineated by a wide sash. The women's jeogori is tied with an otgoreum that trails over the chima. As Seoul has emerged as a modern metropolis, the brightly coloured hanbok is being revived by young people and designers such as Hwang Yi-seul and being worn by visiting celebrities such as Chloë Grace Moretz (see image 2).

After World War II and the defeat of Japan, Korea was divided along the 38th parallel, with North Korea backed by the Soviet Union and the South by the United States. In 1950 the North Korean People's Army invaded the boundary, thus starting the Korean War, the first serious incident of the Cold War. US troops intervened and after the death of millions and the devastation of Seoul, the countries remained divided.

In Seoul, the presence of American GIs brought the latest Billboard hits from American Forces Network Korea radio. Cover versions were played in GI clubs by Korean musicians such as the Kim Sisters (see image 3), who were spotted by GI Bob McMackin and exported to the United States. After establishing themselves in Las Vegas as

nightclub performers, the Kim Sisters appeared on *The Ed Sullivan Show* more than 20 times. Beatlemania hit South Korea in the 1960s and created two home-grown versions: beat combo Add 4 (named after a guitar chord) formed by singer-songwriter Shin Joong Hyun, and the legendary Key Boys who performed and released records across South East Asia. In 1964 Add 4's first album was a major breakthrough because it had no cover versions of Western hits.

Music continued to be the conduit through which Western fashions penetrated Seoul. 2NE1 (to anyone) arrived on the K-pop scene (see page 304) in 2009 with their uber-catchy single 'Lollipop'. They were known for their styling as much as for their songs and wore Mishka, Balmain and Givenchy both on stage and off. They also collaborated with Jeremy Scott in 2011 on a pair of shoes – the JS Collage Wings x 2NE1 – through the Adidas Originals line. Also on the K-pop scene, PSY (real name Park Jae-sang) has had more than two billion hits for his gently subversive parody 'Gangnam Style' (2012), a reference to an upmarket area of Seoul that is home to South Korea's biggest brands. The absurdist pony-step dance – poking fun at K-pop's precise choreography – became a global craze.

In 2012 the fashion concert K-Collection was staged at the Olympic Park Gymnasium Stadium in Seoul. It combined performances by Girl Generation, Big Bang and Tiger JK with collections by fashion designers such as 2PLACEBO, 8Seconds and ippngirl. In the same year, fashion designer Yong Kyun Shin dressed Icelandic singer Björk for her

Biophilia tour and opened his own space, Alogon, in Seoul's Doota department store. He made his debut at London Fashion Week with 'The Broken' (S/S 2014), a dystopian, futuristic collection playing with combinations of materials to imitate damaged forms. Seoul first held its own fashion week in 2000 and it was strategically placed to follow New York, Paris and London. The city's goal to host one of the most prominent fashion weeks in the world was given a boost by Karl Lagerfeld's 2016 Cruise Collection for Chanel (see image 4), which debuted on a polka-dotted catwalk at Zaha Hadid's Dongdaemun Design Plaza. K-pop's premier league stars, CL of 2NE1 and G-Dragon of Big Bang, were in the front row, transmitting the looks – graphic riffs on the Korean hanbok or kimono and the strapless chima dress – directly to their millions of Instagram followers.

K-POP

K-pop (Korean pop) is a musical genre that combines Eastern and Western sounds with perfectly synchronized dance moves. Its modern form is derived from trot, a musical genre that originated in Korea in the 1920s. Marrying the lyrics of the Korean love song with the two-beat rhythm of the foxtrot, trot's syncopated torch songs expressed the heartfelt emotion of a country under authoritarian rule. Hits included Lee Nan-yung's 'Tears of Mokpo' (1935) and Sim Soo-bong's 'Men are Ships, Women are Harbours' (1984).

The 1990s marked the golden age of modern K-pop, as government censorship over lyrical content was lifted and artists were allowed more creativity. When former rock musician Seo Taiji enlisted two dancers to create Seo Taiji and Boys, the best-known K-pop stars were spawned. Their combination of innovative rap/pop mash-ups and exuberantly choreographed hip hop moves were ambrosia to a huge youth audience, and their first single – 'Nan Arayo' (1992) – stayed at the top of the charts for 17 weeks.

By the mid 2000s, K-pop had gone corporate and the packaging of artists was big business, with companies such as SM Entertainment scouting potential stars and enrolling them into a five-year training programme. A conveyor belt of 'idol' groups, including Wonder Girls, Super Junior and the nine-member Girls Generation, saturated the market with bubble gum pop, glossy image construction and side projects. K-pop became known for its drilled

1 G-Dragon cosplay, styled by Hiyukiri in imitation of an outfit worn in 2010. 2 K-pop stars JJCC and Boyfriend perform at the K-Pop Party at the Carriageworks in Sydney in 2016. 3 Hiyukiri dresses as G-Dragon, a South Korean rap artist who was originally a member of K-pop band Big Bang. G-Dragon has achieved global status as a fashion icon and is K-pop's most copied star.

4 K-pop band 2ne1 (2009–16) have been a major influence on street fashion trends in South Korea.

5 The 'K-Collection' fashion concert at the Olympic Park Gymnastics Stadium in Seoul. South Korean K-pop stars, supermodels and celebrities attend the K-Collection, an event that combines fashion and music.

6 G-Dragon attends the Chanel show as part of Paris Fashion Week 2014.

choreography, auto-tuning and power to transform brands via product endorsement. Its fan base spread out from the confines of its mother country to Japan, the Philippines and beyond, with fan sites devoted to the key stars' every moves.

Fashion is a key element of the K-pop phenomenon, with the idols constantly pushing the boundaries of style. The clothes and accessories worn by K-pop stars are highly sought after by fans, who copy every aspect of their idol's look, from their hairstyle right down to the brand of cosmetics that they use. With this has come the invention of a whole new genre of cosplay (see page 296), devoted to K-pop stars such as G-Dragon of Big Bang.

STARCRAFT

SEOUL
COUNTRY South Korea
DECADE OF ORIGIN 1990s

'Seoul is nothing less than a PC gaming hotbed of imagination-defying magnitude.' — Mark Donald, editor of *PC Gamer* UK

South Korea was one of the first countries to establish a nationwide Internet broadband network through its state-owned telecoms company – it is now reputed to be the fastest in the world. By 2005 more than 96 per cent of 6 to 19 year olds were using the Internet, and cafés, or PC bangs, became popular meeting places all over Seoul. In 1998 the first game in the StarCraft franchise was launched by Blizzard Entertainment, a science fiction, multi-player, real-time strategy game set in space, in which three alien races – the Zerg, Terran and Protoss – battle to adapt and survive. It became a huge success among South Korean youth and the PC bangs responded

1 A cosplayer dressed as a StarCraft Terran.   2 A printed Lycra catsuit by Living Dead Clothing.   3 Professional StarCraft players.   4 & 5 Ann-Sofie Back A/W 2010.

by installing high-specification PCs on which fans could play outside of the home. The challenging nature of the game appealed because competition is encouraged in South Korea.

The release of StarCraft overlapped with the establishment of South Korea's first gaming league, and pro-gamers organized teams and quickly found sponsors. There are now 12 professional teams, and the pro StarCraft players make significant amounts of money and are viewed as national heroes. The South Korean government has a department for pro-gaming, or e-sport, thereby confirming that StarCraft is deeply embedded within South Korean culture. Games have become an important area of expression in a conformist country and StarCraft has moved from a game to an entertainment industry that includes a subgenre of cosplay (see page 296).

Fashion has flirted with gaming, most notably Ann-Sofie Back's A/W 2010 collection, inspired by the online gaming phenomenon Second Life, in which she had her own avatar. Some gaming companies are recognizing the potential of partnering with fashion designers. For example, 2K Games collaborated with LDC (Living Dead Clothing), a company based in Brisbane, to create a collection in 2016 for BioShock, a game set in an Art Deco-inspired world.

TOKYO

In the 18th century, Edo developed from a small fishing village into a bustling city of more than a million inhabitants. The ruling classes of early modern Japan operated a strict social hierarchy, with the warrior at the top and the merchant classes far behind. During the Edo period (1615–1868), status was enforced through dress, in much the same way as sumptuary laws operated in Europe, and the intricately decorated kimono (see image 1) was an important garment for the display of social status. Edo was renamed Tokyo after the military ruler Tokugawa Ieyasu moved his primary residence there from Kyoto in 1868. The following Meiji era (1868–1912) opened up the country to Western trade and influence after two hundred years of isolation.

A large-scale Westernization of dress began in the 19th century; men were the first to change, cutting off their 'tea whisk' topknots and eschewing the kimono, the hakama (culotte-type trousers) and the tabi (a slit-toe shoe-sock) in favour of Western business suits and bowler hats. Modernity also began to infiltrate traditional Japanese dress and customs, in the form of luxury goods by Louis Vuitton, for example, whose distinctive monogram incorporated Japanese characteristics. (In 2002 the long-standing love affair with the brand

culminated in artist Takashi Murakami reworking the iconic monogram canvas into 33 colours set against a pure white ground.) However, women wore the kimono well into the 20th century and it crossed over into Europe and the United States through the Aesthetic movement's cult of Japonisme. The Western version was sold at Liberty of London and it was worn in the boudoir, revealing the wearer as a woman of education and elegance. Designers such as Paul Poiret and Lucile also incorporated kimono proportions into their designs.

As Tokyo expanded in the 1920s, women moved from the domestic sphere into the workplace and wore Western dress or the kimono in designs featuring contemporary stylistic devices, including Art Deco geometry and colours such as peach, Schiaparelli hot pink and orange. The industrialization of silk democratized the fabric and made the fine yukata, or summer kimono, more affordable. However, in 1923 the Great Kanto earthquake (see image 2) obliterated the city centre and some 140,000 people were killed. It took many decades for Tokyo to be fully reconstructed, especially after the heavy bombardment from Allied troops following the attack on Pearl Harbor during the Pacific War. The 1950s was a period of economic recovery when rationed

subsistence clothing' was the only option after the country had to exchange the best of its domestic production of materials for food. By 1955 restrictions had been abolished and the city became a hive of mass production that continued unchecked until the oil crisis of 1973.

American-influenced fashion was imported via Hollywood films and made a huge impact on Tokyo youth, who created their own version of the US biker or UK rocker known as the kaminari zoku (thunder tribe). They rode illegally customized motorcycles and frequently clashed with police. The preppy or Ivy League style (see image 3, see page 78) was also popular, documented in Teruyoshi Hayashida's study of campus style, *Take Ivy* (1965), which featured photographs of students in checked Bermuda shorts, blazers and Weejuns. 'Shine modo' (cinema mode) was a term used to describe women's fashion that was influenced by female stars: Audrey Hepburn's gamine haircut, capri pants and Ferragamo ballet flats in *Roman Holiday* (1953), for example.

Japanese teenagers began to create their own distinctive style: girls were drawn to the red lipstick glamour of the pan-pan girls – street prostitutes who collected around the American GIs stationed

in the city – combined with the look of the home-grown calypso star Michiko Hamamura (see image 4), whereas boys were influenced by the film *Taiyo no kisetsu* (*Season of the Sun*, 1956) in which Hawaiian shirts were worn with slim Jim ties, skinny suits and Shintaro-style haircuts. The DC burando movement (designer brands with obvious logos) dominated the 1980s, and the kimono was reserved for formal and ceremonial occasions. This was also the decade in which street performers and avant-garde fashionistas began to gather in the Harajuku district of Tokyo on Sundays, when the Omotesando – a long street of boutiques – was closed to traffic. Radical and globally influential street fashions emerged, including gothloli (see page 334), visual kei and ganguro (see page 322), and labels such as Baby, The Stars Shine Bright (1988) and Moi-même-Moitié (1999) emerged to cater to the looks. The fanzine *FRUiTS,* by photographer Shoichi Aoki, has been documenting the scene since 1997.

In the 21st century, canny investments in new technology have made Tokyo a prosperous city that has weathered a global recession and the Tohoku earthquake of 2011. It remains one of the most important centres of radical style tribes and street fashion today.

BOSOZOKU

TOKYO
COUNTRY Japan
DECADE OF ORIGIN 1970s

Like many countries, Japan has a biker culture that dates back to the 1950s. Its military returned to a defeated country, and many young men found solace in rebellion following the lead of stars such as James Dean in *Rebel Without a Cause* (1955). The kaminari zoku, or thunder tribe, named after the sound of their motorbikes, grew exponentially, creating headlines after violent clashes with the police in the 1970s and their dangerous habit of street racing without wearing helmets. A home-grown version of the biker emerged dubbed the bosozoku (speed tribes); they became members of a nationwide street movement revolving around the customization of cars and bikes.

The bososoku wear the tokkofuku (special attack uniform), a biker outfit based on uniforms worn by kamikaze suicide bombers during World War II. Tokkofuku are modified overalls or a one-colour jacket

1 This black overall is based on kamikaze flying outfits.
2 A kamikaze displays the rising sun motif. 3 Kyushakai
with towering pompadours. 4 A bosozoku on a modified
motorbike in 2015.

and trouser combination, with the name of the bosozoku's group embroidered on the back in metallic colours alongside nationalist symbols, including the imperial chrysanthemum and the naval ensign of the rising sun. Underneath is a tasuki, a ritualistic sash tied around the torso in an 'X', taken from the kamikaze, and a hachimaki headband. Long white coats covered in nationalist symbols are also popular, worn with trousers tucked into knee-high pilot boots. The tokkofuku is passed down from generation to generation and, like the Hells Angel (see page 24), the leather jacket can never be washed.

An offshoot of the bosozoku, known as kyushakai, has a more 1950s-oriented look, exaggerated to attract attention: hair is permed and teased into a huge pompadour known as a rizento worn with a black leather jacket and jeans. Bososoku are renowned for meeting in Harajuku Park on a Sunday afternoon; they include the Black Shadows who dress in full leathers and have the highest pompadours. Motorbikes are displayed with amplified exhaust systems, air horns and the distinctive bosozoku turned-down handlebars that make it easier to weave between traffic to evade the police.

SUKEBAN

A member of a vast international network of syndicates involved in criminal activity that has its origins in the 16th century, the notorious tattooed Japanese gangster – the yakuza – cuts a threatening figure. The family-like structure echoes that of the Mafia, with a father/godfather in control and his acolytes beneath. This boss and follower relationship is replicated in other gangs who are regarded with disdain and considered young upstarts by the 'real' yakuza gangsters. The leader of a gang of juvenile toughs was known as the banchou and the female boss was the onna banchou, or sukeban.

The first Japanese girl gangs emerged in the 1970s, breaking out of the constraints of the submissive femininity deemed appropriate for Japanese women, and the term 'sukeban' became a collective description. The largest gang in Tokyo was the United Shoplifters group, which had upwards of 80 members at any one time; the Kanto Women Delinquent Alliance was estimated to have twenty thousand members. The most notorious sukeban was rumoured to be Tokyo's K-Ko, a knife-wielding boss of a 50-strong gang who roamed the district of Saitama shoplifting, fighting and causing mayhem. Allegedly, she was the inspiration for male shojo author and illustrator Shinji Wada, whose 22-volume manga series *Sukeban Deka* (*Delinquent Girl Detective*), created between 1976 and 1982 stars a sukeban turned undercover agent who uses a metal yo-yo as a weapon.

The sukeban customize their sailor fuku school uniforms and wear sunglasses to create a 'bad girl' image. Tops are cropped to expose the midriff; cuffs are turned back to show subversive linings including leopard print; gang-related slogans and motifs such as a thorny rose are embroidered across the back; skirts are lengthened to the ankle. The footwear of choice is Converse sneakers, a classic black-and-white

1 The sukeban figure of the delinquent schoolgirl.   2 High-school girl gang, 1973.   3 Sukeban style in 2016, including eyeball hair ornaments and blood splatter stockings.   4 *Yo-Yo Girl Cop* (2006).

basketball shoe launched after World War II and worn by college and professional players. By the 1950s, Converse Chuck Taylors (after the basketball star) were associated with rebellion when adopted by US teenagers and worn with jeans and a leather jacket. The sukeban love these delinquent associations as filtered through US movies and the GIs stationed in Japan. GIs were also responsible for the sukeban's adoption of the functional black nylon MA-1 flight jacket with its distinctive orange lining.

The 'delinquent girl boss' caught the popular imagination and appeared as a character in many Japanese films throughout the post-war years. Examples include *Zubeko Tenshi* (*Bad Angel*; 1960) starring Mitsue Komiya, the four-picture franchise *Zubeko Bancho* (*Bad Girl Boss*) directed by Kazuhiko Yamaguchi in the early 1970s, and the *Sukeban* series of seven films that ran from 1970 to 1972.

TOKYO
COUNTRY Japan
DECADE OF ORIGIN 2000s

FAIRY KEI

The concept of kawaii, or cutie, has underpinned much Japanese street fashion since the 1980s, influencing hair, make-up, clothing and accessories. It spontaneously erupted out of schools across Japan in the 1970s when, according to Sharon Kinsella in her essay 'Cuties in Japan' (1995), pupils invented a cute form of handwriting, using childish characters interspersed with hearts and exclamation marks, in a rebellion against the formality of traditional Japanese culture. The childlike aesthetic moved into clothing, thus initiating a style originally dubbed burikko (fake children) or kawaiikochan (cutie-pie kid). It was soon picked up by the market and led to the global success of brands such as Hello Kitty. Kinsella sees the rise of the cute in Japan as a way of negotiating city life, describing how the 'consumption of lots of cute-style goods with powerful emotion-inducing properties could ironically disguise and compensate for the very alienation of individuals from other people in contemporary society'.

Pop star and 'idol singer' Matsuda Seiko promoted the look in her performances, presenting herself as an emotional child unable to hide her true feelings when on stage, a lack of artifice that seemed

1 Blogger Florrie wears layers of pastel-coloured clothing with baby pink accessories and a handmade headdress atop her turquoise and lilac curls for London Fashion Week 2013.

2 Fairy kei originated in Japan but has been adopted by young women all over the world. 3 Brazilian fashion blogger and personal stylist Luly Salle. 4 Jewellery designer Roxie Sweetheart from London.

appealing in a strict and seemingly strait-laced society. The enactment of a fantasy childhood to rebel against the obligations of adulthood has created a number of street styles since, including decora, lolita and its subgenres, and the more recent fairy kei (fairy style). Followers of fairy kei wear layers of pastel-coloured clothing mixed with polka dots and flashes of fluorescence. It is a ramped-up version of the A-line dresses, tulle ruffled skirts or tutus usually worn by little girls to birthday parties, with petticoats and bloomers, or pumpkin pants, peeping out beneath. Hair is pastel-coloured, too, although wigs are popular due to the sartorial rules of the workplace. References are made to 1980s fashion and cartoon brands such as My Little Pony, Rainbow Brite and the Care Bears. The look is occasionally referred to as Spank! style, after one of its early adopters, Sayuri Tabuchi, who opened the shop Spank! in Shibuya in 2003.

DECORA

Cuteness dominates the Internet, and countless videos of kittens, pandas and puppies are uploaded as consumer click-bait. Evolutionary biology is at work here, according to Austrian ethologist Konrad Lorenz, who studied the behavioural patterns of animals. He analysed why human beings react positively when confronted with babies and found that certain physical characteristics, which he termed 'baby schema' – large head and high forehead; short nose and big eyes; chubby cheeks and plump body – triggered feelings of nurture because of their cuteness, or 'kawaii' in Japanese culture. Lorenz realized that this was 'an evolutionary adaptation which helped ensure that adults cared for their children, ultimately securing the survival of the species'. The features that render babies 'cute' can also be found in young animals, which explains our predilection for kittens and puppies as well as for fictitious cartoon characters such as Disney's Bambi.

The idea of kawaii dates back to the Edo period, when it was used to describe a superior looking down on his inferior, and it gradually evolved into an affectionate term for something or somebody small, cute and beautiful. Kawaii has been taken to its extreme by the decora (decorative) of Tokyo, who dress like children who have raided a dressing-up box. Their layered ensembles of rainbow-coloured clothing and accessories, including multiple plastic barrettes clipped into hair worn in schoolgirl bunches, conjure a childlike cuteness. Leg warmers are worn over tights and up to three pairs of kneesocks with Mary Jane shoes. Japanese pop star Tomoe Shinohara was one of the first to experiment with the look. She took her cues from Western stars from the 1980s such as Cyndi Lauper and pop group Strawberry Switchblade, wearing childlike colour-clashing clothes. Members of the long-running girl group Morning Masume (Morning Girls), directed by the Hello! Project, are similarly styled.

1 Male decora in Tokyo in 2014.　2 Two examples of Tokyo decora.　3 Dark decora in Harajuku, Tokyo.　4 Pop star Kyary Pamyu Pamyu is decora's poster girl.

Decora style first took off with the launch of *FRUiTS* magazine in 1997. The cover model on the first issue, Aki Kobayashi, had a distinctive hand-crafted aesthetic that was much admired and copied, and her fans — the decora-chan (decora girls) — began hanging out in Harajuku hoping to be photographed for the magazine. Kyary Pamyu Pamyu, known as 'Japan's Lady Gaga', is a former model for Harajuku fashion magazines and a pop star. She became the poster girl for decora after the success of her first single, 'PonPonPon', in 2011 and performs on stage wearing tutus and kneesocks surrounded by giant furry animals.

Today the decora scene has spawned a series of subcategories, including original/casual decora, the first colourful and layered manifestation of the style; pink decora, who wear predominantly pink clothes and accessories; and dark decora/koteosa, which is a monochromatic look that uses a black base with hints of colour. The last is accessorized by 'sad' rather than 'cute' toys, such as Mori Chack's Gloomy Bear, a wild bear that attacks and draws blood. Decololi combines the decora and Lolita street styles.

GANGURO

A delicate fair skin 'as white as snow' is prized in Japan and considered the epitome of female beauty when offset by jet-black hair. The most beautiful geishas had soft pale skin and carried decorative parasols when outdoors for protection from the penetrating rays of the sun, thus marking themselves out from lowly peasants who developed coarse, tanned skin while toiling in the fields. In the 1950s, the popularity of Western stars continued the vogue for pale skin and lightening creams. However, with the global domination of hip hop in the 1990s, young Japanese women around the Ikebukuro and Shibuya districts of Tokyo began to reject the traditional tropes of Japanese beauty by covering their faces in heavy foundation and bronzer, using self-tanning products and going to tanning booths to emulate black stars such as Lauryn Hill and Macy Gray. They were dubbed ganguro, meaning 'black-faced', and included Namie Amuro who modelled herself on the singers in the US band TLC by sporting a tan, long hair extensions and plucked and arched eyebrows.

The ganguro look can also be read as a rebellion against submission in its overt sexuality. Make-up is deliberately exaggerated, the tan offset by white panstick around the eyes, fake eyelashes, black eyeliner, pearlescent eye shadow and highly powdered skin. Hair is obviously bleached, ranging in shades from orange through yellow

1 Members of staff at the Ganguro Cafe & Bar in Shibuya in 2015. The establishment offers special services such as ganguro make-up and the chance to take 'purikura' (photographs in a booth).

 2 3 4

2 A manba ganguro in Shibuya, Tokyo.
3 Ganguro Cafe & Bar staff wear contemporary versions of the original 1990s look. 4 An extreme version of ganguro known as yamanba, with an exaggerated manicure and deep tan.

to silvery-grey, and micro skirts are worn with luuzu (bunched ankle socks) and atsuzoko (high platform shoes). In addition, the ganguro are reacting against the suppression of individuality in Japanese culture and the strict competitive work ethic fostered by parents and the educational system.

The more extreme ganguro look is known as yamanba or manba, after the hags or mountain witches with superhuman strength that appear in Japanese folklore. Fanzines such as *Egg* documented the style, featuring three of its most extreme exponents: Buriteri – named after a type of dark-brown soy sauce – Akoyoshi and Fumikko, all of whom have the darkest tans, the whitest lipstick and apply stickers and glitter to their faces. Lurid plastic accessories, including Hawaiian lei, are also worn.

GYARU-O

TOKYO
COUNTRY Japan
DECADE OF ORIGIN 1990s

The bishonen or 'beautiful boy' is a figure with a long history in Japanese culture, dating back to the Edo period (1615–1868). He can take the form of a pageboy, a young warrior or the more 'feminine' partner in a male-male relationship, as depicted in the novel *Kinsei setsu bishnen roku* (*A Record of Recent Rumours About Beautiful Youths*; 1848) by Takizawa Bakin.

The early 20th-century bishonen was denuded of any gay references and referred to as a fresh-faced schoolboy hero, featuring in literature targeted at adolescents. Boys emulated the bishonen and girls fell in love with him in a relationship that was spiritual rather than physical. He appeared in early manga, including Tezuka Osamu's *Astro Boy* (1952–68), and in the 1970s yaoi genre by women manga

1 The highlighted and ironed hair of the gyaru-o.
2 Gender-fluid street fashion.   3 The demeanour of
the gyaru-o is a studied pose of 'coolness'.   4 A fashion-
forward, less exaggerated male version of the ganguro.

1 2 3 4

artists who featured relationships between men as a 'safe' area in which young girls could explore their own sexual yearnings. The bishonen became a figure of transgression who mixed gender markers and blurred boundaries, showing that the binary oppositions of masculinity/femininity were not necessarily fixed, but in a constant state of flux.

The gyaru-o ('girl man' or 'pretty boy') is street fashion's version of the bishonen, the male counterpart of the gyaru or 'gal' (English idiom of 'girl'). He is typically a peroxided college student with coloured contact lenses who buys into the brands with the most cachet – Louis Vuitton and Chanel, for example – and hangs out in Shibuya, Tokyo's fashion district where the vista is dominated by an

eight-storey shopping mall with a myriad of outlets. By the end of the 1990s, the gyaru had morphed into a more exaggerated version, the ganguro (see page 322), while substyles of the gyaru-o look included the rocker gyaru-o, the military gyaru-o, the biker gyaru-o and the surfer gyaru-o. Stores such as Vanquish and Lumine Man target the gyaru-o who are considered the most fashion-forward men in the city, known for their 'cool' demeanour even when dressed in the most outlandish of outfits. They have deep tans and high-volume, brightly coloured hair, reminiscent of 'hair metal' bands of the 1980s such as Bon Jovi. Clothes are minimal, as the shock-chic of the hair draws the eye, and include open shirts worn over a vest and skinny jeans.

1 Two Japanese high-school girls in uniform with umbrellas, eating toffee apples.   **2** School uniforms took over from the traditional kimono in Japan in the late 19th century and the sailor suit became its most popular form.

KOGAL

Groups of kogal, a moniker derived from 'kogyaru' (small/little girl), can be seen loitering around fashion outlets in the Shibuya area of Tokyo wearing their school uniforms out of hours. Uniforms are ubiquitous in the city as the majority of schools require them, and they are a mark of social status if the wearer comes from one of the elite. Some girls sport outfits that are a little more curious, known as 'nanchatte seifuku' (just kidding uniforms), fantasies worn as street fashion and designed by brands such as Conomi of Harajuku, whose best-selling item is a large ribbon neck-tie emblazoned with crests to imitate the insignia of top private schools. Kogal ensembles are made up of blazers and pleated skirts, with navy kneesocks or loose socks bunched around the legs and kept in place with roll-on glue.

School uniforms replaced the Japanese kimono as the appropriate daywear for school in the 1880s. By the 1920s, the two-piece sailor suit with a blouse had become popular as the country assimilated more Western influences, including the US Ivy League or preppy look (see page 78) in the 1960s. Middy blouses were worn under a jumper with a pleated skirt and generic Weejun loafers, an American classic designed by the Maine-based G H Bass & Co. in 1936. The shoes have a hand-sewn front, leather soles and heels, and a leather band with a diamond cut-out across the front. In the 1980s the effects of the declining birth rate began to impact on private schools and they competed to attract pupils. Tactics included remodelling their school uniforms using the country's best fashion designers.

The archaic sailor suit began to lose its appeal when compared with a well-cut blazer worn with the haute couture flair of Alicia Silverstone in the US high school comedy *Clueless* (1995), for example.

3 Kogal wear loose socks bunched around the lower half of the leg in the manner of leg warmers. They are kept in place with roll-on glue. 4 A cosplayer portrays popular manga character Sailor Moon. Sailor Moon's costume is derived from the Japanese school uniform.

On the streets of Shibuya the rebellious kogal hitched up her skirt and flirted, embodying contemporary stereotypes found in UK culture and seen in the *St Trinian's* movie franchise. A schoolgirl in a sailor suit also appeared on TV Tokyo in the anime series *Neon Genesis Evangelion* (1995–96) and in the global manga and anime hit *Sailor Moon* (1991–97).

The kogal created a moral panic in Japan and parents became frantic in case their daughters were spirited away for so-called 'enjo kosei', or compensation dating, in which girls are paid to spend time with older men, a fear that found expression in the movie *Baunsu ko gaurusu* (*Bounce KO Gals*; 1997) by Masato Harada. However, the kogal is more likely to be found in a group of like-minded schoolgirls clinging to her fleeting freedom before the responsibilities and obligations of adult life become overwhelming.

OSAKA

The port of Osaka has been Japan's gateway to traders for thousands of years, as it lies where the River Yodo meets the Inland Sea. As the Yodo ran through the city in a series of canals, goods could be transported to each district with ease. In 1583 the feudal lord and chief imperial minister Toyotomi Hideyoshi unified the warring factions across the country and chose Osaka as his base, building a five-tiered, two-moated castle on the site of a temple called Ishiyama Hongan-ji. When the capital moved to Edo, or Tokyo as it was later known, Osaka remained a hub of domestic and overseas trade and gained its reputation as the 'kitchen of the nation'. Today Osaka is regarded as the 'foodie' capital of Japan where visitors are encouraged to kuidaore (eat until you drop).

With mercantile money came crime, including a group of 17th-century hoodlums known as the kabuki-mono (crooked people; see image 1), who deliberately ignored dress codes. They shaved the front part of their heads and left their back hair long and loose, refusing to tie it into the customary topknot. Their short kimonos had weighted hems and imported velvet collars, and they took to the streets in noisy groups, wearing women's kimonos as multi-coloured

cloaks and intimidating passers-by with long swords or katana held in flamboyant red scabbards. Osaka's citizens, whose clothing was regulated by sumptuary laws, regarded such behaviour with dismay, including the merchant class who were forbidden to dress above their station. By the 18th century, a subtle approach came into fashion and men wore brown or navy kimonos with 'secretive' coloured silk linings in a similar vein to the Western business suit. This refined elegant attitude to fashion was given the name 'iki'.

Fashion influence also came from the gender-fluid wakashu (beautiful boys) of the kabuki theatre, whose legacy can be seen in the androgyny of Japanese street style, including visual kei (see image 4), gyaru-o (see page 326) and the recent genderless boys tribe (see page 338) who can be found in Osaka's shopping districts of Minamisenba and Shinsaibashi. Another key area of subcultural style is Amerika mura (American village; see image 2), a bizarre US-influenced shopping district dating back to the 1970s with its own Statue of Liberty and lampposts in the shape of robots. In the centre is Sankaku Koen (Triangle Park), the city's equivalent of Tokyo's Harajuku; every weekend it becomes a temporary catwalk where

1 A kabuki-mono or 17th-century hoodlum.   2 Amerika mura shopping district of Osaka is a subcultural hang-out.   3 Evisu catwalk show, A/W 2007.   4 Cosplayers dress as members of Phantasmagoria, a visual kei band.

rivets, weave and finish that denim aficionados loved were replaced. Denim purist Hidehiko Yamane, who worked in Lapine, a fashion boutique in Osaka, realized that Japanese youth were ignoring these new products and investing in vintage jeans at extraordinary prices. He decided to start a jeans brand that had the quality of the original product. In Okayama Prefecture, vintage denim was created on old power looms that were lying unused in fading factories formerly used to make school uniforms. The result was global jeans brand Evisu (1991; see image 3), followed by Mikiharu Tsujita's Fullcount (1992) and the Shiotani brothers' Warehouse (1995).

Nipponbashi, also known as 'Den-Den Town', is a district in Osaka that began selling electrical imports after World War II. It has developed into Japan's major outlet for anime, manga, gaming and cosplay (see page 296) cafés, where waitresses dress as anime characters. Furthermore, Nipponbashi is *the* destination for anime and manga fans known as otaku. The term was originally pejorative, the equivalent of the socially awkward 'computer nerd' who was single-minded in his passions wherein he found his escape from conformity. In his essay 'The City is Full of Otaku' (1983), Nakamori Akio described the typical otaku as having 'rumpled long hair parted on one side, or a classic kiddie bowl-cut look. Smartly clad in shirts and slacks their mothers bought off the "all ¥980/1980" rack at Ito Yokado or Seiyu discount retailers, their feet shod in knock-offs of the "R"-branded Regal sneakers that were popular several seasons ago, their shoulder bags bulging and sagging.' As gaming gained cool credibility, otaku became a means of self-identification by the 2000s and they were recognized by the Japanese government as a 'soft' power in 2014. In a complete turnaround, the otaku were harnessed to promote the country as 'Cool Japan'.

punks (see page 360) with rainbow-coloured mohawks, goateed hipsters and hip hop fans stroll side by side with uber-tanned ganguros (see page 322) and gothlolis (see page 334), the last Osaka's home-grown version of the much-debated Lolita street style.

The city is also the home of the vintage stores that helped establish the post-war cult of US denim in Japan. Iconic jeans brands such as Levi's and Wrangler were much sought after, but by the 1980s mass production and new loom technology had changed the design details; zinc buttons were substituted with plastic and the copper

GOTHLOLI

In the 1980s the post-punk gothic style reached Japan, where it was given a contentious twist. The penchant for black clothing and religious ephemera persisted but it was mixed with Japan's kawaii or 'cute' aesthetic. The G&L, or gothloli street fashion as it became known, gained its name from the combination of 'gothic' and the infamous novel *Lolita* (1955) by Vladimir Nabokov, which tells of the protagonist Humbert Humbert's obsession with a young girl. However, sexual references were absent in the gothloli fashion, and the fetish references of the original London look were discarded for a whimsical, childlike, asexual appearance recalling Victorian porcelain dolls, 19th-century mourning dress and the work of book illustrators such as John Tenniel for *Alice's Adventures in Wonderland* (1865).

Early Lolita style, now known as sweet Lolita, developed in Tokyo in the 1980s and followed a strict taxonomy of pastel-coloured, layered clothing; dresses had high necklines, full-length sleeves and bow sashes tied at the natural or slightly higher waistline. Hemlines hung below the knee, with bell-shaped skirts held out by petticoats to give an exaggerated Victorian-inspired silhouette. Legs were fully covered with long socks and tights, or a combination of both, and hair was worn in ringlets with an Alice band or poke bonnet. Many sweet Lolitas carried dolls that wore replicas of their own outfits, thereby reinforcing the notion of a 'living doll'. The original members of the style tribe made their own clothes, but as the look gained popularity brands were set up to cater to its fans. These included Angelic Pretty (1979) and Akinori Isobe's Baby, The Stars Shine Bright (1988).

1 Children's book illustrator Kate Greenaway portrayed children in a fantasy version of 18th-century dress that was adapted by Liberty's for a range of children's clothes. The mop cap, pinafore and dress inspired the Lolita look.   2 The sweet Lolita style developed in Tokyo in the 1980s and uses layers of pastel clothing to give a nostalgic, childlike effect.   3 The gothloli look evolved in Osaka and marries the black of goth style with Lolita's Victorian and Edwardian references.

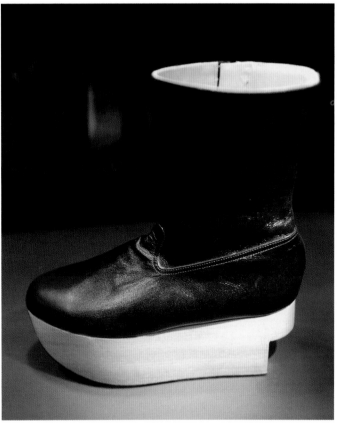

4 A Lolita wears a pink mini-crini skirt, held out with petticoats, and matching pink accessories.   5 The use of black gives a funereal quality to the look.
6 The Rocking Horse ankle boot, with an extreme wooden platform, was devised by Vivienne Westwood in 1985 for her Mini-Crini collection.

The goth element was added by Osaka fans of the UK-based style, and designers such as alice auaa, Marble/Visible and Victorian Maiden who introduced gauze blouses and skirts, puffed sleeves, mourning veils and funereal black top hats, all rendered in black instead of pastel. The childish Mary Jane shoe was supplanted by the platform, an elevated sole deriving from the ancient Japanese geta that underwent a revival in the late 1980s after Vivienne Westwood launched her Rocking Horse shoe for her Mini-Crini spring/summer 1985 collection. Westwood's abbreviated crinolines, the eponymous mini-crinis, with plastic hoops inserted into the fabric to hold out the shape, were also taken up in gothloli.

Osaka designer Kazuko Ogawa was an important link in the spread of the style as a result of his stage costumes created for visual kei band Malice Mizer (1992 – 2001). Guitarist Mana had two alternate personas – gothloli and vampiric aristocrat – and went on to found his own successful fashion label, Moi-même-Moitié, in 1999. As with decora (see page 320), the gothloli look can be read as escapist, a yearning or mourning for a fantasy childhood that keeps the overwhelming societal pressures at bay in an unstable post-recession economy.

OSAKA
COUNTRY Japan
DECADE OF ORIGIN 2010s

GENDERLESS KEI

"Masculinity is not connected to the clothes you're wearing – it's in the mind." — Jean Paul Gaultier

Genderless clothes are some of the earliest forms of fashion. The ancient Egyptian shendyt (sash skirt) denoted class rather than gender. It offered ease of movement and was perfect as hunting garb, but when pleated and draped in the finest linen it was the stuff of pharaohs. Androgynous fashion blurs the boundaries of gender and it has been posited by many designers since the 1960s, when masculinity – or at least masculine clothing – was being redefined in an era of liberalized sexual expression, the acknowledgment of gay identity and the rise of radical feminism. Fashion pioneer Jacques Esterel was prepared to enter dangerous sartorial waters in 1966 with the 'skirt suit' for men, featuring a Bermuda short with front flap in a snazzy Dacron check. Austrian designer Rudi Gernreich used the figure of a man in a skirt to presage a space age unisex Utopia, believing that, as women achieved liberation, male dress would emerge from the aesthetic exile into which it had been cast in the 19th century. In 1984 Jean Paul Gaultier began dismantling the clichés of masculine styling and debuted the man-skirt in his And God Created Man collection (1985), ostensibly inspired by 'the long apron of the Parisian bistro waiter'. In the same decade, Japanese designers Yohji Yamamoto and Rei Kawakubo mixed Japanese and European fashion traditions to create clothing with an androgynous appeal.

Japan's tradition of beautiful boys, or gyaru-o (see page 326), dates back to the kabuki theatre, in which men customarily took on female roles. It is also reflected in visual kei, a glam rock-influenced theatrical style worn by pop and rock bands in Osaka from the 1980s onwards.

1 Designer Rudi Gernreich at the Fashion Fantasy Show in New York in 1975.
2 & 3 Pop star G-Dragon is renowned for his play with gender and fashion and presents an evocative image of ambiguous sexuality.

4 Genderless kei wear deliberately non sex-specific clothes to create an image of gender fluidity. 5 Model Genking wears a Louis Vuitton blanket coat at the A/W 2015 Kansai collection in Osaka. 6 Swedish singer and songwriter Yohio is inspired by Japanese street fashion and notes, 'A guy wearing a dress is not a sexual thing, it's just a stage show.'

A recent manifestation of visual kei in Osaka and Tokyo is genderless kei, an expression of modern gender fluidity, a notion that has been preoccupying fashion designers in the 2010s. When Hedi Slimane took over the reins at YSL menswear in 2012, he used model Saskia de Brauw as his muse. The press dubbed the trend 'New Androgyny', reading it as a disruption of sartorial codes and a precursor of cultural change, although Slimane was also looking at 'le smoking', YSL's iconic tuxedo design for women in the 1970s.

Japanese model Genking and model and idol star Yohdi Kondo are the popular faces of the contemporary genderless kei street fashion, which gained media attention after Genking and other genderless models appeared on the catwalk for the Tokyo Girls Collection autumn/winter 2015 show. The rule is to look androgynous, neither male nor female but elements of both, so genderless kei boys wear make-up and nail varnish with non sex-specific clothes. Genderless kei frees up the traditional assumptions of dress as a marker of gay or straight identity. Toman of XOX (Kiss Hug Kiss) explains, 'What we genderless boys have in common is flamboyant hair, coloured contacts, wearing ladies' clothes and platform shoes. There's also our sophisticated aesthetics and the fact that we wear make-up.'

TAQWACORE

LAHORE
COUNTRY Pakistan
DECADE OF ORIGIN 2000s

'A lot of Muslim kids are tired of being told what to do, how to think, what to believe in, and how to act, by their parents.' — Sabina England

Punk (see page 360) remains an important conduit for rebellion in the world's most oppressive and reactionary regimes. As writers Stephen Duncombe and Maxwell Tremblay explain in *White Riot: Punk Rock and the Politics of Race* (2011), 'There is something in punk – how it operates and what it does – that provides effective tools for social organization and the negotiation of racial identities.' The Muslim punk music scene, or Taqwacore (Taqwa, or 'Allah-consciousness', plus hardcore), drew its inspiration from Michael Muhammad Knight's novel *The Taqwacores* (2003). Knight, who converted to Islam from Christianity as a teenager, detailed the exploits of a group of punks in a shared house in Buffalo, New York, who rejected any form of authority – whether parental, political or religious – and included

Rabeya, a feminist Riot Grrrl who played guitar on stage wearing a burqa. Knight's work of fiction gave birth to reality when Kourosh Poursalehi, a Sufi Muslim in San Antonio, Texas – believing the fictional scene to be fully functioning – set Knight's poem 'Muhammad was a Punk Rocker' to music. He sent the track to Knight, who then played it to two Pakistani Muslims based in Boston: Basim Usmani and Shahjehan Khan. Inspired, they decided to form their own Muslim punk band, the Kominas ('bastards' in Urdu). The scene slowly grew with like-minded Muslim musicians, including the first all-female band Secret Trial Five. In 2007 a tour was organized in which the bands and Knight travelled through the United States and Pakistan, mobilizing musicians in cities such as Lahore. Writers, bloggers and fans from the diaspora met online, drawn by the number of relatively uncensored spaces in which to interact. As explained by academic Dhiraj Murthy in his essay 'Muslim Punks

1	2
	3

1 The animated film *Persepolis* (2007), based on Marjane Satrapi's graphic novel of the same name, depicts a young girl against the backdrop of the Iranian Revolution where punk, as in many geographies, has become a locus of dissent.   2 Michael Muhammad Knight, author of *The Taqwacores* (2003), a novel that created a subculture.   3 Basim Usmani from Muslim punk band the Kominas performs at La Casa Maladita, Chicago.

4 The moral outrage that it inspires ironically makes the burqa the most 'punk' item of clothing one can wear today, seen here with a niqab at Graduate Fashion Week, 2014.   5 A hijab worn with G-Star jeans, an Alexander McQueen belt and a BCBG Max Azria jacket during New York Fashion Week 2016.   6 A model in a niqab walks the runway at the Cavalera show at São Paulo Fashion Week A/W 2014.

Online' (2010), 'Muslim youths...feel unable to be fully expressive in both mainstream public culture (due to Islamophobia), as well as within dominant Muslim communities (especially orthodox Muslim communities who would consider the scene to be blasphemous).'

Today, Muslim punks are still fighting back against Islamaphobia, but the scene has all but disappeared in the United States. Conversely, it has strengthened in Lahore after Usmani moved to the city from Boston and started Pakistan's first punk band, Noble Drew. The burqa, worn throughout Knight's novel by Rabeya, has become a site of contestation and in some countries causes more outrage than a dyed mohican haircut. The moral outrage it inspires ironically makes the burqa one of the most 'punk' items of clothing worn today.

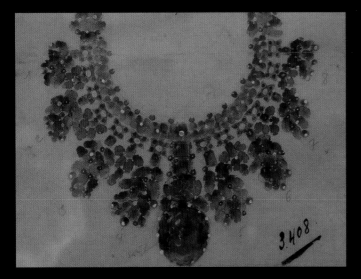

1 Cartier's design for Daisy Fellowes's Hindu necklace, 1936.
2 Jawaharlal Nehru with President John F Kennedy at the White House in 1961.   3 The Beatles in India in 1968.   4 Designer Gaurang Shah shows at Bangalore Fashion Week 2015.

BANGALORE

'Our parents' generation was completely subdued to authority and respect for the British Empire. But India has opened up, things are changing.' — Manou Singh

Bangalore, capital of the Karnataka state, became one of India's centres of trade after the city's founder, Kempe Gowda I, took control in 1537. As there was no river or coast nearby, he created a series of lakes by damming three natural valley systems: the Koramangala-Challaghatta, Hebbal and Vrishabhavathi. The city changed hands several times, including being captured by the Moguls, until it came under British colonial rule from 1806 and was made the administrative centre for the region until independence in 1947.

Influences from the traditional dress and jewellery of India began to filter into Europe. In 1911, for example, Jacques Cartier visited the country and was inspired by the Mogul aesthetic of carving brightly coloured precious gems into fruit and flowers. He began to collect the stones and created the 'tutti frutti' style of jewellery much beloved by Hollywood stars and socialites in the 1930s. In 1936 Daisy Fellowes commissioned from the firm a huge flexible collar of emeralds, diamonds and rubies, dubbed the Hindu necklace (see image 1).

The post-colonial city of Bangalore was absent of youth subculture; partition had disrupted the economy, illiteracy was high and basic amenities, including food, were scarce throughout India. As the country emerged into democracy after World War II detached from the Cold War superpowers, the first independent prime minister, Jawaharlal Nehru, took to the world's stage wearing a front-buttoned knee-length tunic with a stand-up collar (kurta) over a vest (bundi).

Nehru visited the United States several times (see image 2), and after China attacked India's border in 1962 he sought allies to halt the rise of communism. Jackie Kennedy, the decade's style icon and wife of the US president, visited Nehru the same year. The world's lens was focused on her fashion but Nehru's jacket also drew attention, especially after a version was designed by Pierre Cardin in 1964 and worn by the Beatles. The Beatles' love affair with Indian fashion did not stop there. After a visit to Rishikesh in northern India in 1968 to study transcendental meditation at the ashram of Maharishi Mahesh Yogi (see image 3), they wore kaftans, paisley shirts, beads and Kolhapuri sandals, clothes that became the mainstay of the hippy movement.

Traditional forms of dress such as the sari – a draped strip of cloth up to 9 m (30 ft) in length and worn to expose the belly button, a zone of the body considered the source of life and creativity – remained dominant in India's cities, including Bangalore. Saris and the short-sleeved undergarment known as the choli can be minimalist or lavishly mirrored and embroidered. For example, in Bangalore the regional kasuti style of embroidery is done entirely by women using motifs of temples, lotus flowers and peacocks. Traditional weaves and dyes are also incorporated into the work of fashion designers such as Deepika Govind, Neelima Lal Hembram who works under the label Aakarr) and Gaurang Shah (see image 4).

In the 1980s Bangalore emerged as a global city as a result of its high-tech software industry; from 1985 to 1996 multinational companies such as Microsoft and Hewlett-Packard invested in Bangalore followed by the establishment of Indian-owned software companies. With IT came young entrepreneurs and college graduates who emigrated from all over the country to the city known as the Silicon Valley of India. Bangalore was redrawn as youthful, with inhabitants whose musical tastes – hip hop (see page 46) and heavy metal (see page 352), for example – began to shape its nightlife. Venues opened up catering to each fan base, but many club and bar owners found the city's restrictions on drinking and late night licensing difficult to negotiate. In 2016 the hours of clubs and bars were extended and Bangalore was able to revel in its reputation as the 'pub city' and rock capital of India.

Bangalore was once known as the Garden City because of its many parks and green spaces. Today, globalization and rapid growth has caused air pollution, congested roads and the disappearance of many lakes and jacaranda trees after building encroached on the lakebeds. There is a vast difference between rich and poor, from those who spend lavishly on wedding garments to the shalwar kameez and saris worn on the streets. The moneyed middle class has made the city a destination for luxury brands, but the tailors (darzi) still survive, happy to copy the clothes worn by the stars of the Kannada film industry based in Bangalore since 1934. In *The Powder Room: The Untold Story of Indian Fashion* (2012), Shefalee Vasudev writes of shops booking advance tickets for the opening of a big Bollywood movie and sending a tailor army to take extensive notes on the outfits so exact copies could be made. It is also common practice for clients to commission so-called darzi couture or replicas of designer garments

DESI RAP

'Desi' originally derives from the Hindi 'from the country' or countryman. By the 1980s it was being used to describe South Asians living outside of the Indian subcontinent. In the 1980s, after the popularity of bhangramuffin star Apache Indian, the term Desi boy was used to describe a young Indian-American or Anglo-Indian as an equivalent of 'homeboy' and became a means of self-identification. Desi boys had double identities; they lived within traditional homes and communities but embraced hip hop, rap and graffiti culture. The gangsta Desi boy was described in the novel *Londonstani* (2006) by Gautam Malkani and by the academic Sunaina Maira whose *Desis in the House* (2002) documented Indian-American youth in New York City and the rise of Desi parties where bhangra (a musical genre traditionally sung at harvest festivals that dates back to 14th-century Punjab) and Hindi film soundtracks were mixed with hip hop. Labels catered to this subcultural fusion, including Desiwear whose designs mixed urban street fashion with South Asian colours and print. There was even Desi Bling, not surprising as India has such a culture of status jewellery dating back to the Mogul Empire. By the 2000s Desi boy street fashion had moved back to the homelands and an important Desi hip hop culture emerged in Delhi, where bhasha rappers followed the blueprint of US ghetto fabulous style by rapping about girls, guns and bling in their vernacular language. Baba Sehgal was the first to rap in Hindi; Bohemia was the first Punjabi rapper and rap was incorporated into Bollywood films through commercial stars Hard Kaur and Yo Yo Honey Singh.

1

2

3

1 Taru Dalmia, Indian hip hop artist and performance poet.   2 Punjabi rap artist Sukhbir Singh, in 2000.   3 A breakdancer from the SlumGods crew.

4 Badshah is a well-known Desi rap artist who performs in Hindi, Haryanvi and Punjabi. 5 Mir Gazanfar, a Kashmiri rapper, performs on stage in 2012.

In Mumbai, conscious rap emerged; Abhishek Dhusia, aka ACE, was a founding member of the city's first rap crew – Mumbai's Finest and Divine – and Naved Shaikh, aka Naezy, provided the breakthrough track, 'Mere Gully Mein' (2015). The duo rapped about the banality of 'thug life' in comparison to living in the chawl, one of the infamous dilapidated tenement blocks in Mumbai where each floor is divided into small kholis that house up to 15 family members. Chawls have become havens for drugs, prostitution and organized crime, the equivalent of Rio's favelas and the ghettos of Compton. This was the authentic voice of India and paved the way for the urban Desi genre that includes the SlumGods of Dharavi and Swadeshi, a collective

named after the Swadeshi movement for independence in the early 20th century. Lyrics are combative, rapped in regional languages and concerned with drawing attention to political corruption and gender inequality rather than the sex, money and status of US rap. Indian rap fashion is not local; street fashion choices are about maintaining a global hip hop solidarity that makes links with black identity in a post-colonial world rather than referencing indigenous clothing. Bangalore has seen important developments in Indian rap, including the first rap-cypher led by Sumukh Mysore, aka Smokey, and Vighnesh Shivanand, aka Brodha V. Urban Lads are exponents of a subgenre, Kannada rap, which uses Kannada, the classical language of India.

METALHEAD

BANGALORE
COUNTRY India
DECADE OF ORIGIN 1970s

'He could be a geek with short hair, an old school leather wearing guy, a teenager in a black T-shirt with explicit graphics or a scary man with a long gruff beard. The Indian metal head is likely to have an identity as diverse as the country.' — The Hindu, 2013

India has a long tradition of classical music that stretches back three thousand years. Most Indian classical music combines rag (melodic form), tal (rhythmic form) and drone (sustained note). The other dominant cultural production is Bollywood, whose movies and saccharine soundtracks are a romantic escape from the teeming streets of the country's cities and the harsh reality of the rural poor. These two aesthetics dominate the country, leaving little room for young people to create their own forms of personal expression. Rebellion is difficult to maintain within the confines of huge parental expectations regarding education and career and the dictats of religion. Nevertheless, a large metalhead movement has grown

1 Metalheads in the 1970s wear double denim and bullet belts and play air guitar. 2 The classic metalhead long-haired look, as worn by Alvina Gonson of White Fire, a rock band from Imphal, the capital of Manipur, India.

3 Accessories include the typical skull motif worn by bands such as Black Sabbath and Iron Maiden.   4 Bangalore fans described by Venkatram as 'geeky-looking yuppies'.   5 Music director and heavy metal fan Jianngam Kamei.

within the city of Bangalore, inspiring devotion in its followers who wear the standard uniform in the main – black T-shirts, jeans and leather jackets. Vibhas Venkatram of Eccentric Pendulum says there are two types of fans, those 'who believe metalheads are supposed to be [a certain] way. Even if they're working in a software company or a bank they have long hair...and head bang. But there are these other guys who are short-haired, with glasses, completely geeky-looking yuppies.'

Bangalore provided the right cultural context for a series of serendipitous reasons. In the 1990s the city became a haven for IT start-ups and international companies, providing employment opportunities for graduates fresh out of college who brought their rock fandom with them. The city's pubs and clubs provided the venues for bands such as Millennium, India's first home-grown rock band who, after forming in 1986, gigged around Bangalore playing metal standards before composing their own tracks. This was the cradle of India metal, and the spark that lit the flame was Iron Maiden's show in March 2007 in the Palace Grounds. It is estimated that forty thousand fans turned up, some ticket holders, others content to stand outside the fences just to be in the vicinity of such rock gods. This was the first time an international metal band had toured India, and Iron Maiden had little inkling there was such a huge fan base. Home-grown bands began to rise, showcased at the so-called 'Woodstock of India', the Independence Rock festival held each year since 1986 at Chitrakoot Grounds in Mumbai, including Parikrama, Pentagram, Them Clones and Brahma. As Nitin Malik, lead vocalist of Parikrama puts it, 'Heavy rock in India has been the preserve of the young intelligentsia until now. It's filtering down to the blue-collar workers, becoming the music of a new generation in a new kind of country.'

SKINHEAD

Skinheads are a tribe who developed out of 'hard mods', an offshoot of the early 1960s mod movement (see page 112) and members of street gangs who fiercely patrolled their territories against incursions from rival 'firms'. Hard mods wore the rolled-up jeans and pork pie hats of West Indian rude boys (see page 130), plus the Fred Perry polo shirt of the mod. Skinheads ditched the hat but kept the rest and added a touch of Jamaican ska. They also wore the Dr Marten, a stout eight-laced working boot with distinctive yellow stitches and heel loop that went on to be worn by labourers.

Skinheads had a working-class credential that seemed fresh after the foppish peacock fashions and laid-back hippy vibe of the late 1960s. Fashionable masculinity was in flux, toughening up as recession began to bite. As the peace and love optimism of psychedelic counter-culture started to fade, skinheads gained a reputation as aggressive, confrontational and violent, especially after right-wing groups began to infiltrate the movement as the 1970s wore on. Hair was buzzed off and braces were worn with bleached jeans, rolled up to showcase the Dr Marten or 'bovver' (bother) boot, so named because the wearers were out to create trouble by beating up other gangs, gay men and ethnic minorities. Skinheads also transported street fighting to the terraces of England's football grounds, where the implicit link between fighting factions, allegiance to a team, masculine fashion and intimidating violence was made. The skinhead look became more visible on the streets of the United Kingdom and caught the attention of film director Stanley Kubrick, who provided a futuristic version for his charismatic delinquent protagonist, Alex DeLarge, in *A Clockwork Orange* (1971).

4 Skinhead girl wearing Fred Perry polo shirt in London in 1980. Her feathered fringe is the female version of the cropped haircut. 5 A skinhead gathering in Kuala Lumpur in 2015. 6 Malcolm McDowell as Alex in *A Clockwork Orange* (1971), wearing futuristic skinhead gear.

In the late 1970s, the rise of Oi! music in the United Kingdom, a punk-derived genre in which white right-wing sentiments were expressed throughout the lyrics of bands such as Skrewdriver, led to a skinhead revival that infiltrated other parts of the world, including Malaysia. In Kuala Lumpur, skinheads reverted to the original Jamaican-influenced style, with the distinctive combination of shaven heads, Lonsdale jackets and Dr Marten boots. However, they vociferously rejected the racist overtones of the Oi! revival. Rozaimin Elias, a member of the Kuala Lumpur-based band Street Boundaries, explains, 'Being a skinhead in Malaysia means embracing positive, anti-racist ideas of sociopolitical change to challenge our racist government', and his progressive Muslim followers make up the Malaysian chapter of SHARP (Skinheads Against Racial Prejudice), an international group founded in the United States in 1987. Like the Jakarta punks (see page 360), Kuala Lumpur's skinheads use gigs and lyrics as a way of voicing their dissent and promoting social change.

1 Punk style is a form of visual dissent against regimes all over the world. Here, Burmese punks drink beer during the 2013 Myanmar New Year Water Festival in Rangoon. 2 Marjinal punk band singer MIKE celebrates Indonesian Mother's Day in Jakarta in 2011. 3 Punks protest in Jakarta in 2011 after the arrest of 65 punk rock fans in Aceh province. They were forced into 'rehabilitation' by the police, including having their hair cut, bathing in a lake, and changing their clothes.

JAKARTA
COUNTRY Indonesia
DECADE OF ORIGIN 1970s

PUNK

The youth of Indonesia have been active for many decades in the political struggle against authoritarian regimes, whether in the 1940s at the front line of the independence movement or in the 1990s when engaged in widespread protest in Bali, Bandung and Jakarta against the oppression wrought by President Suharto. Punk concerts became covert locations for the underground network of protesters and a way of publicly voicing protest from the stage.

The belligerence of Western punk has its roots in the anti-art exploits of early 20th-century Dada, the agit-prop montages of John Heartfield who influenced the punk graphics of Jamie Reid, designer of the Sex Pistols' artwork, and the Situationist rioters of May 1968 in Paris. In 1976 punk developed a visible set of sartorial symbols that soon appeared on the streets of major cities. Vivienne Westwood was a fashion designer of uncompromising confrontation who, with Malcolm McLaren, displayed her creations in her subversive shop at 430 King's Road, London. She used restrictive straps, metal buckles and exposed zips, black studded leather and trashy leopard print to create outfits that shocked Middle England. The image of the dominatrix led to the use of rubber and leather, fishnet stockings and killer heels, and Westwood's Bondage Collection of 1976 made the relationship with punk and fetish-wear clear. Stateside, 'Blank Generation' (1977) by US punk innovator Richard Hell was the song that launched a generation of nihilists, but his influence did not stop there. When Hell's girlfriend left him, cutting up his clothes in angry protest at his junkie habits, he held the tatters together with safety pins. McLaren happened to be in the same club and the rest is history.

4 Death punk in Camden, London, in 2016.   5 From Vivienne Westwood's A/W 2015 at London Fashion Week.   6 A punk in Jakarta tends to his friend's spiked mohican.   7 Three punks in Jakarta with bleached mohicans. Punks help raise money to assist the homeless street kids of the city.

The 1980s are marked by punk's second wave: the mohican hairstyle morphed into its most extreme form, the kingfisher, and UK bands such as Discharge from Stoke-on-Trent and Derby's Anti-Pasti began to penetrate the Iron Curtain and beyond. Punk's angry stance and politics of protest made sense in Eastern Europe where the music was used to condemn injustice. In Indonesia, where Suharto's New Order regime cracked down on the country's youth to prevent the uprisings for which they were traditionally known, punk became the voice of activism. In Jakarta, Movement Records was the meeting point of the city's punk rock scene where bootleg tapes and fanzines such as *Submissive Riot* were exchanged and new bands formed. Protest songs were recorded by Superman is Dead and Puppen to help mobilize fans against Suharto, thereby making punk an important factor in toppling the regime. One of the most significant bands is Marjinal, whose work with street kids was publicized in the documentary *Jakarta Punk: The Marjinal Story* (2012). In 2011 protests were held in Jakarta after 65 punks in the Muslim province of Aceh were arrested and forced to have their hair cut and change their clothes after the authorities dubbed punk 'a disease of the moral'.

SCOOTERIST

BANDUNG
COUNTRY Indonesia
DECADE OF ORIGIN 1950s

The first motor scooters were manufactured after World War I and they were targeted at women as a more feminine equivalent of the 'masculine' motorbike. Scooters had a flat platform at the front on which to rest the feet and an enclosed engine fixed over the rear wheel. They were designed to cover short distances at a moderate speed, with no need for protective clothing. The image of the scooter underwent considerable change in the 1950s after the launch of the Vespa or Wasp (1946) and the Lambretta (1947). The contemporary styling and thus modern image of the Italian scooter made it a huge success among young people and it became an object of desire in many subcultures, including the mods (see page 112), paninaro (see page 240) and scooterists of Bandung.

Mods fetishized Italian design and the image of *la dolce vita* that was spread by movies from the mid-1950s onwards. A rich fantasy of Continental life was sold to a global audience through films such as *Roman Holiday* (1953) and *Three Coins in the Fountain* (1954) and a

1   An extreme Vespa modification.   2   A scooter enthusiasts' meet-up in Pangandaran.   3   A scooter festival in 2013 in Cibeureum.   4   A female member of the Scooter Brotherhood of Indonesia.

popular visual culture was born, encapsulated as design consultant Stephen Bayley describes in 'evocative symbols [such] as the Vespa, the sharply tailored mohair suit and the hissing Gaggia coffee machines'. By the mid-1950s, scooter clubs such as the Epping Forest Rakes had been set up where like-minded enthusiasts could meet and go to rallies en masse. Mods adopted the scooter by the end of the decade and gave it a new branding through customization, including extra mirrors, aerials, modern upholstery and the ubiquitous foxtail.

In Indonesia, the scooter is one of the main modes of transport and the Vespa has been produced under licence there since 1967. The island has an extensive network of scooter clubs that hold regular rallies. Customization includes the use of indigenous wax resist-dyed batik cloth, but the most extreme customization is done by the anti-establishment scooterists of Java, who take elements of Jakarta punk (see page 360) and mix it with a post-apocalyptic aesthetic akin to the *Mad Max* franchise and the New Age traveller style (see page 206). Parts are sourced from scrap dealers, motor shops and dumps, and refashioned into drag racers and multi-seated vehicles that are almost unrecognizable as original Vespas. The aesthetic continues in the heavily embroidered and appliquéd denim vests as well as jackets with patches on the back displaying the name of the owner's club. Denim is popular in Bandung; it is cheap, readily available and more suited to the climate than the usual biker leather. Home-grown denim brands in the city include Wingman, Pot Meets Pop, and Lea.

AUSTRALIA AND NEW ZEALAND

TENTERFIELD SYDNEY
HAWKES BAY OAMURU NAPIER

FERAL SURFER SHARPIE MONGREL MOB STEAMPUNK VINTAGE

In Australia and New Zealand, tribal groups lived along the rivers and foreshores of the land, fishing and hunting, and conducting their own rituals in which dress and body adornment played an intrinsic part. Clothing was deeply rooted in the landscape; in Western Australia belts were fashioned from pearl shells and suspended from the waist. The Maori made all types of clothing and adornment from local plants, bird plumage and animal skin. Status was confirmed through the fineness of the material or the abundance of feathers woven into a cloak. Skin was intricately decorated in body paint or tattoos.

The arrival of Captain James Cook in Australia and New Zealand in the 1770s and the subsequent colonizations led to the decimation of indigenous Aboriginal and Maori culture. As land was dispossessed and many were forced to live on government reserves, European notions of modesty and dress meant the original inhabitants of the so-called 'New World' were coerced into acculturation. In Tasmania, for example, Aborigines were persuaded to wear a 'peasant' costume that included checked gowns and tam-o'-shanters in order to assimilate them into white culture and designate them a lowly status.

Colonial suits and gowns were either imported from Europe or made by the local tailor and dressmaker. By the end of the 19th century, made-to-measure clothes were available in department stores such as David Jones and the work of Paris couturiers remained a dominant influence on women's fashion into the 20th century. As Margaret Maynard writes in *Out of Line: Australian Women and Style* (2008), 'The modernism that arrived in the guise of luscious designer clothing, geometric shapes, bold French fabrics and colourful cosmetics was soon absorbed into the wider marketplace.'

Colonial dress also developed in response to the climate and geography of the city and its surrounds. The bushmen, a collective name given to stockmen, shearers and rural workers, were seen as a mateship of 'blokes' who could survive harsh conditions. Hard-wearing bush clothing included cotton drill or moleskin trousers, worsted wool vests, oilskin coats, Akubra hats in rabbit-fur felt and elastic-sided boots. These last were originally invented in 1837 by J. Sparkes-Hall of London, and a heavier version evolved in Australia known as the 'blunnie' or Blundstone boot. Beach culture and the surfing community (see page 374) were responsible for the popularity of Hawaiian shirts, board shorts and rubber flip-flops, manufactured by John Cowie in Hong Kong and imported in New Zealand by Morris Yock under the name 'jandals' or Japanese sandals. Manufactured in the bright bubble-gum palette of the post-war years, flip-flops perfectly encapsulated the New World lifestyle of outdoor living,

barbecues and beach culture. Champion swimmer Annette Kellerman wore the first one-piece swimsuit without a modesty skirt in 1903. (Four years later, she wore the same outfit in Boston and was arrested for indecent exposure.) The swimwear company Speedo was founded in Sydney in 1928, when the concept of beachwear was beginning to be fully integrated into fashion. Aboriginal and Polynesian motifs became popular for use in informal forms of beach attire.

The mateship of the original bushmen underpinned the gangs of rebellious larrikin (derived in 1868 from 'larking about'), who evolved out of the urbanization of Australia. Larrikins were fly-by-night figures who, according to historian Manning Clark, were known for 'bending rules and sailing close to the wind, avoiding rather than evading responsibility'. Larrikins had an in-built distaste of colonialism, dating back to the years of transportation, which morphed into rebellion against authority, traceable through the street fashion of the street gangs, or push, of the 19th century to the bodgies of the 1950s and beyond. The bodgie and his female counterpart, the widgie, took inspiration from African-American GIs stationed in Australia and New Zealand during the Pacific War of World War II. Surry Hill teenagers, who felt rejected by their parents' generation and impelled to rebel, admired the GIs' zoot suits, key chains and duck-tailed pompadours. Garments were sourced directly from GIs at Sydney's Woolloomooloo docks or made by local tailors.

The post-war landscape of New Zealand was particularly oppressive; the islands lived in fear of the spread of communism and juvenile unrest. Hanging was reintroduced and young men were conscripted to fight with the United States in Korea in an attempt to rein in crime, prevent rebellion and prepare a youthful army for what seemed an inevitable nuclear war. By the 1950s, clothing was influenced by an array of street styles from the United States, including James Dean's threads from *Rebel Without a Cause* (1955). The star's jeans, white T-shirt, red windbreaker jacket and messy pompadour were copied by bodgies, whereas the widgies were influenced by Natalie Wood's circle skirts, neckerchief and ballet pumps, as well as by the bobbysoxer's ponytail and the Beat's duffle coat and capri pants. The bodgie became a figure of moral outrage, his skirmishes, petty crime and promiscuity detailed in the New Zealand press. In 1958 psychologist A E Manning published his analysis of the phenomenon, *The Bodgie: A Study in Abnormal Psychology*, concluding that the bodgie was indeed a problem. However, it has been shown by modern historians that these particular teenagers were, in fact, more moderately behaved than the generations before the war.

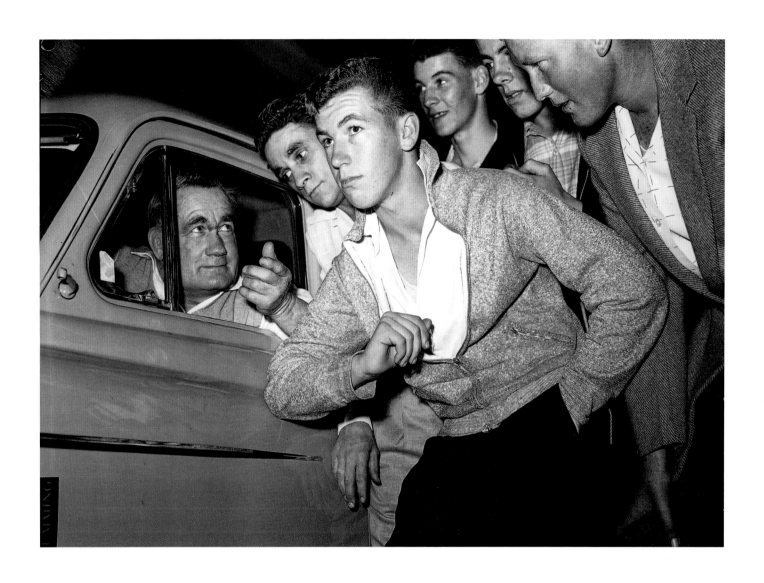

New Zealand has become a haven of steampunk (previous page), with its own festival held every year at Oamuru. The rebellious bodgies (above), here seen in 1958, copied the look and demeanour of stars such as James Dean and Elvis Presley.

FERAL

TENTERFIELD
COUNTRY Australia
DECADE OF ORIGIN 1980s

The Australian hippy movement was firmly established in the Northern Rivers area of north-east New South Wales, also known as the Rainbow Region, and by the 1990s the original members had opened New Age businesses and created comfortable communities at Margaret River and Byron Bay akin to Glastonbury in the UK. In 1973 hippy activists settled in the town of Nimbin after the Aquarius Festival, also known as Australia's Woodstock, was staged by the Australian Union of Students. The hippies had a legacy of activism dating from the 1970s. This included the anti-logging campaign mounted by Nimbin residents in protection of the rainforest at Terania Creek in 1979 and the blockade of Errinundra forest in 1984. ConFest, the long-running 'spontaneous' music, dance and clothes-optional festival, was established in 1976.

The environmental activism stimulated by disasters such as Bhopal in 1984 and Chernobyl in 1986 that led to the emergence

1 Nudity is seen as the ultimate in 'authenticity' and closeness to one's natural state.   2 Accessories sourced from thrift stores and festivals.   3 A dreadlocked resident of Nimbin in 1995.

of the New Age travellers in the UK (see page 206) had the same effects in Australia. As the urban squatters, also known as crusties, left the UK's cities to travel to festivals and demonstrations, so did the Australian ferals. Their name was allegedly bestowed on them by the media after a group of twenty-somethings with piercings and dreadlocks were forbidden to board an aeroplane in Queensland because of their appearance. The first feral community was Om Shalom, established near the town of Tenterfield, New South Wales, and the first feral camp of young protesters, also known as 'forest punks', was set up in the Chaelundi Forest in 1991. Feral style was a wild pick and mix of hippy, punk (see page 360), Rastafarianism and

paganism, described by Kevin Hetherington in 'Identity Formation, Space and Social Centrality' (1996) as 'recycled garb, dreadlocked, adorned with multiple piercings and folk jewellery: feathers, birds feet, skulls and umbilical-cord necklaces (feralia)...fabrics fade and hair tangles in unkempt locks. The feral rig is an ensemble of materials discovered dada-esque in garage sales, op' shops, or fashioned from the hide of road-kill or dead animals found in the bush. Outfits range from the sartorial splendour of brightly imbued and offbeat garments, to dirty green and brown-hued favourites. Army great coats with personalized patches sewn on the rear are not uncommon, nor are silken night dresses and fairy wings.'

SYDNEY

The city of Sydney was named after the British Secretary of State Thomas Townshend, Lord Sydney (1733–1800, see image 1), who had gained his honorary title in recognition of his work negotiating the peace treaty with America after the War of Independence. He advocated a policy of transporting convicts to British colonies as an alternative to hanging; it was cheaper than having to pay for criminals to languish for years in overcrowded, privately run gaols or in prison hulks, the huge rotting man o' war ships beached along the Medway Estuary where prisoners were chained to their beds at night. Transportation meant that nefarious criminals were no longer on British soil, and new colonies needed a workforce. After the Declaration of Independence in 1777, convicts could no longer be transported to America, so the first penal colonies were established in Australia under the governorship of Arthur Phillip, a British admiral. The initial fleet of convict ships landed first at Botany Bay (see image 2), then sailed on to Port Jackson, settling in Sydney Cove because,

as Phillip described, 'It has the best spring of water. And ships can anchor so close to the shore that, at a very small expense, quays may be made at which the largest ships may unload.' The cargo comprised prisoners, guards, livestock and enough food supplies to last two years. From 1788 to 1868, it is estimated that 160,000 men, women and children were sent to Australia in this fashion, and they settled in wooden huts working as servants or on chain gangs under the threat of the lash. After sentence was served, the free men and women received a 'ticket of leave', which allowed them to seek paid work in the colony and to apply for their families to be sent out.

The colonists began to systematically dispossess the indigenous people of their land, and a smallpox epidemic in 1789 killed many Wangal, a clan who lived and fished along the Parramatta River, and the Wallumedegal, or snapper clan, from its north shore. One Wangal, Woollarawarre Bennelong, was abducted by Phillips from a gathering on a beach and forced into the role of interpreter and mediator for all

| 3 | 4 |
| 1 | 2 |

1 Thomas Townshend, Lord Sydney.   2 The arrival of the first prisoners at Botany Bay in 1788.   3 Richard Neville, editor of *Oz* magazine with his girlfriend Louise Ferrier, 1966.   4 Launched in 1969, Rip Curl is now a global brand.

the coastal clans or Eora people. Bennelong became a figure of curiosity and was dressed in European fashion, including a ruffled shirt, frock coat and breeches, and paraded in London. The iconic Sydney Opera House (1973) designed by Danish architect Jørn Utzon sits on Bennelong Point.

In the 19th century, the city of Sydney saw a period of rapid growth, under the governorship and civic planning of Lachlan Macquarie alongside architect Francis Greenway. Roads were paved and public buildings lit by gaslight from 1841. Like every city, Sydney had its slums. These included Surry Hills, which was vividly depicted by author Ruth Park in her first novel, *The Harp in the South* (1948). Surry Hills was the centre of the rag trade, where local dressmakers did piecework for small-scale manufacturers. The department store David Jones opened 'large and commodious premises' on the junction of George Street and Barrack Street. David Jones sold silks, cotton, gingham and buckskin to its customers from the city and the bush. The majority of clothing was homemade or stitched by the local dressmaker and tailor, dependent on patterns and fabrics that were imported from the UK. In 1887 the premises were transformed into a department store with a hydraulic lift based on the European model, and in 1890 the first mail-order catalogue was printed and goods were sent to customers all over Australia. In the early 20th

century, David Jones set up a factory on Marlborough Street to manufacture 'a huge variety of goods from clothing to cabin trunks'.

The Rocks, one of the city's earliest settlements, was a notorious area of Sydney, the place for sailors to seek out prostitutes and gambling. In the 1870s, it was run by a street gang – the Rocks Push – described by Andrew Barton 'Banjo' Paterson in *An Outback Marriage* (1906) as wearing 'black bell-bottomed pants, no waistcoat, very short black paget coat, white shirt with no collar, and a gaudy neckerchief round the bare throat. Their boots were marvels, very high in the heel and picked out with all sorts of colours down the sides.' They also adopted the cabbage palm hat, a distinctively Australian style woven from the leaves of the Australian cabbage tree and often worn in the bush. The Rocks Push were the instigators of the first of many indigenous street fashions in Sydney, the appearance of which was determined by geography. For example, an urban bohemian style was embraced by the Sydney Push in the 1960s, whose members included Richard Neville (see image 3)– founder of *Oz* magazine – and Germaine Greer, whereas the Sydney Rockers followed the classic Brando mode, prompting the name 'sandkickers' from their enemies the surfies (see page 374). All have spawned a variety of labels that have influenced global fashion, including Blundstone boots, Rip Curl board shorts (see image 4) and the humble flip-flop, or jandal.

SURFER

The original Hawaiian surfboard was made of hardwood and its length reflected status, with the island's chiefs cresting unbroken waves on olo: heavy wood boards that were 0.6 m (2 ft) wide and 6 m (20 ft) long. The thinner alaia was for riding the curl and was the genesis of the modern surfboard. After colonization, the practice of surfing declined in Hawaii until visiting US author Jack London enthusiastically described it in his article 'A Royal Sport', published in *Women's Home Companion* (1907). London described surfer George Freeth 'tearing in on the back of [a wave] standing upright with his board, carelessly poised, a young god bronzed with sunburn'.

Hawaiian swimmer and Olympic medallist Duke Paoa Kahanamoku introduced surfing to Australia after being invited by the New South Wales Swimming Association to put on a swimming exhibition. After his performance at Sydney's Domain Baths, Kahanamoku planed a board of Queensland sugar pine from a local timberyard and in February 1915 surfed the waves at Freshwater Beach, Manly, thereby inspiring new life-guarding techniques. A new age of surfing began, and the coastline around Sydney became its playground. At first, there were curfews on bathing, sexes were separated and women had to wear knee-length, skirted, woollen swimsuits for modesty. By the 1930s, elasticized bathing costumes had taken over from the uncomfortable waterlogged sag of wool, but men could not expose their upper torsos through most of the decade.

The culture of the beach developed with Sydney's inhabitants travelling to Bondi Beach and beyond every weekend. Surfing clothing evolved out of functionality; knee-length baggy shorts, or boardies, prevented abrasion when sitting astride the board, for example. However, the sense of subcultural cool emerged in the 1960s as Sydney surf culture moved from its association with the heroism

1 High fashion surfer style: stylist Kelly Saks in a wetsuit top by We Are Handsome, her own vintage Levi's cutoff shorts, Manolo Blahnik shoes and Torch Burch sunglasses. 2 Surf fashion evolved out of functionality but has become a popular street fashion. 3 The culture of the surfie developed at Sydney's Bondi Beach, earning subcultural cool from the 1960s onwards.

4   5   6

4 Board shorts allow ease of movement.   5 Print detail from DSquared2 in 2015 references the construction of the wetsuit.   6 Beach culture on the DSquared2 catwalk.

of life-saving to become a hedonist escapist activity of 'beachniks'. The soul surfers merged with hippy culture in the late 1960s, sporting long sun-bleached hair and psychedelic board designs and travelling around in Kombi vans.

In 1973 Australian Shane Stedman created a version of a traditional sheepskin drovers' boot for surfers. Worn without socks, it could be pulled on and off, and the fleece absorbed moisture from damp feet between surfing sessions. The boots gained a rebellious reputation when worn with football jerseys and ripped Levi jeans, and they were banned from Sydney's cinemas and nightspots. Girls wore

their boyfriend's boots as a mark of being one half of a cool couple. In 1978 enterprising surfer Brian Smith began importing and selling a similar sheepskin boot to Californian surf shops under the label Uggs Australia. Many key Australian surfing labels began to emerge as surfers created products of their own, including boards, board shorts and clothing for the sport's slouchy downtime. They include Quiksilver (1969), Rip Curl (1969), Hot Tuna (1969), Billabong (1973) and Mambo (1984). By the 1980s, surfing clothes had become mainstream fashion for non-participant 'city surfers' in the same way that hip hop (see page 46) transformed sportswear.

Fashionable menswear from 1973. **2 & 4** Sharpies wore tightly fitting cardigans or Connies several sizes too small. **3** Sharpie style was strongly macho, rejecting the perceived femininity of hippy street fashion.

SHARPIE

'We're in revolt against the femininity of long hair and sissy clothes.'
— Sharpie, 1966

The Sydney sharpies formed one part of a larger style movement that emerged in Melbourne in the 1960s and grew in popularity throughout the 1970s. Sharpies looked 'sharp', hence the name, and the initial look was influenced by preppy (see page 78) and mod (see page 112) styles imported into the country with the latest wave of immigration. US and home-grown brands were favoured over UK and the Sydney sharpie eschewed cotton Fred Perrys in favour of wash-and-wear Ban-lon polo shirts, a synthetic yarn popular in the 1950s. They were worn in one colour, with the buttons fastened to the neck, and tucked into tailored cuffless trousers made to measure by Zink & Sons tailors in Oxford Street. The initial look was sleek, but by the late 1960s the cut of sharpie trousers reflected fashions in menswear by being worn ultra tight and high at the top and flared below. The sharpie flags, a distinctly Australian take on Oxford bags, were minimalist in design detail save for a flapped fob pocket at the front and rear pocket flaps. The requisite flash came through the choice of bold houndstooth or Prince of Wales check and the wide two- or four- button waistbands. Flags were worn with skintight Crestknit

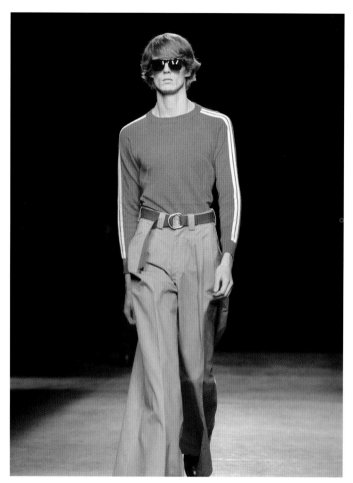

5 The subcultural silhouette, as worn by
the sharpies and exponents of Northern
Soul, is being revived by fashion brands
such as Topman Design, S/S 2016.
6 A bold check trouser and basket-weave
shoes worn with no socks reference sharpie
style for a modern audience.   7 A modern
sharpie look for 2016, featuring an overly
tight cardigan, jeans and braces.

polos or Venito knit tops in conservative maroon, mustard or bottle
green and Italian basket-weave shoes and no socks or lace-up
platforms to lengthen the leg. Sharpie girls, also known as 'brush',
wore early mod-inspired twinsets with accordion-pleated sunray
skirts and flat shoes, or flatties.

The look became progressively glam rock, influenced specifically
by the early styling of the UK group Slade. Levi, Lee and, by 1975,
high-waisted wide-legged Australian Staggers jeans were worn with
braces and custom-made cardigans in a variety of colours and stripes
from F & L Conte Knitwear, aka Connies. Sharpies were known to
wear knitwear two sizes too small to get the tightest fit. Hair was
not buzzed off in skinhead (see page 356) mode; instead, the sharpie
introduced an alternative 'tennis ball' haircut that was short on
top and long at the back, thus anticipating the mullet by many years.
The exposure of the ears drew attention to another innovation, the
male pierced ear.

MONGREL
MOB

HAWKES BAY
COUNTRY New Zealand
DECADE OF ORIGIN 1960s

'Being Maori meant nothing to us even though the majority of us were Maori; the only culture worth anything to us was Mob culture.'
— Tuhoe 'Bruno' Isaac, gang leader

In the 1950s the migration of rural white and Maori workers to Auckland caused significant housing shortages. The construction of cheap housing contained the problem in the short term, but also created ghettos in which crime flourished. US culture started to infiltrate New Zealand and the authorities were shocked by its brash vulgarity. They reacted by confiscating pulp fiction, and *The Wild One* (1953) — a touchstone for rebellion in many geographies — was banned from cinema release until 1977. Despite this, a group of bikers dubbed the 'milk-bar cowboys' regularly met up along Auckland's Queen Street. They were the start of New Zealand's biker culture and were

1   2   3

1   Black Power gang members, rivals to the Mongrel Mob.
2   A member of the Mongrel Mob in gang colours.
3   Facial tattoos refer to the status and ancestry of the wearer.

followed by gangs such as Currie's Cowboys in Auckland, the Saints in Wellington and the Coffin Cheaters in Dunedin. Auckland also had its own chapter of Hells Angels (see page 24) by 1961.

Maori biker gangs emerged around Hawkes Bay, including Napier and Hastings, on the east coast of North Island. The main industry there was horticulture and the predominantly Maori workers suffered mass layoffs every time seasonal work ended. Consequently, they found themselves living in poor conditions in the crime-ridden ghettos of a colonial city. The structure of a gang helped assuage their feelings of alienation and provided a respite from everyday racism.

The most infamous Maori gang in Hawkes Bay and beyond remains the Mongrel Mob, formed in 1962, who took their traditional culture and merged it with biker culture, thereby creating a hybrid dubbed 'Mongrelism' or 'Dog Culture'. Today, there are estimated to be at least one thousand patched members all over the islands. The Mongrel Mob present a fearsome sight dressed as neo-warriors in black leather with red bandanas and Maori ta moko (tattooing), including facial tattoos relating to the status and ancestry of the wearer. Patches feature deliberately confrontational imagery, some with references to Nazism such as swastikas.

1 Steampunk image of author G D Falksen in an arm mechanism created by Thomas Willeford. 2 Steampunk incorporates technology and clothing to create a retro-futuristic street fashion inspired by 19th-century and early 20th-century fashion and industry. 3 A steampunk shoe that uses modern materials and a retro-futuristic style to create a design that is difficult to date.

OAMURU
COUNTRY New Zealand
DECADE OF ORIGIN 1980s

STEAMPUNK

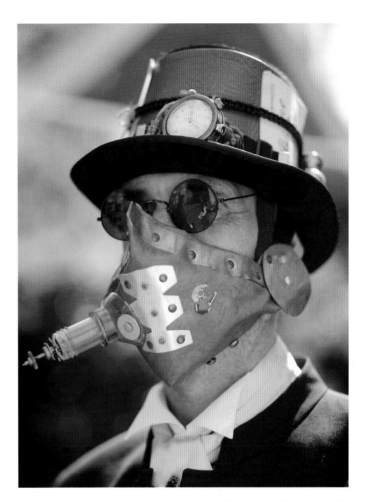

In 1987 science fiction author K W Jeter coined the term 'steampunk' in a letter to *Locus* magazine, saying, 'Personally I think Victorian fantasies are going to be the next big thing, as long as we can come up with a fitting collective term...based on the appropriate technology of that era, like "steampunks" perhaps.' Jeter was trying to differentiate his novel *Morlock Night* (1979) – together with Tim Powers's *The Anubis Gates* (1983) and *Homunculus* by James Blaylock (1986) – from the dystopian human-machine hybridization portrayed in the cyberpunk genre. Jeter and others depicted a retro future inspired by the classic science-fiction novels and Victorian and Edwardian settings of H G Wells, Jules Verne and Arthur Conan Doyle. Academic and steampunk aficionado Lisa Hager noted, 'Much like a seamstress ripping out stitches on a garment and putting it all back together again with a few key additions that entirely alter the effect of the item, steampunk takes apart the 19th century to see what makes it tick and then, turning it just so, gives us a transformed and newly unfamiliar past and present.'

Modern technology was given a whimsical historic 'retro-tech' aesthetic in the vein of the fantasy machines of Caractacus Potts, played by Dick Van Dyke in the film *Chitty Chitty Bang Bang* (1968), rather than the streamlined minimalism of industrial design. Costume designer Kit Stolen of New York, also known as Anachrønaut, is generally recognized to be one of the prime movers of steampunk fashion after posting his Victorian-inspired looks on the Internet in the late 1990s, although British designers Vivienne Westwood and John Galliano had experimented with similar references in the 1980s.

Salon Con, the first steampunk convention, was held in 2006, and steampunk street fashion began to evolve, mixing recognizably Victorian garments and accessories such as top hats, fob watches, frock coats, corsets and crinolines with imaginary Victorian technology. Goth (see page 164) influences can be traced in the look, including lace, leather, fetish and vampiric references. Outfits also reference the mechanical, using cogs, gears, wire and brass piping alongside the ubiquitous goggles that variously recall explorers when worn with pith helmets, 'mad scientists', airship pilots or early motorists. The popularity of steampunk among millennials can be read as a reaction against the overly casual nature of modern clothing in a similar stance to the chap (see page 188).

New Zealand has embraced steampunk and every year hosts a large gathering of fans at the Steampunk Festival held in Oamaru, a small coastal town on the South Island known for its Victorian architecture. In 2006 the steampunk gothic vampire film *Perfect Creature* was shot in the town and in 2010 Iain Clark (Agent Darling) staged an exhibition with the help of Weta Workshop, the special effects company that worked on the *Lord of the Rings* franchise. It drew a surprisingly large audience of local farmers, as Helen Jensen (La Falconesse) explained, 'New Zealanders are great creators and inventors, especially if they can make inventions from the junk collected in their garden sheds. I think the inventive side of steampunk is something Kiwis are particularly open to – making things from nothing makes sense to them.' In 2011 the mayor announced that 'Oamaru has become a centre of steampunk and the movement has taken on a literal "head of steam".' Today the Steampunk HQ, an exhibition centre and art gallery, is situated in the original Meeks Grain Elevator building of 1883, designed by Forrester & Lemon for the grain traders and millers J. and T. Meek.

4 A model on the runway at Prada's A/W 2012 show inspired by steampunk. 5 Chanel haute couture S/S 2013, held at the Grand Palais, Paris, shows a range of historical influences that tap into steampunk's vision of a dystopian retro-future. 6 Steampunk's visual aesthetic is eclectic. Here, a feather headdress is mixed with a gothic mask, crinoline skirt and utilitarian saddlebag, as well as the ubiquitous clock face.

NAPIER
COUNTRY New Zealand
DECADE OF ORIGIN 1960s

VINTAGE

The concept of vintage is a modern one. Formerly, second-hand clothes were worn by the poor and sourced from markets, second-hand shops and the local ragpicker. In the post-war years after austerity, clothes rationing and make-do-and-mend, the idea of wearing the clothes of the dead was highly unappealing. Consumers wanted brand-new fashion and looked to the Paris collections for inspiration. Outside of mainstream fashion, bohemian counter-culturalists began to take delight in the threads of the past and in the 1960s looked to wear antique clothing as a form of romantic rebellion. Edwardian stoles, 1930s bias-cut satin dresses and 1940s fox fur could be bought from Portobello Market in London, and labels took inspiration from the past, too – most notably Biba, for whom Barbara Hulanicki designed bias-cut liquid satin or panne velvet gowns that evoked the sirens of Hollywood's golden age. She revived other retrospective styles such as the Art Deco clutch bag and 1930s peep-toe shoe.

By the 1980s, vintage stores and markets were firmly established in cities all over the world, and well-known faces such as Madonna, Courtney Love and model Kate Moss helped make a niche activity mainstream through their habitual wearing of vintage. New Zealand also became a vintage haven, but unlike in other countries designer labels were rare and finds tended to be the products of home dressmakers and those who supplied department stores. The country has a long tradition of dressmaking dating back to the wives of 19th-century missionaries who introduced the indigenous Maoris to needlework. Rural isolation led to the practice of women making their

1 One of the many vintage outlets in Napier.   2 Barbara Hulanicki, founder of Biba.   3 Mischa Barton in an Art Deco beaded dress.   4 Kate Moss in a chiffon 1950s gown.

own clothes, and magazines such as the *New Zealand Woman's Weekly* provided a free pattern service to its subscribers during the post-war years. The country's greatest contribution to menswear is bush clothing, which includes the sought-after label Swanndri, an iconic Kiwi brand established in 1913. In recent years, the products of the Pacific Islands have become collectable, including the traditional 'tapa' textile designs.

The cities of Auckland and Dunedin have a variety of vintage boutiques, including Victorian Gilt, one of the first ports of call for fashion shoots and film costume. Napier is the most original destination for vintage street fashion, a unique and complete Art Deco town and World Heritage Site that was completely rebuilt after the devastating Hawkes Bay earthquake of February 1931, which claimed 256 victims. Rather than building the town in its original form, the decision was made to follow the progressive architectural flourishes of European Art Deco, down to its ziggurat details and Cubist motifs. Every February, for five days, Napier travels back to the 1930s, and inhabitants and forty thousand visitors dress in 1930s clothing to watch classic car parades and to attend Gatsby-themed picnics and Depression-era parties. The town even has its own 'McDeco McDonald's' in a 1931 Taradale hotel.

5 & 6 Dressing in vintage clothes was formerly a niche activity but has now become mainstream. 7 The Art Deco town of Napier in New Zealand has an annual festival that attracts more than forty thousand vintage enthusiasts.

GLOSSARY

Anime
A style of Japanese animation in which the characters have exaggerated eyes.

Beatnik
A young person in the 1950s who, inspired by philosopher Jean-Paul Sartre and writer Jack Kerouac, sought a sartorial expression that symbolized the lack of understanding they found in the adult world. The pristine grooming and bandbox neatness of 1950s fashion was avoided in favour of a casual relaxed bohemian style. The beatniks were the first teenagers to wear jeans.

Booty bass
Aka Miami bass. A subgenre of hip hop featuring the Roland TR-808 drum machine. Dating from the 1980s and 1990s, the style was notorious for its sexually explicit lyrics.

Chinos
A khaki-coloured trouser. Its name derives from the Spanish for 'Chinese', in referrence to the Chinese cotton cloth it was originally made from. Chinos first became popular in the 1890s, when they were adopted by US soldiers stationed in the Philippines.

Conk
Hair straightened with a DIY mix of lye and potatoes (aka conkolene, hence 'conk') and pressed into waves. Worn by urban black men from the 1920s to the 1960s, it created an air of rebellion when mixed with the zoot suit. Many black entertainers sported the look, including Nat King Cole and Duke Ellington.

Cumbia
From the African *cumbe*, meaning 'to dance'. A musical form combining styles from three cultures – African drum rhythms, Columbian flute and European melodies – that dates back to the slaves of the late 17th century and is accompanied by a distinctive 'shuffle-step' dance.

Crust punk
Originally a 1980s musical form that fused hardcore punk and extreme metal, which spawned its own scene and look influenced by the black paramilitary clothing of anarcho-punk. In the UK, the look was more overtly unkempt and associated with the movement for squatters rights and anti-capitalist protest in the 1990s.

Dashiki
A multi-coloured patterned tunic, with flared, elbow-length sleeves, that originated in Africa. The dashiki was adopted by militant civil rights protesters and hippies in the United States in the 1960s and stood out as a rebellious alternative to the suburban suit and tie. It became an important symbol of black affirmation and of pride in African roots.

Deathhawk
A variation on the Mohawk hairstyle recognizable by its feathery volume, rather than the usual straight spikes. It often has tufts resembling sideburns pointing down at the sides, and is commonly associated with the gothic/industrial music scene.

Deshabille
Derived from a casually wrapped look that appeared in 17th century portraiture and evolved into a self-consciously disordered and seductive form of dress worn in the 18th-century boudoir. A state between dress and undress, accessorized with the artifice of 'bedhead' hair.

Flaca
Aka scrawny. Can be used as a term of abuse or endearment in Latino culture, depending on the context and tone of voice.

Froufrou
A 19th-century term used to describe the sound of rustling petticoats, and now used to describe highly decorative clothing with the overuse of ribbons, tulle, lace and layers of net underskirts.

Manga
A generic term for Japanese comics, whose rich and complex history dates back to the 12th century *Choju-giga* picture scrolls. Demand for manga soared in Japan after World War II and one of the most popular titles was Osamu Tezuka's *Astro Boy*. The distinctive large eyes in Tezuka's work were inspired by Disney characters, and remain a key stylistic feature in present-day genres of manga.

Mary Jane
A broad, closed-toe shoe with a flat single strap that fastens across the instep with a button to the side and a low heel. Originally a child's shoe, its meanings were subverted when worn by Courtney Love in the 1990s as part of the grunge look.

Queercore
A DIY scene that arose as a rebellion against those who espoused the bourgeois gay metropolitan lifestyle and the rabid heterosexuality of hardcore punk. It was originally a literary movement, out of which emerged the homocore bands Fifth Column, Comrades In Arms, and Anti Scrunti Faction.

Roustabout
A black itinerant worker who was employed on the levees of the Mississippi and Ohio rivers in the 19th century. The black dance bands of riverboat culture had a profound effect on the development of US jazz. The term was later used to describe itinerant workers in the United States during the 1930s Depression, and those who worked on the drill pumps of the US oilfields and wore heavy workwear including black leather jackets and original Chippewa and Dayton boots.

Slacker
A 19th-century term used to describe the lazy or workshy, which was revived in the 1990s to refer to the cynical underachieving youth of Generation X.

Snapback
A baseball cap with a large flat 'bill' or brim, popular in hip hop. The name derives from the adjustable strap at the back, which is comprised of two pieces of plastic that snap together.

Soukous
A genre of Congolese dance music popularized by Congolese musicians Franco, Kanda Bongo Man and Koffi Alomide. Soukous was originally influenced by the Cuban rhumba but developed a more pop-influenced sound from the 1950s, using repeated guitar riffs with a simple chorus.

Techno
A form of fast, rhythmic electronic dance music that originated in Detroit clubs during the 1980s.

Trailer trash
A pejorative term that originated in Baltimore, Maryland in the 1820s to describe newly arrived immigrants. Today it is a term of abuse for white working-class inhabitants of mobile homes or trailers in the United States.

Ultrasuede
A synthetic textile invented by Dr Miyoshi Okamoto in 1970 and described by *Time* magazine as 'the most innovative material since the fig leaves worn by Adam and Eve'. It was used by many fashion designers during the 1970s, including Issey Miyake.

Vaporwave
A genre of sampled ambient eerie music that emerged in the 2010s, parodying the generic muzak of the corporate world. It is most commonly associated with seapunk.

Visual kei
A mode of performative dressing developed in the 1980s by Japanese bands such as X Japan and Malice Mizer, which was later copied by fans. It involves elaborate androgynous make-up, teased hair and extravagant outfits that meld elements from US rock, UK punk, goth and glam rock.

READ UP!

Brake, Michael
Comparative Youth Culture: The Sociology of Youth Cultures and Youth Subcultures in America, Britain and Canada, London, Routledge, 1985

Brewster, Bill and Broughton, Frank
Last Night a DJ Saved My Life: The History of the Disc Jockey, Croydon, Headline Books, 2006

Epstein, Jonathon S
Youth Culture: Identity in a Postmodern World, (Ed.), Oxford, Blackwell, 1998

Feldman, Christine Jacqueline
We Are the Mods: A Transnational History of a Youth Subculture, New York, Peter Lang, 2006

Gibson, William
Neuromancer, New York, Ace, 1984
Pattern Recognition, New York, G.P Putnam's Sons, 2003

Gondola, Ch. Didier
Tropical Cowboys: Westerns, Violence and Masculinity in Kinshasa, Bloomington, Indiana University Press, 2016

Hebdige, Dick
Subculture: The Meaning of Style, London, Routledge, 1979
Cut 'n' Mix: Culture, Identity and Caribbean Music, London, Routledge, 1987
Hiding in the Light: On Images and Things, London, Routledge, 1988

Hodkinson, Paul
Goth: Identity, Style and Subculture, Oxford, Berg, 2002

MacInnes, Colin
Absolute Beginners, London, MacGibbon & Kee, 1959

Moynihan, Michael and Soderlind, Didrik
Lords of Chaos: The Bloody Rise of the Satanic Metal Underground, Port Townsend, Washington, Feral House, 1998

Noble, Denise
'Ragga Music: Dis/Respecting Black Women & Dis/reputable Sexualities' in Barnor Hesse (Ed.), *Un/settled Multiculturalisms: Diasporas, Entanglements, Transruptions.* Ed. London, New York: Zed Books, 2000, pp. 148–69

Freitas, Frederico and Kuhn, Gabriel (Ed.)
Sober Living for the Revolution: Hardcore Punk, Straight Edge, and Radical Politics, Los Angeles, PM Press, 2010

McCormick, Sran
'Gothicism in Hip Hop', www.academia.edu

Nowell, David
The Story of Northern Soul, London, Portico, 1999

Packard, Vance
The Status Seekers, New York, D. McKay Co, 1959

Polsky, Ned
Hustlers, Beats and Others, London, Pelican, 1971

Riordan, Jim, Ed.
Soviet Youth Culture, London, Macmillan, 1989

Root, Regina A
Couture and Consensus: Fashion and Politics in Postcolonial Argentina (Cultural Studies of the Americas) USA, University of Minnesota Press, 2010

St John, Graham
Ferals: Terra-ism and Radical Ecologism, Australia, Journal of Australian Studues, 64, 2000

Taylor, Tadhg
Top Fellas: The Story of Melbourne's Sharpie Cult, Melbourne, Surefire Productions, 2013

Thompson, Hunter S
Hell's Angels, USA, Random House, 1966

Thornton, Phil
Casuals: Football, Fighting and Fashion, Lytham, Milo Books, 2003

Wilson, Peter J
Crab Antics: The Social Anthropology of English-Speaking Negro Societies of the Caribbean, USA, Yale University Press, 1973

Wolfe, Tom
The Electric Kool-Aid Acid Test, USA, Farrar Straus Giroux, 1968

Yska, Redmer
All Shook Up: The Flash Bodgie and the Rise of the New Zealand Teenager in the Fifties, Auckland, Penguin, 1993

ACKNOWLEDGEMENTS

To Lionel and Paul with love

Aeron Willey, Ales@dustoashes, Anna Mavridis, Amigo Skate, Astrid Kearny, Baybe Champ, Bianca Saunders, Blue@ Rivithead, Bob Masse, Bobby Raffin, Bobby Tarlton, Brando Von Badsville, Celestial Darkness, Colin Roy, Courtney@HempHugs, Chloe Kerosene, Crystal@ Cryoflesh, Dana Suchow, DJ Phroh, Doris Yeh, Elspeth Beidas, Eurobeat Kasumi, Fiona Cartledge, Florence Berrier, Gabriela Giacoman, Galina Sherri, Geena Matuson, Isabel Eeles, Isabel Tinkler, Jamie Balbuena, Jane Brown, Jesseca@Sea Dragon Studio, Jessica Knipprath, Josh Gibson, Julian Kubel, Karl Fox, Karolina Stromgrem, Lady Mella, La Goony Chonga, Lauren Spike, Lionel Marsden, Lindsey @ Cyberdog, Loli Lux, Lovina Yavari, Lua P., Luana Gabriella, Luis Amella, Luly Salle, Lupa@ thegreenwolf, Martyn Hallam, Max Reyenders, Michelle Kliem, Michelle Meijer, Mona Bitter, Neandro Ferreira, Nicole @ ku Ibiza, Nixi Killick, Northern Soul Girl Levanna, Ollie @ toohotlimited.com, Pascal Martin Saint Leon, Paul Conrad Schneider, Philip Cooper, Princess Chaos, Rafael Ambrosio, Raphaelle Leboeuf, Richard Kaby, Roland Hyams, Rose Van T., Roxie Sweetheart, Rupert Hitchcox, Ruth Patrick, Sabrina Tan, Sando Dal Bianco, Sarah Dee, Sarah@ Menagerie Workshop, Sbro Castil, Scottie D., Sheila Ableman, Shiya Wind, Sho Tatsuishi, Sofia Holmberg, Soyeon Choi, Stephen Myhill, Stuart McDowell, Susie Mutch, Thomas Keenes, Tom Ingram, Vanessa Hartley, Yinka Germaine, Zektor Zero

INDEX

PICTURE CREDITS

2 Cultura/REX/Shutterstock **6** LYNN BO BO/EPA/REX/Shutterstock **8** Junior D. Kannah/AFP/Getty Images **11** Jonas Gratzer/LightRocket via Getty Images **12** Paper Boat Creative/Getty Images **15** Hulton Archive/Getty Images **16** 1 Everett/REX/Shutterstock 2 Ebet Roberts/Redferns/Getty Images **17** Mick Hutson/Redferns **18** Luanna Perez-Garreaud/Le Happy Blog **19** 5 Kyle Ericksen/Penske Media/REX/Shutterstock 6 Kyle Ericksen/Penske Media/REX/Shutterstock **20** 1 brand: UEG Warsaw, photographer: Sandro Dal Bianco, model: MXDVS, styling: MXDVS 2 brand: UEG Warsaw, photographer: Sandro Dal Bianco, model: MXDVS **21** 3 REX/Shutterstock 4 Ray Tang/REX/Shutterstock **22** 1 Malcolm Lubliner/Michael Ochs Archives/Getty Images 2 Library of Congress, LC-DIG-ds-07750 3 Elijah Nouvelage/Getty Images **23** 4 Caroline Culler/Wikimedia Commons, CC-BY-SA-3.0 5 Rolls Press/Popperfoto/Getty Images **24** Central Press/Getty Images **25** 2 Daniel Zuchnik/Getty Images 3 Julien Boudet/BFA/REX/Shutterstock 4 Paul Conrad Schneider **26** Melodie Jeng/Getty Images **27** 6 Bettmann/Getty Images 7 Chris Jackson/Getty Images **28** Hulton Archive/Getty Images **29** 2 Dana Suchow @DotheHotpants www.DoTheHotpants.com 3 PETER BROOKER/REX/Shutterstock 4 Courtney Schindler/HempHugs **30** 1 Roger Cracknell 01/classic/Alamy Stock Photo 2 © Ted Streshinsky/CORBIS/Corbis via Getty Images **31** Adrian Sherratt/Alamy Stock Photo **32** 4 WENN Ltd/Alamy Stock Photo 5 DOMINIC FAVRE/AFP/Getty Images **33** Piedmont Boutique, Kelly Pacamarra **34** 1 Erol Birsen 2 Erol Birsen **35** © PYMCA/Photoshot **36** 1 Dino Graniello; www.dinograniello.com 2 Dino Graniello; www.dinograniello.com 3 Dino Graniello; www.dinograniello.com **37** Dino Graniello; www.dinograniello.com **38** 1 SNAP/REX/Shutterstock 2 Library of Congress, LC-DIG-highsm-24420 **39** Ann Summa/Corbis via Getty Images **40** REX/Shutterstock **41** Purestock/Alamy Stock Photo **42** Geoff Pugh/REX/Shutterstock **43** Sipa Press/REX/Shutterstock **44** evan Hurd/Alamy Stock Photo **45** 2 Michael LeSage 3 © PYMCA/Photoshot 4 PYMCA/UIG via Getty Images **46** © PYMCA/Photoshot **47** 2 Kevork Djansezian/Getty Images 3 © PYMCA/Photoshot **48** 4 Jennie Baptiste/PYMCA /REX/Shutterstock 5 Julien Boudet/BFA/REX/Shutterstock **49** Benjamin Lozovsky/BFA/REX/Shutterstock **50** 1 amdophoto/luis amella 2 David Corio/Michael Ochs Archives/Getty Images **51** amdophoto/luis amella **52** 2 GERARD DECAUX/REX/Shutterstock **53** 1 REX/Shutterstock 2 Carol M. Highsmith/Buyenlarge/Getty Images **54** 1 Martin Norris Travel Photography/Alamy Stock Photo 2 Michael Ochs Archives/Getty Images **55** Mike Harrington **56** 4 Robin Preston 5 Robin Preston **57** MonikaBatich/Getty Images **58** 1 © PYMCA/Photoshot 2 © PYMCA/Photoshot **59** 3 © PYMCA/Photoshot 4 © PYMCA/Photoshot **60** 1 Bettmann/Getty Images 2 Everett Collection Historical/Alamy Stock Photo **61** REUTERS/Henry Romero **62** REUTERS/Henry Romero **63** REUTERS/Henry Romero **64** 1 REUTERS/Alamy Stock Photo 2 snapshot-photography/ullstein bild via Getty Images **65** 3 Frazer Harrison/Getty Images for IMG 4 PYMCA/UIG via Getty Images 5 jay goebel/Alamy Stock Photo **66** 1 Niday Picture Library/Alamy Stock Photo 2 Library of Congress, LC-USF33- 016122-M2 **67** 3 Horst P. Horst/Condé Nast via Getty Images 4 John Lamparski/Getty Images **68** 1 Zoonar GmbH/Alamy Stock Photo 2 Wayne Tippetts/REX/Shutterstock **69** 3 Wayne Tippetts/REX/Shutterstock 4 Mat Hayward/Getty Images **70** Nixi Killick/www.nixikillick.com **71** Nixi Killick/www.nixikillick.com **72** 3 Julien Boudet/BFA/REX/Shutterstock 4 Victor Boyko/Getty Images **73** 5 Nixi Killick/www.nixikillick.com 6 Nixi Killick/www.nixikillick.com **74** Lupa **75** 2 Silmaril 3 Lupa 4 Silmaril **76** 1 Jet Yonkin of Faygoluvers Heaven 2 Jordan Kinnear **77** 3 Jet Yonkin of Faygoluvers Heaven 4 Jet Yonkin of Faygoluvers Heaven **78** Cultura RM/Alamy Stock Photo **79** 2 Alfred Eisenstaedt/The LIFE Picture Collection/Getty Images 3 AF archive/Alamy Stock Photo **80** 4 Sarah Vickers/www.classygirlswearpearls.com 5 Sarah Vickers/www.classygirlswearpearls.com **81** Silvia Olsen/REX/Shutterstock **82** 1 Bettmann/Getty Images 2 Granger Historical Picture Archive/Alamy Stock Photo **83** 3 WENN UK/Alamy Stock Photo 4 Bettmann/Getty Images **84** 1 Bettmann/Getty Images 2 Eugene Adebari/REX/Shutterstock **85** Andrew Chin/Getty Images 4 Peter Muller/Getty Images 5 Cultura/REX/Shutterstock **86** 1 Peter Anderson/PYMCA /REX/Shutterstock 2 PYMCA/UIG via Getty Images **87** 3 Said Karlsson **89** 2 brand: MXDVS, model: Олд Ник 3 Benjamin Lozovsky/BFA/REX/Shutterstock **90** 4 Victor VIRGILE/Gamma-Rapho via Getty Images 5 Melodie Jeng/Getty Images **91** brand: MXDVS, photographer: Sandro Dal Bianco, model: Kofi Von Ohene **92** 1 Melodie Jeng/Getty Images 2 Vanni Bassetti /Getty Images **93** 3 Melodie Jeng/Getty Images 4 anni Bassetti/Getty Images **94** 1 Jens Wolf/DPA/PA Images **95** Mike Schiller/Geisler-Fotopress/DPA/PA Images **96** 1 © PYMCA/Photoshot 2 © PYMCA/Photoshot **97** 3 Sofia Holmberg 4 Kirstin Sinclair/Getty Images **98** 1 Jamie Balbuena/www.vivabandida.com 2 Jamie Balbuena/www.vivabandida.com **99** 3 Luca Ghidoni/FilmMagic 4 lemonade/Alamy Stock Photo **100** City of Vancouver Archives City of Vancouver Archives **101** Dayton Boots Topical Press Agency/Hulton Archive/Getty Images **102** 1 John Willie/© Bélier Press Inc. John Willie/© Bélier Press Inc. **102** 2 Santiago Felipe/Getty Images **103** DreamPictures/Getty Images **104** 4 dpa picture alliance/Alamy Stock Photo 5 nullplus/Getty Images 6 PYMCA/UIG via Getty Images) **105** 7 Andre Titcombe/Sasha Louise 8 Jim Smeal/WireImage **106** Eric Charbonneau/REX/Shutterstock **107** MCPIX/REX/Shutterstock **108** Albert L. Ortega/Getty Images **109** Jake Warga/Getty Images 5 Eurobeat Kasumi Photography **110** © PYMCA/Photoshot **111** Photographer Eric Beckstead **112** 1 Popperfoto/Getty Images 2 Image: Courtesy of Sassoon **113** TS/KEYSTONE USA/REX/Shutterstock **114** Silvia Olsen/REX/Shutterstock **115** Photograph courtesy of ©Derek D'Souza **116** PYMCA/UIG via Getty Images **117** 2 PYMCA/UIG via Getty Images 3 © PYMCA/Photoshot **118** Mar Photographics/Alamy Stock Photo **119** Photographer: Jean-Frédéric Mongeon Model: Sandrine Brisebois **120** PYMCA/UIG via Getty Images **122** Jose Luis Quintana/LatinContent/Getty Images **124** AP Photo/Dario Lopez-Mills/PA Images **125** 2 AP Photo/Dario Lopez-Mills/PA Images 3 AP Photo/Zacharie Scheurer/PA Images **126** 1 Ozge Elif Kizil/Anadolu Agency/Getty Images 2 AP Photo/Franklin Reyes/PA Images **127** 3 Amigo Skate 4 age fotostock/Alamy Stock Photo 5 AP Photo/Franklin Reyes/PA Images **128** 1 Wikimedia Commons 2 James Hakewill/Wikimedia Commons **129** 3 NY Daily News Archive via Getty Images 4 Giles Moberly/PYMCA /REX/Shutterstock **130** 1 George W. Hales/Fox Photos/Getty Images 2 Larry Ellis/Daily Express/Hulton Archive/Getty Images **131** David Corio/PYMCA /REX/Shutterstock **132** Yinka Jermaine/yinkajermaine.com **133** 5 Pictorial Press Ltd/Alamy Stock Photo 6 Bianca Saunders **135** © PYMCA/Photoshot **136** © PYMCA/Photoshot In Pictures Ltd./Corbis via Getty Images **138** AP Photo/Felipe Dana, File/PA Images 2 In Pictures Ltd./Corbis via Getty Images 3 AP Photo/Felipe Dana, File/PA Images 4 Mario Tama/Getty Images **140** 1 Earl Leaf/Michael Ochs Archives/Getty Images 2 Moviestore Collection/REX/Shutterstock **141** 3 Giambalvo & Napolitano/Redferns 4 MARIE HIPPENMEYER/AFP/Getty Images **142** Axel Bueckert/Alamy Stock Photo **144** 2 joSon/Getty Images 3 Joey Foley/Getty Images 4 Christian Vierig/Getty Images **145** Ian Ross Pettigrew/Getty Images **146** 1 Rafael Ambrosio 2 Rafael Ambrosio **147** 3 Rafael Ambrosio 4 Rafael Ambrosio 5 Rafael Ambrosio 6 Rafael Ambrosio **148** Rafael Ambrosio **149** Rafael Ambrosio **150** PYMCA/UIG via Getty Images **151** 2 © PYMCA/Photoshot 3 TarpMagnus/Getty Images 4 © PYMCA/Photoshot **152** Andrew Pini/Getty Images **154** Mondadori Portfolio via Getty Images **156** PYMCA/UIG via Getty Images **158** Chtonic **159** Vassil/Wikimedia Commons, CC-BY-3.0 **160** Bettmann/Getty Images **161** 2 Ola Billmony Photography 3 Ola Billmony Photography **162** Ola Billmony Photography **163** 5 John Kobal Foundation/Hulton Archive/Getty Images 6 Ola Billmony Photography **164** 1 Pictorial Press Ltd/Alamy Stock Photo 2 Gus Stewart/Redferns **165** Martin SoulStealer from London, England/Wikimedia Commons, CC-BY-2.0 **166** Rachel Torres/Alamy Stock Photo **167** 5 Said Karlsson 6 Euan Cherry/Alamy Stock Photo **168** 1 Richard Peel/Alamy Stock Photo 2 Alan Wilson/Alamy Stock Photo **169** © PYMCA/Photoshot 4 © PYMCA/Photoshot 5 © PYMCA/Photoshot **171** Jonas Unger/PYMCA /REX/Shutterstock **172** 1 Classic Image/Alamy Stock Photo 2 Bob Thomas/Getty Images **173** 3 Richard Creamer/Michael Ochs Archives/Getty Images 4 Peter J Walsh/PYMCA /REX/Shutterstock **174** Br/Everett/REX/Shutterstock **175** David Corio/PYMCA /REX/Shutterstock **176** 3 Vertigo Films/REX/Shutterstock 4 Adidas 5 Snap Stills/REX/Shutterstock **177** 6 Slaven Vlasic/Getty Images 7 Randy Brooke/Getty Images **178** 1 © Photoshot/TopFoto 2 Melodie Jeng/Getty Images **179** Daniel Zuchnik/Getty Images **180** Julien Boudet/BFA.com/REX/Shutterstock **181** 5 Estrop/WireImage 6 Estrop/Getty Images **182** 1 Popperfoto/Getty Images 2 Ian Dickson/Redferns **183** 3 SSPL/Getty Images 4 Michael Putland /Getty Images **184** Mirrorpix **185** 2 Ted Polhemus/PYMCA /REX/Shutterstock 3 Alex Dellow/Picture Post/Getty Images **186** 4 Victor VIRGILE/Gamma-Rapho via Getty Images 5 Victor VIRGILE/Gamma-Rapho via Getty Images **187** 6 Stephen Coke/REX/Shutterstock 7 Mirrorpix **188** Courtesy of Vidal Sasson **189** 2 Ali Winstanley/PYMCA /REX/Shutterstock 3 Stephen Myhill **190** 4 Matthew Chattle/REX/Shutterstock 5 Nick Mann Photography **191** Said Karlsson **192** 1 PYMCA/UIG via Getty Images 2 Ben Pruchnie/Getty Images 3 PYMCA/UIG via Getty Images **193** RoBeDeRo/Getty Images **194** 2 Georgia Kuhn/Getty Images 3 Georgia Kuhn/Getty Images **195** 7 Wayne Tippetts/REX/Shutterstock 8 Cultura/REX/Shutterstock 9 Ali Winstanley/PYMCA /REX/Shutterstock **196** 1 Shane Drummond/BFA/REX/Shutterstock 2 Chris Jackson/Getty Images **197** Lionel Marsden **198** 4 Neil Rasmus/BFA/REX/Shutterstock 5 Angela Pham/BFA/REX/Shutterstock **199** Shane Drummond/BFA/REX/Shutterstock **200** Simon Wheatley/PYMCA/Photoshot Simon Wheatley/

First published in Great Britain in 2017 by Mitchell Beazley
A division of Octopus Publishing Group Limited
Carmelite House
50 Victoria Embankment
London EC4Y 0DZ
www.octopusbooks.co.uk

An Hachette UK Company
www.hachette.co.uk

ISBN: 978-1-78472-242-5

10 9 8 7 6 5 4 3 2 1

A CIP catalogue record for this book is available
from the British Library.

This book was designed and produced by
Quintessence Editions Ltd
The Old Brewery
6 Blundell Street
London N7 9BH

Senior Editor	Elspeth Beidas
Lead Designer	Michelle Kliem
Designers	Isabel Eeles, Thomas Keenes
Picture Researcher	Isabel Tinkler
Production Manager	Anna Pauletti
Editorial Director	Ruth Patrick
Publisher	Philip Cooper

Jacket front: Sapeur © Hector Mediavilla / Picturetank
Jacket back: Cosplayer © Marlo Cueto / Pacific Press / Getty Images

Printed in China